ALAIN MARCHADOUR, A.A., is former
Dean and Professor of Scripture at L'Institut
Catholique de Toulouse, and now superior
of Saint Peter in Gallicantu in Jerusalem. He
is the author of numerous exegetical studies,
particularly on the Gospel of John.

DAVID NEUHAUS, S.J., is Professor of
Scripture at the Catholic Seminary of the
Holy Land and at Bethlehem University. He
is active in Jewish–Catholic dialogue and
the struggle for peace and justice in Israel
and Palestine.

The Land, the Bible, and History

The Abrahamic Dialogues Series
David B. Burrell, series editor

Donald Moore, *Martin Buber: Prophet of Religious Secularism.*

James L. Heft, ed., *Beyond Violence: Religious Sources of Social Transformation in Judaism, Christianity, and Islam.*

Rusmir Mahmutćehajić, *Learning from Bosnia: Approaching Tradition.*

Rusmir Mahmutćehajić, *The Mosque: The Heart of Submission.*

The Land, the Bible, and History

Toward the Land That I Will Show You

ALAIN MARCHADOUR, A.A.
DAVID NEUHAUS, S.J.

FORDHAM UNIVERSITY PRESS
NEW YORK   2007

Copyright © 2007 Fordham University Press

Library of Congress Cataloging-in-Publication Data

Marchadour, Alain, 1937–
   The land, the Bible, and history : toward the land that I will show
you / Alain Marchadour, David Neuhaus.—1st ed.
        p.   cm.—(The Abrahamic dialogues series ; no. 5)
   Includes bibliographical references and index.
   ISBN-13: 978-0-8232-2659-7 (cloth : alk. paper)
   ISBN-10: 0-8232-2659-X (cloth : alk. paper)
   1. Bible—Geography.   2. Bible—History of biblical events.
3. Bible—History of contemporary events.   4. Palestine—
Church history.   5. Israel—Church history.   6. Palestine—
History.   7. Israel—History.   8. Catholic Church—Doctrines.
9. Bible—Criticism, interpretation, etc.   I. Neuhaus, David,
1962–   II. Title.
BS635.3.M37 2006
231.7'6—dc22

                                                    2006037392

Printed in the United States of America
09 08 07   5 4 3 2 1
First edition

Contents

List of Framed Texts   vii

Foreword   ix
   Carlo Maria Cardinal Martini, S.J.

Acknowledgments   xv

Introduction   1

PART I: INTERPRETING THE LAND IN THE BIBLE

1 The Land in the Old Testament   9

2 The Land in the New Testament   63

PART II: THE LAND IN CHRISTIAN TRADITION

3 Visiting the Land   89

4 A Christian Reading of the Land until Vatican II   108

5 Shaking Up a Familiar Landscape   125

PART III: THE LAND IN THE CONTEMPORARY
DOCUMENTS OF THE CATHOLIC CHURCH

6 Traditional Christian Attachment to the Land   147

7 The Interpretation of the Bible   151

8 Interreligious Dialogue   160

9 Peace and Justice   177

Conclusion—Holy Lands: Yesterday and Today   187
Appendix: *Redemptionis anno:* Apostolic Letter of Pope
    John Paul II (April 20, 1984)   203
Notes   209
Selected Bibliography   223
Index   227
Index of Biblical Citations   233

List of Framed Texts

1. A Note on the Use of the Term *Holy Land* 5
2. Babel and Jerusalem 13
3. In the beginning . . . 14
4. The Town of Shechem 16
5. The Price of the Land 19
6. The Tent, Where God Meets Man 22
7. The Gift of the Land and Its Obligations 24
8. The Violence of God 25
9. The Dream of Moses 30
10. The Deuteronomist: A Reading of Seven Centuries of History 31
11. Land of Dreams, Land of Violence 45
12. Justice (*Mishpat*) and Righteousness (*Tsedaka*) in the Land 49
13. Jeremiah, the Poet of the Land 53
14. The Changing Borders of the Land 60
15. Blessed are the meek, for they shall inherit the Land (Mt 5:5) 76
16. The Land and Christ 86
17. Pilgrimage in the Bible 92
18. The Holy Spirit and the Holy Places 98
19. The Land and the Rabbinic Tradition 100
20. The War for God 103
21. The Land and the Muslim Tradition 105

22. Christian Reading of the Old Testament   111
23. The True Land   114
24. The Myth of the Wandering Jew   121
25. Judaism, Zionism, and the State of Israel   127
26. Zionism and the Biblical Heritage   130
27. Palestine, Palestinian Arabs, and Palestinian
    Nationalism   131
28. The Surprise of the Excavations in Jericho   141
29. The Official Status of the Churches   150
30. What Is Christian Zionism?   198

Foreword

Carlo Maria Cardinal Martini, S.J.

Anyone even vaguely familiar with the Bible realizes how important the Land is in the Scriptures. In general terms, the Land refers to space created by God for the human person. In more specific terms, it designates the strip of territory once inhabited by the Canaanites, then promised to Abraham on the occasion of his call, becoming for many centuries the residence and homeland of the Jews, only to become, later on, booty divided up among many different peoples.

This portion of the earth that would become known as the Holy Land or, alternatively, as Palestine or Israel, is not only sporadically mentioned in the holy books but has an almost omnipresent quality. This book bears witness to the constant interest in this theme of the Land as it appears in all the books that make up the Holy Scriptures. The authors of the present work have deemed it fitting to read the diverse books of the Bible according to their order in the Christian canon, reviewing and weighing up all of the numerous times that the Land is mentioned almost in each and every page of the Holy Book.

The survey begins in the first chapters of Genesis, with the creation and the ordering of the land inhabited by human beings. However, the theme becomes a burning issue with the call of Abraham, to whom a particular Land is promised, a land in which he and his descendants shall dwell. From this point on the reader is accompanied through the pages of the Bible in studying and analyzing the diverse ways in which this fundamental theme is present. This book proposes not only a synchronic reading of Scripture but also a diachronic one. It demands of the reader the patient discipline of listening to the sacred books in order to discover a thread that indicates the significance of the space in which God places human beings and, in particular, the significance of that particular space in which God placed the chosen people.

The subsequent reading of the Land touches upon almost all the books of the Bible, taking into account their variety and the diversity of points of view expressed as the biblical reader moves from one book to another. Thus, for example, the book underlines the fact that in the historical books the land loses some of its importance in favor of the city of Jerusalem, which is presented, especially after the exile, as the center of religious practice. The exile is in fact an important time of trial, during which a new sensibility comes to the fore with regard to the Land. This sensibility is expressed by the original and innovative way in which life is conceived as faithfulness to the Torah, a conception that remains vibrant and operative in the memory and the practice of the Jewish people until the present day. Thus, the mission of this people becomes ever clearer, being that of witness to the nations of the world. After the exile, the centrality of the Land, with its specific sovereignty and its well-defined borders, is no longer experienced in exactly the same way.

This can be seen, for example, in the books of the Maccabees. The focus is more on the defense and purity of religious practice than on sovereignty or the borders of the land of Israel. Other books, like Esther and Tobit, present life that is lived in foreign lands, but is regulated by Jewish practice and piety, in faithfulness, and in a spirit of prayer, even though the Land and the Temple are absent.

The authors do not ignore the difficult passages in the Bible, especially some in the historical books, where what seems to be excessive cruelty is shown toward the conquered populations. The reader of the Bible might have the impression that it is God who commands such violence. The book, however, not only provides the necessary historical-critical, literary, and theological indications that are necessary in order to make sense of these texts, but it also seeks to impede the improper use of these texts in order to justify violence in our own times.

In the wisdom books, the authors draw attention to the focus on the universal rather than on the particular. In contrast with the historical books, concerned with the contingent history of Israel, wisdom literature deals with human experience that is relevant always and everywhere. The Land, obviously, is also present here as it is the space in which human beings live and observe the law and the precepts of reason and common sense. What is noteworthy is that the particular makes room for the universal. The Book of Job, about a man who is probably not a son of Israel, places him in direct relationship with God and with the problem of evil without dealing with the specific issue of the land of Israel.

In the rich diversity of the Psalms one does find echoes of the specificity of the territory in which many of them were, in fact, composed. However, what seems evermore important is the global dimension of the divine norm, the vocation of Jerusalem and of the Temple in promoting the universal appreciation of the Law of God. Furthermore, one notes here too a transformation, moving from the theme of political sovereignty to that of religious practice regulated by the law, focused on the city of Jerusalem and the Temple. This is also noteworthy in the message of the prophets, in particular, the last prophets in the canonical list, namely Haggai, Zechariah, and Malachi. These prophets, writing in the period after the exile, focus their prophecies on Jerusalem, which must become a city of faithfulness and a holy mountain (Zec 8:3). The promise of the restoration of the Land takes on cosmic proportions, so that what is at stake is no longer a geographically limited space that must be reestablished but rather a new creation that restores the original creation. Thus, the entire surface of the earth becomes once again privileged space for intimate relationship between God and humanity.

The dynamic found in the diverse books of the Bible opens up to include all of humanity, of which Israel is a representative. All persons are, in fact, called to live a divine filial relationship and the whole earth is the space given to live this relationship. What remains always intact is divine faithfulness to the ancient promise by which a precise geographical space was assigned to the Jewish people, even if its exact proportions are obscure. The contemporary problem is how to interpret these ancient passages in the light of the successive historical developments. Do these passages signify a broader spiritual horizon for a geographical space that remains limited or do the passages permit a new reading of the meaning of this specific geographical space? Directly related to this dilemma there has been an outpouring of much violence; grave injustices have been committed and many open wounds still fester and seem to us without hope of healing. What is at stake here is neither the legitimate right of the State of Israel to exist nor the right of the Palestinian people to have their own territory and their own homeland, but rather the theological interpretation of these facts and, consequently, the measure of sacredness or secularity with which they must be considered.

In the New Testament, alongside continuity with the past, there are also elements of newness, moving toward a further spiritualization of the Land. In particular, it is the resurrection of Jesus that constitutes the decisive point in this dynamic transformation. The victory of Jesus over death gives a new meaning to the land of Israel, stretching it evermore toward a universal dimension, by which every land on the surface of the earth is called to become a holy land. Thus, for Christians, Jesus Christ assumes in his person the entire sacred history, including the relationship between land and covenant. The land of the covenant becomes concrete in the kingdom of Christ that extends beyond every human or geographical border. "Blessed are the meek for they will inherit the earth" (Mt 5:5).

The research of the authors of this book continues way beyond biblical times, especially focusing on the continued reflections found in the documents of the Fathers and the ancient, medieval, and modern Church. Here too, we are struck by both the continuity and the openness toward an ever-greater universality. The authors do not attempt to hide the judgments and criteria of the past, which, today, we can only deplore because they are unjust and oppressive with regard to the Jewish people. However, the authors draw attention to the fact that in the past century there has been a profound change of direction, consolidated by the Second Vatican Council and the work of recent popes, especially of John Paul II.

In order to comprehend how Christians see the contemporary issues, one must take into account the diversity of elements, resumed and explained by the authors, who base themselves, in particular, on the important 1984 letter of John Paul II, *Redemptionis anno*. The basic data that must be taken into account might be summarized thus:

(1) The traditional attachment of Christians to the Holy Land, whether as a historical heritage or as a sacramental figure in the history of salvation. From this derive both the growing importance of biblical pilgrimage and the love that binds Christianity in its entirety to the holy places that are foundational for its birth and history.

(2) The biblical interpretation of the Land, in particular the Old Testament passages that speak of the promise and the gift of the land of Israel as well as the question of their validity for today.

(3) The necessity for interreligious dialogue and its conditions, first and foremost with both the Jewish and the Muslim worlds.

(4) The search for peace and justice in the Middle East in general and in Israel and Palestine in particular.

Many important and urgent questions emerge from all of this. How should one respond to Jewish claims to the Land, based as they are on the Scriptures? How should one make sense of the fact that a part of this land became the State of Israel in 1948? How can one recognize the legitimate rights of the Palestinian people, deprived of sovereignty and liberty and undergoing unjust oppression, within a faithful reading of the Holy Scriptures? How can Christians commit themselves to the search for peace and justice in the Holy Land? How should they react to the claims of both Israelis and Palestinians without denying the legitimate rights of each side?

The authors examine the positions of the Church on each of these issues in order to evaluate their coherence and seek to open up possibilities for solutions that pave the way toward dialogue and peace.

These few words show the importance of the theme discussed in this book and the need to publicize these facts to all who hold dear the future of the Land of the Bible, as well as the future of both Jews and Palestinians and the peace of the world. I am thinking here especially of Christians who are neither always aware of all the necessary facts nor of the most recent teachings of the Church concerning these matters. However, I believe that other religious and political groups involved in these issues might derive great benefit from the reflections in this book, which are systematic and comprehensive, balanced and ever mindful of respectfully and delicately maintaining the rich diversity of interpretations.

Acknowledgments

The authors would like to express their gratitude to:

His Eminence Carlo Maria Cardinal Martini, S.J., who graciously agreed to read our manuscript and write a foreword to this book.

Rev. Robert Fortin, A.A., who generously and painstakingly reread the English and French versions of our text and helped correct them.

The Shalom Hartman Institute in Jerusalem, in whose precincts much of this book was originally conceived and where some of it was written.

To our Assumptionist and Jesuit communities in Jerusalem, whose fraternal support and sharing made this book possible.

To the Church of Jerusalem, whose questions provoked our own and whose longing for justice and for peace, for pardon and for reconciliation, echoes throughout this work.

Alain Marchadour, A.A.
David Neuhaus, S.J.

Introduction

This book was born in an encounter between two Catholic exegetes, both formed biblically in the same academic institutions (the Pontifical Biblical Institute in Rome and the École Biblique in Jerusalem). Alain Marchadour is a French Assumptionist priest, who taught for many years in the faculty of theology in Toulouse, France, where he was professor of Scripture as well as dean of the faculty. For the past six years he has been living in Jerusalem, where he has continued his biblical research as well as serving as the religious superior of the Assumptionist community at the shrine of Saint Peter in Gallicantu. David Neuhaus is an Israeli Jesuit priest. Having completed his doctorate in political science at the Hebrew University of Jerusalem, he went on for further theological and biblical studies in Paris and Rome. In the Holy Land, he is professor of Scripture at the diocesan seminary and at the Catholic University of Bethlehem. He is engaged in biblical research and interreligious dialogue with both Jews and Muslims.

Although quite different in our backgrounds, culture and history, we have worked together in Jerusalem and on numerous occasions have shared our opinions on the most burning issues that face the peoples of the Holy Land, including the questions of the Land and its history and meaning. The history of this particular land has been almost uninterruptedly agitated over the past several millennia, and this is particularly true in our own times. It is the Bible, both Old Testament and New, which bears witness to the influence that the history of this little strip of territory has had on the entire world for the past two thousand years through the influence of Judaism, Christianity, and Islam—all having emerged, partially or fully, out of the biblical narrative.

We are clearly identified as Catholics and Christians and addressing ourselves primarily to Christians, have witnessed on numerous occasions how much of what goes on in the Land divides and creates conflict among Christians. The events that have taken place in the Land in the twentieth century, notably the creation of the State of Israel and the birth of the Palestinian refugee problem, are disputed issues that are not easy to understand. This difficulty might be particularly acute for Western Christians, who carry a painful heritage of centuries-old anti-Semitism, on the one hand, coupled with a history of colonialism, on the other. The result is that Christians today, often inspired by fiery passions, take contradictory positions on the issues at stake in the Holy Land, positions born of particular sensibilities, favoring one side or the other. This book poses the question of the Land afresh: is it possible to develop a coherent Christian understanding of the Land that takes all the various diverse and complex factors into account and moves beyond partisan and, consequently, partial perspectives?

For Christians, the first illumination regarding the Land must come from the Book itself. This book, in its reading of the Bible, reflects the traditional saying: *scriptura interpres sui* (Scripture interprets itself). For this reason, an important part of this study is devoted to *the Land as it is presented throughout the biblical narrative*. From Genesis right through to Revelation, the Land constitutes an essential and omnipresent reference point, with important nuances of meaning from one book to the next, from period to period, from the Old Testament to the New. In this interpretation of the Bible, we propose a reading of the Land that purports to be both coherent and dynamic. It is, however, only one possible reading. Furthermore, it has the specific characteristics of a Christian biblical reading as performed in the Land today. The Land, created by God, is a space offered to humanity so that all might live there, putting into practice the covenant with God and establishing fraternity and justice with all who are brothers and sisters. In this way, people can pursue the work of preserving and ordering the Land, a work initiated by God in the creation. Tragically, the first attempt was a failure but then Abraham, considered father of the three monotheistic religions that are tied to the Land today—Judaism, Christianity, and Islam—was called by God in order to become a blessing for all nations, beginning in a particular Land, defined geographically. This Land that

is promised, given, conquered, threatened, lost, and eventually regained, is the concrete backdrop to the covenant between God and the
people chosen to be "a light to the nations." The history of this people
and their relationship with the Land plays itself out through the long
centuries reflected in the Old Testament. In this story, God is constantly
faithful to his promises while the people vacillate between exemplary
faithfulness to God and stiff-necked resistance and infidelity.

For the Christian, the death and resurrection of Jesus is a decisive
stage in this unfolding story. Jesus' victory over death gives a new character to the land of Israel, opening up a universal dimension by which
every land, across the entire face of the earth, is called to become a
"holy land." The essential dialectic of continuity with the old and dis-
continuity in the new is communicated by Jesus to the Samaritan
woman: "Woman, believe me, the hour is coming when you will worship the Father neither on this mountain nor in Jerusalem. You worship
what you do not know, we worship what we know, for salvation is from
the Jews. But the hour is coming, and is now here, when the true wor-
shipers will worship the Father in spirit and truth for the Father seeks
such as these to worship him. God is spirit and those who worship him
must worship in spirit and truth" (Jn 4:21–24). For Christians, Jesus
Christ assumes in his person all of sacred history, including the inviola-
ble link between land and covenant. At the same time, he gives to both
land and covenant their ultimate meaning. The land of the covenant,
geographically localized, takes body in the kingdom of Christ which
extends beyond every boundary: "Blessed are the meek for they will
inherit the earth" (Mt 5:5).

Although the Bible presents a normative teaching about the Land,
the adventure of the Book does not end with writing the experiences of
Israel, of Jesus, and of the early Church. Once the writing has been
completed and the Book brought into existence, a time of *readings and
interpretations* begins, never completed but rather beginning afresh
with each generation of Christian readers. From the time of the birth
of Christianity, the Holy Land, although clearly maintaining a specific
exemplary value for Christians, is no longer the central reference point.
The land of Israel, sacred space where revelation was given, becomes
one symbolic holy place. For all Christians, Jerusalem represents the
mother Church of all churches, a place to which Christians might desire
to come on pilgrimage. However, Christians do not seek to stay in the
Land but rather, after having experienced the immediacy and grace of

the holy places linked with "the history of salvation," they go back into the wide world, reinvigorated in their Christian lives. After the Resurrection, all lands are called to become holy because they are sanctified by the presence of Christian believers in whom the Spirit resides.

The dispersion of the Jewish people from the Land was a focal point in the teaching of the Old Testament prophets. However, in the way that Christians interpreted the dispersion after the destruction of the Second Temple (in A.D. 70), a fundamentally new situation had developed. There was no longer one religious group, the Jews, meditating on the Bible but two, Jews and Christians. The Christian biblical readers combined the theme of the exile, traditionally understood in the Bible as a consequence of Israel's sin, with the condemnation of the Jews for their rejection of Christ and their responsibility for his death on the cross. Without seeking to be exhaustive, this book presents a brief selection of Christian interpretations of the Jewish dispersion, particularly from among the Church Fathers. This traditional Christian teaching, often embarrassing to hear today, bears the marks of its time, and one should not forget this. These readings also represent an ever-present danger in biblical and theological interpretation: they transform the tragic history of the Jewish people into a Christian theological and sociopolitical attitude that smacks of fundamentalism.

This study reflects on the events that have led to the present situation of ongoing conflict in the Land. The rise of modern anti-Semitism in the nineteenth century and the catastrophe of the Shoah resound in Western Christian memory today, as does the history of the European colonial conquest of far-off lands. The creation of the State of Israel and the birth of the Palestinian refugee problem have also left their distinct marks on any contemporary reading of the Land. An important part of the book is devoted to a study of the evolution of the position of the Catholic Church from the Second Vatican Council until the beginning of the twenty-first century.

This biblical and theological reading of the Land seeks to help Christians reflect on the important questions raised by the complex past, conflicted present, and insecure future of the land known today as Israel and Palestine, claimed by two peoples (Israelis and Palestinians) and by faithful from three religions (Jews, Muslims, and Christians). Although it is certainly true that other peoples and other lands have known protracted conflicts regarding identity, territory, and borders, comparable to that between Israelis and Palestinians, this particular conflict in the Holy Land has special significance for Christians because it unfolds in the very land that is a sacred geographic space and it involves two peoples that evoke the protagonists in the biblical saga. This land saw the development of the history of Israel, reaching its summit, for Christians, in the incarnation of Jesus Christ Son of God and son of Mary. God became man in this land and not somewhere else. For Jews too, this same Land is central to their identity and history and they have prayed throughout the long centuries: "Next year in Jerusalem." And for Muslims also, the attachment to this land has a special importance because it has been sanctified by the succession of prophets that lived here and finally by the Night Journey of the Prophet Muhammad to "the furthest mosque" (*al-Aqsa*) in Jerusalem.

The Land is the land of God, but also the land of men and women. This is the land that "flows with milk and honey," but also the land that is awash in "tears and blood." It is this land of breathtaking beauty and mind-boggling diversity, of troubling complexity and intense passions, of mystical attachment and blood-curdling claims of exclusivity, a fascinating land because of its history, both human and divine, that provokes the reflections in this book.

A Note on the Use of the Term *Holy Land*

What should the land of the Bible be called? Today, two groups call the Land by different names, each evoking political aspirations and claims. Palestinians call this land Palestine, while Jews call it the land of Israel or the Promised Land. Through the centuries, Christians have called it the Holy Land. This term is used only once in Scripture, in Zechariah 2:16 (Hebrew: *admat haqodesh,* Greek: *he ge he hagia,* Latin: *terra sancta*) but is adopted often in this book as best evoking the Christian attachment to the Land and what it represents. However, most often the authors refer to this land simply as the Land.

Part I

Interpreting the Land in the Bible

The first part of this book surveys the theme of the Land from Genesis to Revelation, following the canonical order of the books of the Bible according to the Catholic tradition. Our study in this part does not deal with historical issues concerning the production of the texts, their date of composition, their authors, or their addressees. Although historical-critical research is essential in order to understand the texts within the context of the universe in which they were produced, these issues do not concern us here as we follow the logic of the presentation of the Land in these texts within the Bible. In focusing on the theme of the Land, we shall be especially attentive to the continuity, to the repetitions, but also to the transformations and moments of rupture in the development of this theme throughout the Bible. With regard to the Old Testament, we will follow the order of the four major parts of the Christian Bible: the law (*torah*), history, wisdom, and the prophets. At the outset, it is important to note that the Jewish tradition presents a different organization of the material: Torah, Prophets, and Writings, thus providing a different framework and context for the interpretation of the Land.[1]

In our study, the theme of the Land is omnipresent and structures the biblical account in its entirety. At the one extreme we find the Land as the space afforded Adam at the time of creation (Gn 1–2) and at the other extreme we find the Land as the heavenly Jerusalem descending to earth, the home of the saints (Rv 21–22). The presentation of the theme of the Land in the New Testament and the newness it proposes are incomprehensible without the backdrop of the Old Testament.

This synchronic survey of the Bible is an essential first step in our proceeding. We set off with the Bible as a starting point, taking the time to listen to the Word of God in the Bible. We will attempt to trace a coherent meaning to be attributed to the space in which God placed humankind, a meaning worked out through the long centuries of the history of salvation, despite contradictions and resistance all along the way. After this first step, we will then proceed to examine how the biblical narrative was received in the successive generations as they read the theme of the Land. Only after the fundamental first step can we present the readings and re-readings of this theme in the Church from the time of the Church Fathers until the Second Vatican Council and right up until our own day.

1. The Land in the Old Testament

The Land of God (Gn 1–11)

"In the beginning when God created the heavens and the Land" (Gn 1:1).[1] In the creation narrative with which the Bible begins (Gn 1:1–2:4a), the Land refers to the entire surface of the earth, separated from the all-encompassing waters (Gn 1:9–10). After each creative act, God looks at the Land (*ha-aretz*) and sees that it is good. Progressively, the Land emerges from the primordial, chaotic waters, becoming an accommodating terrain, ready to be cultivated and populated by living creatures and finally by human beings. The Bible describes, day by day, an orderly emergence from the "*tohu-bohu*" (Gn 1:2) through a series of successive separations and orderings. In this unfolding work, the creation of humankind (*adam*) on the sixth day constitutes a turning point in the narrative, though not its culmination, because God remains its main actor from beginning to end. Treated differently than all other creatures, *adam* is the object of a solemn, deliberative act on the part of God, an act he does not perform before undertaking his other works of creation. "Let us make *adam* in our image, according to our likeness" (Gn 1:26). One might suppose that this creation in the image and likeness of God constitutes beyond all else a mission that must be accomplished. "God blessed them and God said to them: Be fruitful and multiply and fill the Land and subdue it and have dominion over the fish of the sea and over the birds of the air and over every living thing that moves upon the Land" (Gn 1:28). This series of punctual orders is

presented not only as law (*torah*) but also as blessing. The Land belongs to God, its management is entrusted to *adam*, and *adam*'s success
will depend on his faithful obedience to the Word of God.

God can now conclude the work of creation and rest. He blesses the
seventh day, presented as *shabbat*, a day of rest (Gn 2:3). In the list of
Ten Commandments, where the *shabbat* is instituted as an obligatory
day of rest, it is written: "For in six days the Lord made heaven and
Land, the sea and all that is in them, but rested the seventh day; therefore the Lord blessed the Sabbath day and consecrated it" (Ex 20:11).
Here the word "rest" translates the Hebrew *nah* that, in the Bible, refers
to a cessation of human activity. Thus, a person interrupts work on the
seventh day in order "to imitate God" who first took the time to contemplate and celebrate creation. The Land offers a person a place where
he or she is called upon to imitate God the Creator and to live in obedience as a child of God. Sabbath rest and life on the Land are linked
from the very beginning.

The second account of creation (Gn 2:4–3:24) uses the word
"earth" (*adamah*) instead of Land (*aretz*). *Adamah* designates the very
substance from which *adam* is formed and from which apparently he
derives his name.[2] *Adamah* has the vocation to become a garden, a cultivated place, through the nurturing care of Adam. He is placed in the
garden "to till it and keep it" (Gn 2:15). Within the creation narrative,
Adam has a particular place. The Land is blessed and Adam is the culmination of this blessing. Through his actions, he has the power to prevent the world from returning to the chaotic state. However, the
continuation of the story shows that a descent into chaos is, unfortunately, not precluded. Adam's behavior must conform to the law of God
(*torah*). In Genesis 2:16, for the first time in the biblical text, we find
the verb *tsivva* (give a commandment, from which the word *mitsva*—
commandment—is derived). The law is breathtakingly simple, precise,
and unconditional. "The Lord God commanded Adam: You may freely
eat of every tree of the garden; but of the tree of the knowledge of good
and evil you shall not to eat, for in the day that you eat of it you shall
die" (Gn 2:16). If Adam obeys God, he will be blessed along with the
entire Land entrusted to his care. Should he disobey, the blessed life on
the Land will come to an abrupt end.

The following nine chapters of Genesis (3–11) tell the tragic story
of how this land of blessing becomes a Land of curse because of the
infidelity of *adam* to God's law, condition for all blessing. *Adam*'s sin

interrupts his relationship with God as well as with his brothers and sisters and with creation itself. When Adam contravened the law (*torah*) and ate of the forbidden fruit, he broke the covenant God had offered him.[3] It is striking that Adam does not die immediately after his sin, a punishment clearly laid out by God (cf. Gn 2:17). Instead, God continues to seek him out, calling to him: "Where are you?"(Gn 3:9). It is Adam, however, who distances himself from God by trying to hide. Adam experiences fear for the first time, thereby indicating that he had lost trust in God. The first covenant is torn asunder. Quite naturally, the result is expulsion from the land of blessing into an arid wilderness. Because Adam was not to eat of the fruit from the tree of life, he now finds himself in a hostile place covered with thorns and thistles, a place where he must earn his bread by the sweat of his brow. The original blessed harmony is lost. The Land itself participates in the curse, no longer offering him the abundant fruit of the first garden. Sin entailed the loss of hospitable Land and exile to a hostile wilderness. The symbolic dimension of these chapters evokes the destiny of Israel that is traced in the later books of the Bible.

Cain, Adam and Eve's son, after having soaked the earth with the blood of his brother, Abel (Gn 4:1–16), is condemned to wander on the Land, homeless and unprotected. Like the serpent and the Land (Gn 3:14.17), Cain is cursed, cut off from his community of origin, banished from the nurturing Land from which he had drawn his subsistence. For him, this is tantamount to a death sentence. All at once, Cain lost the privileged space in which he lived in the presence of God and the particular relationship suggested by his name: "(Eve) conceived and bore Cain, saying, 'I have produced a man with the help of the Lord'" (Gn 4:1). From being a close and privileged son he becomes "a fugitive and a wanderer." The punishment meted out by God appears to be the consequence of Cain's own choices. His responsibility is highlighted more than his guilt. In Gn 4:14, the Hebrew text contains a striking parallelism between "the face of the earth (*adamah*)" and "the face of God." The face is the surface that reveals the living presence of a human being as well as his dignity of having been created in the image of God. Thus, God and the Land are presented as two interconnected realities. To sever one's relationship with one party is to cut oneself off from the other. The "face of the earth" is a human being's living space, somewhat in the image of the "face of God."

In the time of Noah, the connection between sin and Land is clearly expressed. "The Lord said, 'I will blot out from the earth the *adam* I have created—*adam* together with animals and creeping things and birds of the air—for I am sorry that I have made them'" (Gn 6:7). The connection between sin and habitable Land is expressed here in God's decision to open the floodgates, thereby reversing the creative act, because of the perversity of human beings. The ordering of the universe that God had overseen during the first six days of creation is undone. The *tohu-bohu* returns, bringing in its wake the destruction not only of all habitable space but also of humanity that has shown itself unfaithful to its mission.

However, God does not completely put an end to the project of the world and of humanity. Noah, his family, and representatives from all living things are saved from death. Restraining partially this destructive impulse, God calls out to Noah and makes a covenant with him. The word *berith* (covenant) appears for the first time in the Bible in 6:18 with regard to Noah. The covenant here constitutes a re-creation. While the Land reverts back to primitive chaos, the ark, constructed by Noah who follows the orders of God, carries off Noah and the creatures that accompany him. Only Noah and his family survive. On emerging from the ark, God is ready to begin again. This time however, he does not fully entrust the Land to a human being, promising instead never to destroy the Land again because of human sinfulness. "I will never again curse the ground because of the *adam*, for the inclination of the human heart is evil from youth; nor will I ever again destroy every living creature as I have done" (Gn 8:21). Noah, however, receives the same blessing as Adam and a similar *torah*: "Be fruitful, multiply and fill the Land" (Gn 9:1).

In this new creation, however, an important shift occurs. The Land (*ha-aretz*), until this point considered as a unified whole, is now divided into diverse territories. Chapters 10 and 11 are devoted to the story of the splintering of the human race into diverse peoples, languages, and cultures. The origin of this division is also linked to human sin. In Genesis 11, the story of the Tower of Babel tells how humanity, instead of accepting a name from God, seeks "to make a name" for itself. The narrative equates building "a city and a tower with its top in the heavens" with the refusal to fill the Land. "Then they said, 'Come, let us build·ourselves a city and a tower with its top in the heavens, and let us make a name for ourselves; otherwise we shall be scattered abroad upon the face of the whole Land'" (Gn 11:4). The inhabitants of Babel seek to remain in one place, contravening God's call to fill the earth. The human person, created in the image and likeness of God, is commanded to fill the earth with the image of God. God punishes the builders in Babel by confusing their language in such a way that they can no longer understand one another. Dispersion, desired by God but refused by humanity, now becomes a necessity. From Babel, whose very name is linked to the act of confusing the languages, they are dispersed over the face of the Land.

Babel and Jerusalem

Throughout the biblical narrative, Babel and Jerusalem (and the Land of Israel) represent polar opposites. Babel, or Babylon, is portrayed as a sinful city whereas Jerusalem is called to be the city of God. This is resumed at the end of the Bible, in the Book of Revelation, where Babylon is named "Babylon, the great mother of whores and of earth's abominations" (Rv 17:5) and Jerusalem, descending out of heaven "has the glory of God and a radiance like a very rare jewel (Rv. 21:11).

The sinful city in the biblical account has various names and locations: Babel, Sodom and Gomorrah, Egypt, Nineveh, etc. Despite the diversity, the city described represents the place of humanity's refusal of the sovereignty of God. The destruction that is regularly wreaked on the sinful city (Babel in Gn 11, Sodom and Gomorrah in Gn 19, Egypt in Ex 14, Nineveh in the Book of Nahum, Babylon in Is 47 and in Rv 18) is understood as divine punishment.

The great tragedy though is that Jerusalem, called to become the city of God, often chooses the way of the sinful city rather than obedience to God. It is at these times of profound crisis that Jerusalem will be called by the names of the sinful city, evoking the destruction that often follows. Isaiah castigates Jerusalem, saying: "How the faithful city has become a whore" (Is 1:21). Thus, the prophets address Jerusalem as Sodom and Gomorrah (cf. Is 1:10, 3:9, Jer 23:14, 49:18, 50:40, Ez 16:46–56, Am 4:11). And in the Book of Revelation, the earthly Jerusalem in which the Lord was crucified "is prophetically called Sodom and Egypt" (Rv 11:8).

From this understanding of the Land, as reflected in the first eleven chapters of Genesis, it emerges that the Land belongs to the Lord.

Though this is true for all the lands of the world, in the Bible Israel is the first to be called to put this into practice: "The Land shall not be sold in perpetuity, for the Land is mine, with me you are but aliens and tenants" (Lv 25:23).[4] It is God who places Adam in the Garden, giving him the Land to cultivate and preserve in God's own name. For Adam, Land is an inheritance and a place of rest. In this original context, Land clearly means Land that is fertile, life giving and sustaining. From the Land, the human person eats his or her fill, conscious of the blessings showered on him or her by God. Ultimately, the Land is a place of rest where human beings are called to live in harmony with God, fellow human beings, animals, and the earth itself. However, when human beings, through their behavior, forget that the source of this blessing is God, the Land becomes wilderness, barren and foreboding, evoking a return to primordial chaos. The Land is transformed into a place of unrest, violence, and, ultimately, death. Land and wilderness, somewhere and nowhere, fertility and barrenness, these are the two poles that oppose each other in the first eleven chapters and throughout the biblical text.

In the beginning when God created the heavens and the Land, the Land was a formless void and darkness covered the face of the deep, while a wind from God swept over the face of the waters. Then God said, "Let there be light"; and there was light. And God saw that the light was good; and God separated the light from the darkness. God called the light Day, and the darkness he called Night. And there was evening and there was morning, the first day (Gn 1:1–5).

And the Lord God planted a garden in Eden, in the east; and there he put the man whom he had formed. Out of the ground the Lord God made to grow every tree that is pleasant to the sight and good for food, the tree of life also in the midst of the garden, and the tree of the knowledge of good and evil. . . . The Lord God took the man and put him in the garden of Eden to till it and keep it. And the Lord God commanded the man, "You may freely eat of every tree of the garden; but of the tree of the knowledge of good and evil you shall not eat, for in the day that you eat of it you shall die" (Gn 2:8–9.16–17).

And the Lord said, "What have you done? Listen; your brother's blood is crying out to me from the earth! And now you are cursed from the earth, which has opened its mouth to receive your brother's blood from your hand.

When you till the earth, it will no longer yield to you its strength; you will be a fugitive and a wanderer on the Land." Cain said to the Lord, "My punishment is greater than I can bear! Today you have driven me away from the face of the earth, and I shall be hidden from your face; I shall be a fugitive and a wanderer on the Land, and anyone who meets me may kill me." Then the Lord said to him, "Not so! Whoever kills Cain will suffer a sevenfold vengeance." And the Lord put a mark on Cain, so that no one who came upon him would kill him. Then Cain went away from the presence of the LORD, and settled in the land of Nod, east of Eden (Gn 4:10–16).

"As for me, I am establishing my covenant with you and your descendants after you, and with every living creature that is with you, the birds, the domestic animals, and every animal of the Land with you, as many as came out of the ark. I establish my covenant with you, that never again shall all flesh be cut off by the waters of a flood, and never again shall there be a flood to destroy the Land" (Gn 9:9–11).

So the Lord scattered them abroad from there over the face of all the Land, and they left off building the city. Therefore it was called Babel, because there the LORD confused the language of all the Earth; and from there the Lord scattered them abroad over the face of all the Land (Gn 11:8–9).

THE PROMISE OF THE LAND (GENESIS 12–50)

We have seen how the biblical narratives, strongly symbolic in character, tell of the development of sin in the Land (Gn 1–11). They also emphasize, for good or bad, the solidarity of the human person with the Land.

In chapter 12 of Genesis a new narrative begins with Abraham. Abram (he is not renamed Abraham by God until Gn 17:5) receives a call from God to radically change his life. This call, addressed to Abram as a solitary man of faith, envisages, however, the entire human race. In calling Abraham, God promises him that he will become the father of a nation and the source of blessing for many peoples. Abram is the incarnation of what relationship with God should be: he is the man of faith par excellence. God commands Abram to be a blessing for all peoples: "be a blessing" (Gn 12:2).[5] The original blessing, lost by Adam, now rests on Abram. Through him all the peoples of the earth will be blessed.

Abram is called to leave his land and to go to a land "that I will show you" (Gn 12:1). For the first time, the Bible speaks of a particular land (the Land), as distinguished from all other lands. For now, this land is not explicitly named or defined but rather signified by a promise. Abram is invited to associate himself with God's plan, which directs him toward a land where he might fulfill his mission to be a blessing for all peoples. The land promised must become exemplary for the entire face of the earth. This is no longer the history of the beginnings, where blessing depended solely on the unilateral action of a God who placed Adam on the Land. Abram is now God's collaborator and bears responsibility for being a blessing for all nations.

What follows in the remainder of the Book of Genesis is the story of the family of Abram, which focuses on the promise of descendants who will form a nation born of Abraham in a Land for that nation. But there are numerous obstacles making the realization of this promise very difficult. Not only is Sarah sterile (cf. Gn 11:30), compromising the promise of a posterity, but also the Land, promised by God, is already inhabited by others. When Abram arrives in the land of Canaan, God makes the promise more explicit: "To your seed I will give *this* Land" (Gn 12:7). Here, the Land is preceded by a demonstrative pronoun, which makes it possible to localize what, until this moment, had been an undetermined promise. After a first stop at Shechem (Gn 12:6), Abram restlessly travels the Land at this initial stage. Shortly after his arrival, Abram is forced to take leave of the Land because of a famine (Gn 12:10). Preceding his future descendants at the time of his grandson Jacob, Abram goes down to Egypt in search of food. The Land of promise can also be a Land of want and famine.

The Town of Shechem

The first town named when Abraham arrives in the Land God has shown him is Shechem. From this point on, Shechem plays an important role in the relationship to the Land. A first violent encounter with the inhabitants of the Land takes place when Shechem, son of a local potentate, kidnaps Dinah, daughter of Jacob. The ensuing massacre of the Shechemites, reeling under the pain of circumcision forced on them by the brothers of Dinah, upsets Jacob, their father, who says: "You have brought trouble on me by making me odious to the inhabitants of the Land" (Gn 34:30).

Jacob sends Joseph to Shechem in search of his brothers, a mission that ends in the tragic sale of Joseph by his brothers to slave traders, who in turn sell Joseph in Egypt (Gn 37:12). When the children of Israel return to the

Land under Joshua, they carry with them the bones of Joseph and bury them in Shechem (Jos 24:32).

Shechem is the place of the covenant for the generation that enters the Land under the leadership of Joshua. Their fathers had made a covenant with God at Sinai and had died in the wilderness; the new generation renews the covenant at Shechem, responding to Joshua's exhortation, saying "we will serve the Lord for he is our God" (Jos 24:18). However, it is at Shechem that Abimelekh, son of the great judge Gideon, becomes a first king in Israel, a disastrous episode of violence and tyranny that bodes badly for the future (Jg 9).

However, it is in 1 Kings 12 that the biblical reader confronts what this has been leading up to. It is in Shechem that Jeroboam son of Nebat comes to confront Rehoboam son of Solomon who has come to Shechem to be made king. The result of this unhappy meeting is the schism of the kingdom, divided into a northern part (Israel) and a southern one (Judah). Shechem is both the point of entry into the Land and the place that marks the slow descent into chaos that will result in the exile from the Land.

A Christian reader, sensitive to intertextual links, will notice that it is in the vicinity of this town of Shechem that Jesus encounters the Samaritan woman and proclaims to her: "The hour is coming when you will worship the Father neither on this mountain nor in Jerusalem . . . God is spirit and those who worship him must worship in spirit and truth" (Jn 4:21.24).

After Abram's return and because of a conflict of shepherds, he himself divides the Land between himself and his nephew Lot (Gn 13:9). Consistent with the classic reasons for quarrels over wells in nomadic society, the account of the separation of Abram and his nephew Lot repeats one of the recurring themes found in the patriarchal narratives: the role of freedom and risk in the unfolding of events. In the present case, the event is a determining factor, namely the gift of the Land. By human standards, the land of the Jordan Valley was more attractive because it called to mind the "garden of the Lord" (cf. Is 51:3), which, in turn, recalled the lost Eden (Gn 2–3). However, instead of invoking the supreme authority of God, who promised precisely this land to the Patriarch, the author focuses on the issue of human choice. Because of his generosity and disinterestedness, Abram takes the risk of letting his nephew acquire the Land that had been promised to him. The reader, needless to say, understands full well that behind these unexpected and collateral events resulting from free and uncertain human choices, it is God who is directing history. After this separation, God once again promises the Land to Abram and his descendants: "Rise up, walk through the length and the breadth of the Land, for I will give it to you" (Gn 13:17).

WHAT ARE THE BORDERS?

In chapter 15, the Land is finally defined and promised in all its vastness. While Abram bemoans the fact that he remains without seed, wondering how the promise might be fulfilled, God tells him that he will have an heir and descendants as numerous as the stars in the sky (Gn 15:4–5). Then, during a strange sacrifice, fraught at times with anxieties and threats, God reassures Abram and in his unlimited generosity, makes a territorial covenant with him and his descendants regarding a vast expanse. "To your descendants I give this Land, from the river of Egypt to the great river, the river Euphrates, the Land of the Kenites, the Kenizzites, the Kadmonites, the Hittites, the Perizites, the Rephaim, the Amorites, the Canaanites, the Girgashites and the Jebusites" (Gn 15:18–21). Indeed, the borders of the Land promised here include the core of the empires of Mesopotamia and Egypt, as if to remind Abram and his descendants of their responsibility to be a blessing well beyond the borders of Canaan. However, this generous promise is immediately tempered by a reminder that the Land being promised is not devoid of inhabitants: ten nations, enumerated one after the other, inhabit it, a reality that has troubled Israel since its origins. How should we interpret this text today and how should the question of borders be understood? Is a literal reading of this text, considered the Word of God, coherent within the context of biblical revelation and of our modern world? We will come back to this issue.

As a sign of the intimacy between himself and Abram, God changes Abram's name to Abraham. This new name, based on a popular etymology, is meant to be a permanent reminder of Abraham's mission to be "the father of a multitude of nations" (Gn 17:5). Again God reiterates the promise of the Land: "And I will give to you and to your offspring after you, the Land where you are now an alien, all the Land of Canaan for a perpetual holding, and I will be their God" (Gn 17:8). The Land is to be the place where Abraham and his descendants live in intimacy with God, a place that guarantees continuity with the lost garden where Adam and God were to have lived together in harmony. However, the universal status of the Land must not be forgotten: it is a place of blessing for all nations. The way that Abraham is called to live in the Land is meant to enlighten all nations because he is the father of a multitude of nations.

This responsibility is underlined in the astonishing exchange between Abraham and God concerning the fate of Sodom and Gomorrah. Abraham's audacity in reprimanding God is explicable only in terms of Abraham's responsibility toward the peoples of the earth. The purpose of Abraham's vocation and mission is to "charge his children and his household after him to keep the way of the Lord by doing righteousness (*tsedaka*) and justice (*mishpat*), so that the Lord may bring about for Abraham what he has promised him" (Gn 18:19). The two virtues, *mishpat* and *tsedaka*, appear time and again throughout the Bible. They summarize the requirements for living out God's will on the Land and they bear witness against and denounce the violations that are too often committed by Israel.

It is interesting to note that after Isaac was bound (Gn 22), God reiterated the fundamental blessing given to Abraham and through him to all peoples. However, there is no mention here of the Land (Gn 22:16–18). In this passage, the focus is on the seed of Abraham, whose continuity has now been guaranteed. When Sarah dies, and for the first time, Abraham buys a portion of the Land in order to bury his wife (Gn 23:1–20). Abraham insists on paying the full price of the Land even though God has already promised him the Land in its entirety. The Hittite owner of the piece of land is even willing to give it to Abraham without payment but Abraham insists, as if to signify that God's promise does not abolish legal rights and social agreements.

The Price of the Land

"Sarah lived one hundred and twenty seven years; this was the length of Sarah's life. And Sarah died at Kiriath-arba (that is Hebron) in the land of Canaan; and Abraham went in to mourn for Sarah and to weep for her. Abraham rose up from beside his dead and said to the Hittites, 'I am a stranger and an alien residing among you; give me property among you for a burying place, so that I may bury my dead out of my sight.' The Hittites answered, 'Abraham, hear us my lord; you are a mighty prince among us. Bury your dead in the choicest of our burial places; none of us will withhold from you any burial ground for burying your dead.' . . . Now Ephron was sitting among the Hittites; and Ephron the Hittite answered Abraham in the hearing of the Hittites, of all that went in at the gate of his city. 'No, my lord, hear me; I give you the field and I give you the cave that is in it; in the presence of my people I give it to you; bury your dead.' Then Abraham bowed down before the people of the Land. He said to Ephron in the hearing of the people of the Land, 'If you only will listen to me! I will give the price of the field; accept it from me, so that I may bury my dead there.' Ephron answered Abraham, 'My lord, listen to me; a piece of land worth four hundred shekels of silver— what is that between you and me? Bury your dead.' Abraham agreed with Ephron, and Abraham weighed out for Ephron the silver that he had named in the hearing of the Hittites, four hundred shekels of silver, according to the weights current among the merchants" (Gn 23:1–24).

———————————————————————————————————

After the death of Abraham, God repeats the promises to his son Isaac (Gn 26:4) and to his grandson Jacob (Gn 28:13, 35:12). The descendants of Abraham will fill the Land and bring blessing. They will "spread abroad to the west and to the east and to the north and to the south and all the families of the earth will be blessed" (Gn 28:14). The narrative of the Patriarchs in Genesis tells the saga of the formation of a family. Jacob's extended family, like that of Abraham before it, goes down to Egypt because of famine. By the end of Genesis, the descendants of Abraham have become inhabitants of Egypt, a prosperous and extended family. It is important to underline, however, that at the end of the first book, the promises to Abraham have not yet been realized. The nation that had been promised is not yet born and the Land that had been promised is not yet acquired.

THE LAND FOR THE TORAH (EXODUS THROUGH DEUTERONOMY)

From the very beginning of the Book of Exodus, the promise that had seemed so distant suddenly becomes palpable. In Exodus 1:1–4, the direct descendants of Jacob, renamed Israel (*benei Yisrael*) are mentioned. However, by verse 7, the same expression, *benei Yisrael*, no longer refers to the children of the patriarch Israel but rather to the nascent nation.[6] In Exodus 1:9 it is Pharaoh himself who says, "Look the Israelite people (*'am*) are more numerous and more powerful than we." Significantly it is Pharaoh who is the first to draw attention to the fact that the promise has been fulfilled—the children of Israel have become a nation. However, the nation that is coming into being is in Egypt, far from the Land it had been promised. Exodus 1–18 recounts the birth of the nation, long promised to Abraham and his descendants. This nation shares in the vocation of the Patriarchs: to be blessing for all peoples. But, for the moment, this nation is born in the pain and hardship of slavery, under the tyranny of a new Pharaoh, "who did not know Joseph" (Ex 1:8).

God reveals himself to Moses, using the new name of "YHWH" and promising life and a future to the nation that was coming into existence (Ex 3). He sends Moses to bring the people out of Egypt. In the midst of the distress and violence of Egypt, God manifests his presence in the person of Moses. Moses is to lead the people out of Egypt, which has become a place of curse, slavery, and death, and to guide them toward "a good and broad Land, a Land flowing with milk and honey" (Ex 3:8). This Land that is the "heritage" (*morasha*) already promised to Abraham, Isaac, and Jacob (Ex 6:8). Threatened with death because of the genocidal madness of Pharaoh, the people are saved through the intervention of their God. The ten plagues inflicted upon Egypt represent a confrontation between YHWH, the God of the infant nation, and Pharaoh, the symbol of tyranny. The people participate in this confrontation whose outcome determines their life and future. After ten plagues inflicted on the Egyptians, the victory of God is spectacular: Pharaoh and his armies, with all the power they represent, are swallowed up in the waters while Israel crosses dry-shod. Then Israel, led by Moses, and having withstood the tyrannical presumptions of Pharaoh, can sing out: "YHWH God will be king for ever and ever" (Ex 15:18). In YHWH, soon to be revealed to them at Sinai, the people have found a king but still have no land. However, they are aware that, when they do reach the Land, toward which Moses is leading them, it must in no way resemble Egypt they have just left behind. "For the Land that you are about to enter to occupy is not like the land of Egypt from which you have come" (cf. Dt 11:10).

The journey from Egypt to the Land passes through Sinai. However, Sinai is not simply a place of transit. The covenant at Sinai, including the gift of the *torah*, is the central event of the Pentateuch. No other event in the Old Testament fills more textual space than the sojourn at the foot of Sinai. The people arrive at Sinai in Ex 19:1 and stay there until Nm 10:10 (most of Exodus, all of Leviticus, and a section of Numbers). And the amount of space given to this topic is even greater when one considers that in Deuteronomy, at the end of the journey through the wilderness, Moses "repeats" the *torah*, for the benefit of the new generation, substituting the name Horeb for Sinai. It is there at Sinai that the people are to meet face-to-face God, who saved them, "the one who brought them out of Egypt." Once he had led the people to this meeting place with God, the sole purpose of his mission (Ex 3:12), Moses' mission is supposedly over. However, after hearing the Ten Commandments (Ex 20:1–17) and witnessing the thunder and lightning, the people feared and trembled, beseeching Moses to be their intermediary with God. "You speak to us and we will listen but do not let God speak to us or we will die" (Ex 20:19).[7] From this point on, communication between the people and God passes through Moses. Sinai is midway between Egypt, land of death, and the Land of the promise. It is a central station along the way, where God makes a covenant with the people. The Torah revealed at Sinai expresses the will of God for his people and sets the conditions that will enable them to live their vocation in the Land fully and forever.

The Tent, Where God Meets Man

In addition to the link between Torah and Land, there are other concepts of sacred space in the Torah. This is especially true in the last section of Exodus (chapters 25–31, 35–40) and in the first part of Leviticus (1–16).[8] The last section of Exodus is concerned with providing a sacred space where God meets man. Chapters 25 to 31 and 35 to 40 describe the construction of the Tent of Meeting, a space that provides continued intimacy between God and Israel after the latter left the precincts of Sinai. The first part of Leviticus focuses on the persons serving as functionaries in the tent, on the conditions required for entering the tent, and on the various rites that facilitate drawing close to God. The tent is not the Land but rather the model for the future temple to be constructed in Jerusalem, at the center of the Land. The tent represents, in some respects, the ideal space, a new world where God lives in intimacy with the people, after the vestiges of sin have been erased. It is interesting to note that some of the details of the construction of the tent recall the Creation narratives.[9] Unlike the Land, the tent is mobile and moves from place to place with the people. The Glory of God that fills the tent once it is in place directs the movement of the people and is the decisive dynamic factor in the journey to the Land.

The historical books take up the theme of the Tent and its transformations into a multiplicity of sanctuaries scattered throughout the Land. This multiplicity will eventually give way to the centralized cult at the temple in Jerusalem, a process finally concluded at the time of King Josiah (621). However, the temple will be destroyed (587) and restored.[10] The Land and the temple are major themes in the historical narratives. In the Torah, the tribe responsible for conducting the cult, the service of God in the tent and later in the temple, does not receive a share in the Land. The Levites are set apart by God "to carry the ark of the covenant of the Lord, to stand before the Lord to minister to him, and to bless in his name to this day" (Dt 10:8). Their heritage is not a parcel of land given by God but rather God himself, the giver of all land. "Therefore Levi has no allotment or inheritance with his kindred; the Lord is his inheritance" (Dt 10:9, 18:2).

A large portion of the Torah concerns the Land and what the people are required to do once they enter it. They must not forget that the Land given to them by God remains his. God has given it to them as space to be used in carrying out their mission of sanctifying time and place. Once they arrive in the Land, three considerations are of prime importance[11]:

(1) The Torah insists that the Land is meant to be space in which the God of Israel is worshiped. This God is not just any god: he is the one who revealed himself to Moses on Mount Sinai. There is a constant temptation to create a god, under human control and serving the human person. Brueggemann points out that this is "transcendence . . . domesticated."[12]

(2) The Land is where the Sabbath is kept not only by men but also by the Land itself (every seven years). According to Brueggemann, "Landed people are tempted to create a sabbathless society in which land is never rested, debts are never canceled, slaves are never released, nothing is changed from the way it now is and has always been."[13]

(3) The Land is where the Torah is fully applied according to all its constraints. This must be clear from the way that justice (*mishpat*) is practiced. Particular attention must be paid to the poor, the alien, the widow, the orphan and the Levite, who has no land of his own. Thus, the Land is the space in which the obligations of the covenant are carried out. But the covenant has two part-

ners: God who freed his people from slavery so they could serve him, and one's neighbor who must be loved in a juridical sense by respecting his dignity and rights.

The Gift of the Land and Its Obligations

"If you obey the commandments of the Lord your God that I am commanding you today, by loving the Lord your God, walking in his ways, and observing his commandments, decrees and ordinances, then you shall live and become numerous, and the Lord your God will bless you in the Land you are entering to possess. But if your heart turns away and you do not hear, but are led astray to bow down to other gods and serve them, I declare to you today that you shall perish; you shall not live long in the Land that you are crossing the Jordan to enter and possess. I call heaven and earth to witness against you today that I have set before you life and death, blessings and curses. Choose life so that you and your descendants may live, loving the Lord your God, obeying him and holding fast to him; for that means life to you and length of days so that you may live in the Land that the Lord swore to give to your ancestors, to Abraham, to Isaac and to Jacob" (Dt 30:16–20).

At its very center, in the texts that speak of how Israel must become "a holy nation" in the Land, the Torah stresses that the Land belongs to God. In these texts, the call to holiness is central: "Be holy, for I the Lord your God am holy" (Lv 19:2).[14] In fact, the Land itself can only tolerate a holy people, "vomiting" out those who live in impurity. The gift of the Land to Israel is firmly linked to Israel's status as a holy nation and, in this context, Israel is reminded that the Land belongs to God: "The Land shall not be sold in perpetuity, for the Land is mine, with me you are but aliens and tenants" (Lv 25:23). God gives the Land to Israel as a locus in which to sanctify time and space and, for the Torah, this sanctification is ultimately fulfilled in the construction of the holy place with its holy rites, personnel, and feasts and the social and economic legislation that derives from this sanctification. The Land belongs to God and has been given to the people sanctified by God for a special purpose.

The Torah as "repeated" in Deuteronomy reaches its conclusion with the laws of Pentecost, the bringing of the first fruits of the Land to the temple. "You will take from the first fruits of the earth that you will produce from your Land that God is giving you" (Dt 26:2). The Land is the occasion to thank God for his gift, thus remembering the saving acts of God that have led the people from Egypt to its resting place. The crime excoriated above all else is to forget that all is gift and the fitting attitude is gratitude. The activity of the human person and the gift of God come together in the Land. Israel participates in its history as an adult. The Land is a space for making choices, choices that necessitate an orientation founded on righteousness and justice.

Blessings and curses refer to the Land (Ex 23, Lv 26, Dt 28). If the Torah is respected, the Land will be fertile and God will live among his people (Lv 26:11–13). However, if the Torah is violated, the Land will be left desolate, and the place of blessing and promise will become an abandoned wasteland. The gripping description of the curses in Deuteronomy 28 already evokes the destruction of the northern kingdom by the Assyrians in the eighth century and of Jerusalem by the Babylonians in the sixth century.

TROUBLING TEXTS

Some of the most troubling texts in the Torah that relate to the Land are undoubtedly those that underline that the Land promised to Israel is already inhabited by various peoples (cf. Ex 3:8, 6:2–4, 23:23–33, 33:1–3, 34:11–15, Nm 21:1–3.21–35, 33:50–56, Dt 2:33–36, 7:1–6.16–24, 9:1–6, 20:16–18).[15] According to Deuteronomy, seven nations are to be driven out of the Land (Dt 7:1). However, in Genesis, when the Land is promised to Abraham, ten nations are mentioned (Gn 15:19–21). The figures of seven and ten might possibly symbolize fullness; that all peoples apart from Israel and Israel's Torah are lost. It is the fate of these peoples that shocks the contemporary reader of the Bible.

The Violence of God

"You shall devour all the peoples that the Lord your God is giving over to you, showing them no pity; you shall not serve their gods, for that would be a snare for you. If you say to yourself, 'These nations are more numerous than I; how can I dispossess them?' do not be afraid of them. Just remember what the Lord your God did to Pharaoh and to all Egypt, the great trials that

your eyes saw, the signs and wonders, the mighty hand and the outstretched arm by which the Lord your God brought you out. The Lord your
God will do the same to all the peoples of whom you are afraid. Moreover,
the Lord your God will send the pestilence against them, until even the survivors and the fugitives are destroyed. Have no dread of them, for the Lord
your God who is present with you, is a great and awesome God. The Lord
your God will clear away these nations before you little by little; you will not
be able to make a quick end of them, otherwise the wild animals would become too numerous for you" (Dt 7:16–22).

God takes the Land from some and gives it to others. And to make matters worse, some passages describe in extremely violent terms the fate
inflicted on the populations that were driven out. "Know then today that
the Lord your God is the one who crosses over before you as a devour-
ing fire; he will defeat them and subdue them before you, so that you
may dispossess and destroy them quickly, as the Lord has promised
you" (Dt 9:3, cf. Ex 23:24, Dt 20:16–18). This theme is lyrically taken
up in numerous psalms that sing of the God of history (Ps, 78:54–55,
80:8, 105:43–44). Is God responsible for this genocidal ethnic cleansing? This question is all the more important that these biblical texts
have sometimes been used by people who have seen themselves as divinely chosen and under a divine mandate to embark on holy war. Although it might not be possible to resolve all of the difficulties posed
by these texts, a more careful reading of them suggests a number of
factors that make it more difficult for anyone to invoke them in order
to justify genocide or ethnic cleansing.

First, it must be underlined that the fate prescribed for these dispossessed peoples is seen as a punishment for their sins (Dt 9:4–5) and as
a preventative measure to stop them from leading Israel astray (Dt 7:4).
The nations are to "be vomited out" because they are not holy (Lv
18:24–30). The worst sin committed by the peoples who live in the
Land is not that they worship false gods but that they sacrifice their own
children to these gods (Dt 12:31). God is presented here not only as a
just God but also as a very demanding God, always concerned about
protecting his people, the object of his love. Furthermore, not all the
peoples encountered by Israel on their way are destined for extermina-
tion, as were the seven nations, or for permanent exclusion, as were the
Ammonites and the Moabites (Dt 23:3–6).[16] Other peoples are de-

scribed as brothers of the Israelites (the Edomites, Dt 23:7) or as close partners (the Egyptians, Dt 23:8). In contrast to the passages recounting wars of destruction, there are others that insist on the love of strangers in memory of Israel's own situation at the time of its foundation. "You shall also love the stranger for you were strangers in the land of Egypt" (Dt 10:19).

Second, the terrible fate of the nations who lived in the Land will be the fate of Israel if Israel follows their way of sin. "If you do forget the Lord your God and follow other gods to serve and worship them, I solemnly warn you today that you shall surely perish. Like the nations that the Lord is destroying before you, so shall you perish, because you would not obey the voice of the Lord your God" (Dt 8:19–20, cf. 4:26–28, 7:4). This fact is strikingly taken up in the legal part of the Deuteronomistic code that legislates the fate of an idolatrous city in Israel (Dt 13:12–18). "You shall put the inhabitants of that town to the sword, utterly destroying it and everything in it—even putting its livestock to the sword" (Dt 13:15). The Land itself can only tolerate a holy people as it vomits out those who live in impurity. The nations who lived in the Land have been vomited out because of their practices that illustrated their lack of holiness and this will be Israel's fate too if Israel does not live according to the Torah of holiness (Lv 18:28).

Third, without justifying these vindictive texts, capable of inspiring violent behavior, one can indeed doubt whether their injunctions were ever put into practice. It seems rather that Israel continued to live in the midst of these peoples and might even have emerged from them as we shall see further on. One cannot forget that the Bible, Word of God, is also the word of human beings with all their limitations. This is one of the great contributions of the historical-critical critique of the Bible, which recognizes its human dimension in order to avoid dangerous fundamentalist manipulations of biblical texts.

CONTINUING ON TOWARD THE LAND

From Sinai the people proceed to the borders of the Land (Nm chapters 11–13). According to Deuteronomy, this voyage took only eleven days (Dt 1:2). The people have already received the Torah, which defines the terms of their relationship with God and with one another. At this point, they are about to receive the Land they were promised. Here they will finally be able to put the Torah into practice. However, the reports made by the spies sent out to reconnoiter the Land are full of fear. The people refuse to obey God's command to enter the Land. Although God describes the Land as a place of blessing and abundance, the giants encountered by the spies inspire fear. God exhorts the people to trust him when the moment comes to enter the Land they had been dreaming of for so long. "If you say to yourself, 'These nations are more numerous than I; how can I dispossess them?' do not be afraid of them. Just remember what the Lord your God did to Pharaoh and to all Egypt. . . . Have no dread of them, for the Lord your God, who is present with you, is a great and awesome God" (Dt 7:17–19.21). The people's lack of faith in God's word provokes his fury and he condemns Israel to wander in the wilderness for forty years. This sinful generation must die out (and Moses too) and a new generation brought forth before the people can cross the Jordan and enter the Land.

The Wilderness: Dream or Nightmare

The wilderness in the Pentateuch has more than one meaning. First, the wilderness is in opposition to cultivated land. Negatively, it represents a place of punishment for the sins of the first generation. During the wandering in the wilderness, the generation that had been slaves in Egypt is deprived of the Land toward which it was headed. For them, the wilderness is a frightening place, a place of hunger and thirst, of scorpions and serpents, the contrary of a Land "flowing with milk and honey." Here, there is no blessing and no rest, as suggested by the Psalmist: "For forty years I loathed that generation and said, 'They are a people whose hearts go astray, and they do not regard my ways.'" Therefore, in my anger I swore, "They shall not enter my rest'" (Ps 95:11). Elsewhere, the wilderness is described as *tohu* (cf. Dt 32:10, Ps 107:40, Jb 12:24) or *bohu* (Is 34:11), evoking the primordial chaos that reigned before creation. Although the period after the sin at Qadesh Barnea lasted forty years, it takes up no more than a few chapters in the Pentateuch.

However, depending on the context, the wilderness can be something other than a fearful place and can take on a more positive aspect. It is a place where God lives close to his people in an intimacy that calls for total dependence on and faith in him. Here, God reveals Himself as Father lovingly educating his son and preparing him to enter the Land that has been promised. "Remember the long way that the Lord your

God has led you these forty years in the wilderness, in order to humble you, testing you to know what was in your heart, whether or not you would keep his commandments. He humbled you by letting you hunger, then by feeding you with manna, with which neither you nor your ancestors were acquainted, in order to make you understand that one does not live by bread alone, but by every word that comes from the mouth of the Lord. The clothes on your back did not wear out and your feet did not swell these forty years. Know then in your heart that as a parent disciplines a child so the Lord your God disciplines you" (Dt 8:2–5). Later, the wilderness will be seen as the place where God and Israel, rediscovering their first love, re-establish a mutual relationship of trust. "Therefore I will now allure her, and bring her into the wilderness and speak tenderly to her" (Hos 2:14).

END OF THE JOURNEY

At the end of the Pentateuch in Deuteronomy, the new generation that has been formed in the wilderness is at the gates of the Land and about to enter it. Moses repeats the entire Torah for this new generation that was not at Sinai. Since their fathers have died, they are the ones called to learn the Torah so that, on entering the Land, they might live it and be blessing. Israel, who was still a child in the wilderness, is about to become a responsible and free adult. The Land just across the Jordan, until now a promise, is about to become a reality. The long discourses of Moses, exhorting the people to live the Torah, are poignant because he stands before the Land that he will not enter. Just before his death, Moses ascends Mount Nebo from where he contemplates the Land toward which he has led the people (Dt 34:1–4).

At last, the long march toward the Land is about to end. The Pentateuch had begun with the expulsion of Adam and Eve from the Garden of Eden. Deuteronomy prepares the people for entry into the Land, describing it in terms that evoke the garden that had been lost and is about to be regained. "For the Lord your God is bringing you into a good land, a land with flowing streams, with springs and underground waters welling up in valleys and hills, a land of wheat and barley, of vines and fig trees and pomegranates, a land of olive trees and honey, a land where you may eat bread without scarcity, where you will lack nothing, a land whose stones are iron and from whose hills you may mine copper. You shall eat your fill and bless the Lord your God for the good land that he has given you" (Dt 8:7–10). Adam lost the Garden through disobedience. Israel stands to regain the Garden through obedience to the Torah.

The Dream of Moses

"Mount Nebo provides not only a hopeful glimpse of the nation's future. It marks the unmistakable fissure that lies between revolutionary dreams—dreams of a just society in a bountiful landscape—and their realization. If Moses' 'eye was not dim, nor his natural force abated' (Dt 34:7) at the moment of his death, it is because he can now see not only the fulfillment of his national dreams but also their shortcomings. Moses is a member of the desert generation, and its critique of national premises is not entirely foreign to him. He realizes, with the ten rebellious spies, that the land of milk and honey may devour its inhabitants, that the fruitful land has its snares, that settling down in Canaan may turn out to be something of a curse rather than blessing. He realizes with the other giants of the desert generation, that a land that is "not sown" leaves more room for dreaming than a tilled land whose boundaries are determined via horrifying wars and bloodshed."[17]

THE LAND GIVEN AND CONQUERED (JOSHUA THROUGH 2 MACCABEES)

"My servant Moses is dead. Now proceed to cross the Jordan, you and all this people, into the Land that I am giving to them, to the Israelites" (Jos 1:2). With this divine commandment, the historical books of the Old Testament begin. The adverb "now" and the use of the present tense of the verb "I am giving" underline that a new period in the history of the people of Israel is about to begin. The Land now appears before them like a long-awaited actor on a stage. Toward the end of the Book of Joshua, the author affirms that "not one of the good promises that the Lord had made to the house of Israel had failed; all came to pass" (Jos 21:45). The gift of the Torah and the entry into a Land where the people are to live according to the Torah given at Sinai, lead again, as at the time of creation, to God wanting to bring his creative work to completion. The people can now expect to rest, as God rested at the end of creation. "And the Lord gave them rest (*wa-yanah*) on every side just as he had sworn to their ancestors" (Jos 21:44).

At the very beginning of the Book of Joshua, after having once again outlined the borders of the Land, the Torah is said to be the reason for possessing the Land (1:7–8). The historical books describe the occupation of the Land, the establishment of authority there and the organization of worship. Several references are made to the various altars erected by the Patriarchs throughout the Land, which has now been divided among the twelve tribes.

At the beginning of the Book of Joshua, the people prepare themselves to enter the Land. But exactly which Land? The beginning of the book reaffirms the vast borders of the Land promised to Abraham in Gn 15:18. However, these borders are clearly not those mentioned further on in the same Book of Joshua. When the people enter it is the Jordan (not the Euphrates) that marks the eastern border of the Land. In fact, at the end of Deuteronomy and just a few verses before the Book of Joshua's extended borders, Moses goes up Mount Nebo to contemplate from afar the Land he will not enter. There God shows him a Land whose borders are quite narrow (Dt 34:1–4, cf. Nm 34:1–12). Exactly what were the borders of the Land God gave to Israel? In the historical books the ambiguity is never fully cleared up. It would seem that the location of the borders is tied to the fidelity of the people, to their vocation and to their observance of the Torah. If indeed they live the Torah in fidelity, then the borders of the blessing are without limit and extend toward all the other nations.

The Deuteronomist: A Reading of Seven Centuries of History

The books of Joshua, Judges, 1 and 2 Samuel, and 1 and 2 Kings present a vast panorama of the history of Israel, beginning with the entry into the Land and ending with the expulsion and exile (at the end of 2 Kgs). Today, exegetes are of the opinion that, together with the book of Deuteronomy, this collection forms what is called the Deuteronomist history, written during or after the exile. At the time of the formation of the Pentateuch, Deuteronomy was detached from the collection. In their present form, these six books constitute a coherent whole. They try to explain how the entry into the Land of promise (Joshua) could end so badly (2 Kgs). Where was the mistake? In order to understand this, one has to reread history, paying particular attention to the discourses and exhortations that the author inserts into the narrative at particularly decisive moments, often the most tragic ones. These discourses are often the commentary of the narrator but are also sometimes placed in the mouths of the important characters in the story.

These seven centuries, as told in Joshua, Judges, and the books of Samuel and Kings, despite some privileged moments, are perceived as a progressive decadence. This begins already in the period of the judges and reaches its peak at the time of the schism between the tribes of the North and those of the South, after the death of Solomon (1 Kgs 12). This leads to a spiritual deterioration both in the society and in worship. The northern kingdom is wiped out in the eighth century, while Jerusalem and the Temple there are destroyed in the sixth century. In fact, the Torah was not lived out as God had expected. The negative evaluation of the historical experience of Israel is particularly striking in a long discourse at the time of the fall of Samaria (2 Kgs 17:7–23). It is further confirmed in 2 Kgs 21:11f. "Because King Manasseh of Judah has committed these abominations, has done things more wicked than all that the Amorites did who were before him, and has caused Judah also to sin with his idols, therefore thus says the Lord, the God of Israel, 'I am bringing upon Jerusalem and Judah such evil that the ears of everyone who hears of it will tingle.' Even the praiseworthy reforms of King Josiah come too late according to the historian. "Still the Lord did not turn from the fierceness of his great wrath by which his anger was kindled against Judah because of all the provocation which Manasseh had provoked him. The Lord said, 'I will remove Judah also out of my sight as I have removed Israel; and I will reject this city that I have chosen, Jerusalem, and the House of which I said: My name shall be there'" (2 Kgs 23:26–27).

The action begins with a request for help from the tribes already settled beyond the Jordan (Jos 1:12–18), followed by the sending of two spies to Jericho to obtain the help of Rahab the prostitute. Before the people cross the Jordan, they are commanded to purify themselves, just as they had done at Sinai (Ex 19:10–11). Their crossing the river, dry-shod, evokes the crossing of the Red Sea (4:23–24) and provokes terror in the hearts of the inhabitants of the area, who see this as a sign that God, the King of Israel, is with his people. The people of Israel, under God, their king, are about to confront the kings in the area. As soon as they have crossed, they circumcise themselves and keep the first Passover celebrated in the Land. This Passover marks the end of the period of manna, the food that had sustained them in the wilderness. The abundant fruits found in the Land "that flows with milk and honey" now replace the manna (5:11–12). This parallelism with the Sinai experience is underlined by Joshua's mysterious encounter with the Godhead recalling Moses' meeting at the Burning Bush (5:13–15). "The commander of the army of the Lord said to Joshua, 'Remove the sandals from your feet for the place where you stand is holy. And Joshua did so'" (5:15).

AT THE CENTER OF THE BOOK OF JOSHUA: THE LAND

In the Book of Joshua, the Land is central; the people enter it (Jos 1–5) and conquer it (Jos 6–12), after which it is divided among the tribes according to the provisions of the Torah (Jos 13–21). The kings of the Land (listed in Jos 12) are no match for the King of the Universe, who fights on behalf of the people he has made his own. Here again the reader is troubled by the spectacle of a God who fights on behalf of one people against others. Before entering the Land, the people have already experienced the conquest of lands beyond the Jordan, Heshbon and Bashan (Dt 2–3). These regions had been conquered and their inhabitants wiped out in order to inspire fear in the peoples living in the Land.

However, one has the feeling that, beyond the shocking orders given by God, the essential is to live in obedience to God's Word that directs history. Nothing can stand in the way of the people of God who pass among these nations petrified by fear. God does not treat all the nations encountered along the way in the same manner. He commands the people to pass peacefully through certain lands, not to enter others and finally to conquer still others. A particularly chilling description of destruction is that of the entire city of Jericho. "Then they devoted to destruction by the edge of the sword all in the city: both man to woman, young and old, oxen, sheep and donkeys" (Jos 6:21).[18] The subsequent destruction of the city of Ai and the annihilation of its twelve thousand residents is equally dramatic (Jos 8:1–29). Later, we will return to these particularly troubling texts, examining both their original meaning and their interpretation today.

Despite the impression that the conquest took place without any particular problems, it seems that the entry into the Land was more difficult than what appears at first sight. "Now Joshua was old and advanced in years and the Lord said to him, 'You are old and advanced in years and very much of the Land still remains to be possessed'" (13:1). The partition of the Land among the tribes and its geographical contours are lovingly described in all their details in the long chapters that follow (13–21). Toward the end of the book, before underlining the importance of the Torah and the covenant (22–25), the narrative tells us that the promises of God have been fulfilled. "Thus the Lord gave to Israel all the Land that he swore to their ancestors that he would give them: and having taken possession of it, they settled there. And the Lord gave them rest on every side just as he had sworn to their ancestors; not one of all their enemies had withstood them, for the Lord had given all their enemies into their hands. Not one of all the good promises that the Lord had made to the house of Israel had failed, all came to pass" (Jos 21:43–45).

Land and Torah come together here in perfect harmony, recalling the original blessing in the Garden of Eden. However, this harmony in the Book of Joshua is deceptive because the story has just begun. As the book draws to a close it reaffirms both the blessing that the Land represents and its obligations for the children of Israel. "I gave you a Land on which you had not labored and towns that you had not built and you live in them; you eat the fruit of vineyards and olive groves that you did not plant. Now therefore revere the Lord and serve him in sincerity and in faithfulness. Put away the gods that your ancestors served beyond the River and in Egypt and serve the Lord" (24:13–14).

FROM JOSHUA TO JUDGES

What is the exact relation between the narratives in Joshua and those in Judges? Though Judges appears to be the sequel to Joshua, its treatment of the Land is fundamentally different. Whereas in Joshua, the people seem to sweep through the Land with little opposition and under divine inspiration, in Judges, the conquest is slow, less successful and, in fact, more uncertain and ultimately tragic. The difference between the two perspectives hinges, in the final analysis, on the obedience to the Torah. In Joshua, the people have stated clearly and repeatedly that they intend to listen to God. In Judges, however, they show themselves profoundly sinful, incapable of living according to the Torah. This is directly linked to their failure in conquering the Land. "Now the angel of the Lord went up from Gilgal to Bokim and said, 'I brought you up from Egypt and brought you into the Land that I had promised to your ancestors. I said, I will never break my covenant with you. For your part, do not make a covenant with the inhabitants of this Land, tear down their altars.'" But you have not obeyed my command. See what you have done? So now I say, 'I will not drive them out before you but they shall become adversaries to you'" (Jg 2:1–3 cf. 2:20–21). The logic is clear. The people abandon God and God abandons the people. In a repetitive cycle throughout the Book of Judges, the people sin. God punishes them by sending oppressors, the people cry out to God, God returns to them by sending a savior (cf. 2:10–16).

The oppressive kings encountered by the people as they arrive in the Land have a lot in common with the Pharaoh of the Exodus. Like Pharaoh, they are unable to resist the God-inspired judges who come to the rescue of the people. Each one is defeated in turn. They are twelve judges, symbolizing the twelve tribes of Israel. A turning point in the story takes place after the death of Gideon, the great judge who liberates the people from the Midianites. At the end of his life, he repeats one of the fundamental principles in the relationship between the people and their God. "I will not rule over you and my son will not rule over you. The Lord will rule over you" (Jg 8:23). Here, Gideon takes up the cry of Moses as he crosses the Sea dry-shod, at the moment of the birth of the people: "The Lord will reign for ever and ever" (Ex 15:18). However, it is Gideon's son, Abimelekh, who imposes himself as king over Israel and provides the first model for a king in the Land. Far from exemplary, he sets the tone for the kings who will succeed him, many of whom will leave bad memories behind them. The picture is not edifying as it was in the time of Joshua. Israel gives the sad impression of having sunk deeply into sin with only a few passing moments of repentance. The Torah is not lived and thus the gift of the Land is threatened. Israel, called to be a model for all peoples, has become like the other nations. What a chasm there is between God's plan to make of the holy people a blessing for all nations and this decadence. Judges ends with an ambiguous statement: "In those days there was no king in Israel; all the people did what was right in their own eyes" (21:25). Clearly, on one level and in contrast to its surrounding neighbors, Israel has no king. However, on another level, the author seems to be saying that Israel has refused to accept the kingship of God. This lucid assessment sets the tone for the subsequent historical books, where, with only a few exceptions, the life of the people is one of sin and infidelity.

The Book of Ruth, which recounts the magnificent tale of the Moabite woman who enters Israel's covenant by choice, provides an introduction to the story of the Kings of Israel (1 and 2 Samuel and 1 and 2 Kings). In the Christian tradition, the choice of this spot for positioning the Book of Ruth is significant.[19] Robert Alter has astutely described how the story of Ruth transforms the motifs of gender and geography that one finds in other love stories that take place at watering spots. Here the hero is a woman not a man and she is a Moabite, making the biblical Land a "foreign" land for her.[20] In this "foreign" land, which is also our biblical Land, Ruth meets her future husband Boaz. Because of her attachment to her mother-in-law Naomi, Ruth follows her to an unknown land that becomes the land of her destiny. Ruth is a Gentile pagan whose faith in the God of Israel provides a model for conversion. "Ruth is conceived by the author as a kind of matriarch by adoption . . . Boaz essentially established that Ruth's courage and her loyalty to her mother-in-law will amply serve in place of a genealogy."[21] Like Rahab before her, at the beginning of the Book of Joshua, she represents the neighboring peoples, which are often represented as a danger to Israel. According to the Torah, they and especially their women must be avoided lest they lead Israel astray. Nevertheless, Rahab and Ruth are models of a perfect faith lived in obedience to a God of their choice. These two women challenge a simplistic concept of a Land said to be inhabited by people fit only for destruction. Israel, who should have been an example for the nations, is unfaithful to its vocation. The nations, called to follow the example of Israel, can in fact offer Israel these two models to be followed in the persons of Rahab and Ruth.

THE RISE OF KINGSHIP

The demand made to Samuel by the elders that he give them a king to reign over them underlines the full extent of Israel's sin. The people want to be like the surrounding nations. "Appoint for us then a king to govern us like other nations" (1 Sam 8:5). For Samuel, the tragedy is twofold. First, he, the exemplary judge, has to endure the disgrace of unworthy sons, incapable of continuing his work. Second, the people themselves reject the kingship of God, preferring a king of flesh and blood. At God's command, Samuel cedes to the people's desire. However, he must warn them of the danger of having a tyrannical and cruel king like Pharaoh. He will then transform the children of Israel into slaves: "he will take one tenth of your flocks and you shall be his slaves" (1 Sam 8:17). Yet the elders insist and repeat their refusal of

God's kingship. "But the people refused to listen to the voice of Samuel. They said, 'No! but we are determined to have a king over us. So that we also may be like other nations and that our king may govern us and go out before us and fight our battles'" (1 Sam 8:19–20).

Thus begins the long history of the kings of Israel. Although some are presented as righteous and just, most of the kings are judged severely by the historian of the books of Kings. Even David, the beloved of God, who replaces Saul, the first king, chosen and then rejected by God, committed a terrible sin.[22] Nathan denounces him in these terms: "Why have you despised the word of the Lord, to do what is evil in his sight? You have struck down Uriah the Hittite with the sword and have taken his wife to be your wife and have killed him with the sword of the Ammonites" (2 Sam 12:9). In the books of Kings, a refrain repeats itself as one king succeeds another: "He did what is evil in the sight of the Lord, walking in the way of his ancestor and in the sin that he caused Israel to commit" (1 Kgs 15:26). Ahab son of Omri, king of Israel, surpasses all his predecessors in his infidelity: He "did evil in the sight of the Lord more than all who were before him" (1 Kgs 16:30).

It is no longer God who rules over the Land through the mediation of a faithful king but rather a man led by his passion for power. To be sure, the king continues the work begun by Joshua and the judges in trying to subdue the Land. However, it is no longer the Torah that inspires his actions. He engages in wars in order to extend his own power rather than the kingdom of God, in faithfulness to the Torah. The Land is ruled according to the will of a human king and no longer according to God's Torah. In terms of the Land, David's conquest of Jerusalem is a defining moment because from then on Jerusalem becomes the center of the Land. After the conquest, the Ark of the Covenant is brought into the city. In some biblical traditions, Jerusalem in itself comes to represent the entire Land. By its practice of the Torah, Jerusalem is to be the glorious and faithful city, a shining example of godly life. However, through its infidelity, Jerusalem is all too often a new Sodom and Gomorrah, locked in sinfulness.

A Temple for God?

The confusion between the two models of kingship, the human king and the kingship of God, is evident in David's decision that the time has come to construct a temple—a holy dwelling place for God. Having pacified the Land and built a palace for himself, the king believes that the appropriate moment has come to construct a temple for God that will serve as God's palace. In the process, he treats God according to human standards. But God will have none of it as he makes known to David through Nathan the prophet. "Go and tell my servant David, 'Thus says the Lord: Are you the one to build me a house to live in? I have not lived in a house since the day I brought up the people of Israel from Egypt to this day, but have been moving about in a tent and a tabernacle'" (2 Sam 7:5–6).[23] It is not David who will build a house for God but God who promises David a house, which is a dynasty of kings open to his inspiration and willing to accept him as their Father.

God's promise to David does not produce miracles among the kings of Israel. Intrigue and sin multiply themselves, beginning with David's own sin of lust and murder. The sons of David revolt against him, compelling him to flee. Eventually Solomon succeeds David amidst all-too-human intrigues. He is the object of both praise and castigation—a more complex model of human kingship than his father. God is pleased with his prayer of supplication: "Because you have asked this and have not asked for yourself long life or riches or the lives of your enemies, but have asked for yourself understanding to discern what is right . . . I give you a wise and discerning mind" (1 Kgs 3:11–12). Later on, however, God reproaches Solomon for his bevy of wives and concubines who spread idolatry in the Land of the covenant. Almost half of the Solomon narrative is, nevertheless, taken up with the construction of the temple. In his letter to Hiram, king of Tyre, explaining his decision to build a temple, Solomon seems to ignore God's objections to being confined to a humanly constructed edifice. He asks Hiram to provide cedars for the temple, just as he had for the palace of David. Hiram, presented as the son of an Israelite mother, plays a central role in a construction project that recalls the construction of the tent in the wilderness (Ex 25–40) as well as the creation of the cosmos. Hiram, a non-Israelite king, and Solomon, king of Israel, collaborate in this project. However, the ambiguity remains because the construction of Solomon's own palace is inserted within the narrative of the construction of the temple (1 Kgs 7:1–12).

The construction of a temple for God in Jerusalem changed the vision of the Land. Jerusalem, the Holy City, is now at the center of the Land that had been promised and conquered. In Solomon's long prayer at the dedication of the temple, he emphasizes the special vocation of this holy place for the pagans who might come there. "Likewise, when a foreigner, who is not of your people Israel, comes from a distant land because of your name—for they shall hear of your name, your mighty hand and your outstretched arm—when a foreigner comes and prays toward this house, then hear in heaven your dwelling place, and do according to all that the foreigner calls to you, so that all the peoples of the earth may know your name and fear you, as do your people Israel, and so that they may know that your name has been invoked on this house that I have built" (1 Kgs 8:41–43). The holy space represented by the temple has a universal dimension. "My house shall be called a house of prayer for all peoples" (Is 56:7).

Solomon's decadence toward the end of his reign throws a shadow on his times of glory. His attraction to foreign women leads him to worship their gods. At the end of his life, he does not escape the same indictment that haunts his descendants and successors: "So Solomon did what was evil in the sight of the Lord and did not completely follow the Lord, as his father David had done" (1 Kgs 11:6). In fact, the description of Solomon at the end of 1 Kgs 10 and 11 evokes exactly the type of king Israel is not supposed to have according to the Torah. "Even so he must not acquire many horses for himself, or return the people to Egypt in order to acquire more horses, since the Lord has said to you, 'You must never return that way again.' And he must not acquire many wives for himself, or else his heart would turn away; also silver and gold he must not acquire in great quantity for himself. When he has taken the throne of his kingdom, he shall have a copy of this law written for him in the presence of the Levitical priests. It shall remain with him and he shall read in it all the days of his life, so that he may learn to fear the Lord his God, diligently observing all the words of this law and these statutes" (Dt 17:16–19).

THE DECLINE

Upon Solomon's death, a major downtrend sets in. The kingdom is divided and thus the Land is dominated not by one human king, but by two. The political division is accompanied by a religious schism. The sanctuary in Bethel now competes with the one in Jerusalem. From this point on the books of Kings follow the story of the kings of the two kingdoms until their ultimate destruction, first of the northern kingdom of Israel in 721 and then of the southern kingdom of Judah in 586. The story of King Ahab and his Sidonian consort Jezebel might well characterize the general pattern of the kings of Israel and Judah. Their lack of righteousness before God is reflected in their lack of justice toward their subjects. This is brutally exemplified in the story of Naboth's vineyard (1 Kgs 21), object of Ahab's coveting. Driven by jealousy and supported by Jezebel, the king succeeds in taking the vineyard away from Naboth: nothing can resist corrupt power. However, confronting him is Elijah the Prophet who, in the name of God, denounces the sin of the king who stole land from one of his own subjects. "You shall say to him, " 'Thus says the Lord: Have you killed and also taken possession?' You shall say to him, " 'Thus says the Lord: In the place where dogs licked up the blood of Naboth, dogs will also lick up your blood' " (1 Kgs 21:19). The indictment of the king echoes the indictment of the nations that Israel drove out of the Land at the time of the conquest.

The indictment reaches fever pitch with King Ahaz in Judah. "Ahaz was twenty years old when he began to reign; he reigned sixteen years in Jerusalem. He did not do what was right in the sight of the Lord his God as his ancestor David had done, but he walked in the way of the kings of Israel. He even made his son pass through fire, according to the abominable practices of the nations whom the Lord drove out before the people of Israel. He sacrificed and made offerings on the high places, on the hills and under every green tree" (2 Kgs 16:2–4). King Manasseh also had his son pass through fire (2 Kgs 21:6 cf. 2 Chr 33:6). This is one of the sins for which the nations that preceded Israel are specifically blamed (cf. Lv 18:21, Dt 18:10).[24] Wars, famines, internecine strife, and disease come to characterize this land, which, according to the promise, was supposed to be a blessed land. Despite the apparent power of the kings, the number of aggressions increased, whether from within (usurpers or upstart pretenders to the throne) or from without (the great Empires of Assyria, Babylonia, and Egypt, or regional potentates).

But the sin of the kings is also the sin of the people. Eventually, the Land will be lost because the covenant has been contravened so blatantly that the relationship between God and Israel has been emptied of all meaning. When the Assyrians invade and destroy the northern kingdom, the biblical historian is quite lucid. "This occurred because the people of Israel had sinned against the Lord their God, who had brought them up out of the land of Egypt, from under the hand of Pharaoh, king of Egypt. They had worshipped other gods and walked in the customs of the nations whom the Lord drove out before the people of Israel, and in the customs that the kings of Israel had introduced. The people of Israel secretly did things that were not right against the Lord their God. They built for themselves high places at all their towns, from watchtower to fortified city" (2 Kgs 17:7–9). "They made their sons and their daughters pass through fire" (2 Kgs 17:17).

The consequence of all this is exile: "Therefore the Lord was very angry with Israel and removed them from out of his sight" (2 Kgs 17:18). In commenting on the meaning of history, the author already foresees the fate that awaits the southern kingdom of Judah some 150 years later. "None was left but the tribe of Judah alone. Judah also did not keep the commandments of the Lord their God but walked in the customs that Israel had introduced" (2 Kgs 17:18–19). God who had hoped to work through Israel for the salvation of the nations now works through the nations to punish rebellious Israel. This is repeated at the end of 2 Kgs. "Indeed, Jerusalem and Judah so angered the Lord that he expelled them from his presence" (2 Kgs 24:20).

During the exile, there was a new awareness of God and the Land. After five decades, the exiles were able to return to their land when Cyrus, the king of Persia, overthrew the Babylonian Empire. However, those who returned were not able to regain the full political autonomy they had enjoyed in the past. The small, reconstituted province of Judah remained under firm Persian and later Hellenistic hegemony. In addition, not all the people returned to the Land. At first, life in exile had been imposed on the people, but as time went on, some chose it of their own free will. The exile gave rise to a new way of living the Torah. Life in exile, therefore, had its positive aspects as well. Remaining faithful to the Torah became a way of bearing witness to the God of Israel before the nations. For those who did not return, the Land, as circumscribed by specific borders, no longer had the same importance as it had had in the past.

JERUSALEM AND THE TEMPLE

In the remaining historical books of the Old Testament, the Land is less important than Jerusalem. Restored after the return from exile, it becomes the center of worship. In the post-Exilic rewriting of the history of the people, in the books of Chronicles, Ezra, and Nehemiah, the focus is on the temple and on the role of the priests in worship.[25] The geographically defined concept of Land is overshadowed because, from then on and for a long time, political authority is in the hands of foreign overlords, first the Persians, then the Greeks, and finally the Romans. In rewriting the history of David and Solomon, the Chronicler emphasizes the centrality of worship, attributing its origin to King David, whose importance is put on a par with Moses in the Pentateuch. The long history of the people contained in 1 and 2 Chronicles ends with the decree of Cyrus sending the people back to their land to rebuild the temple. "The Lord, the God of heaven, has given me all the kingdoms of the earth, and he has charged me to build him a house at Jerusalem, which is in Judah. Whoever is among you of all his people, may the Lord his God be with him! Let him go up" (2Chr 36:23). The importance given to Cyrus, called the "messiah" (the anointed one) by Deutero-Isaiah (Is 45:1), is astonishing. His role resembles that of Hiram in the building of the First Temple at the time of Solomon, recalling once again the universal vocation of Israel regarding the Land and the worship of God.

The building of the temple is recounted in the books of Ezra and Nehemiah. In these writings there are clear references to the Book of Joshua and to the first entry into the Land. The Land must be purified (Ezr 9:10–12) and the Torah obeyed. Both Ezra and Nehemiah forbid marriages to foreign women, a clear reference to Joshua's "cleansing" of the Land as well as to the sinfulness of Solomon with his bevy of foreign wives (Ezr 10:10–11, Neh 13:23–25). The purity of the Land depends on the purity of the people.[26] Likewise, the Book of Nehemiah clearly insists that the Land and the people must both observe the *Shabbat* (Neh 13:15–18) and refrain from enslaving their brothers and sisters (Neh 5:3–5).

With the loss of the Land after the Babylonian invasion, an important period begins, that of the exile. Even though its details are overlooked in the historical books that emerged at this time, the exile is nonetheless a decisive moment in the birth of Judaism. From the Book of Joshua to 2 Kings, the same painful question keeps recurring: how did we get to where we are? How did we lose the Land that we were given? The second series of history books, from 1 Chronicles to Nehemiah, asks the question: how did we manage to return to the Land and rebuild the temple? The fact that the people survive the exile and return to rebuild Jerusalem and the temple shows beyond all else God's eternal faithfulness to his people despite their infidelity. However, the people's survival in exile indicates that the Land is not as essential to the life of the people with God as was previously thought.

The only two books whose setting is the exile are Tobit and Esther. Tobit lives in Nineveh in Assyria, presumably deported there after the destruction of the northern kingdom in the eighth century B.C. (cf. Tb 1:2). Esther lives in Shushan in Persia, her family exiled there by the Babylonians after the destruction of Jerusalem (cf. Es [Gr] 1:3). These two figures exemplify faithfulness to the Torah in the midst of the nations. Though the Land hardly figures at all in these writings, Jewish life is lived to the fullest without the Land or the temple. Nevertheless, the omission of the exile from the conscious recounting of Israel's history is a striking void and suggests that Israel's exile from the Land parallels the wilderness experience in the Torah: a passing experience that is both a punishment and a pedagogy. Even the seemingly "nationalist" wars of Judith and the Maccabees, with their echoes of the books of Joshua and Judges, focus more on the defense, purity, and practice of worship than on the sovereignty or borders of the Land.

THE LAND ALREADY AND NOT YET WON (JOB–ECCLESIASTICUS)

The third part of the canon of the Christian Old Testament is made up of Wisdom literature. In their diversity, each of the books serves as a reminder that revelation does not replace human experience in the life of the believer. Wisdom literature tells of the human search for a better understanding of God, the world, and human beings. To this end, the sages use the tools of human language and culture, particularly the literary styles favored in the ancient Near East: prose, song, poetry, philosophical dialogues, aphorisms, and proverbs. With their specific originality and, sometimes, their contrasts, Wisdom literature, ostensibly a human expression, and Torah, the divinely revealed Law, are always converging; both are parts of the same canon. Even if attained by more belabored ways, true human wisdom eventually blends in with the divine will expressed in the Torah. The blessed person is the one who finds his "delight in the law of the Lord," as underlined in the first Psalm (Ps 1:2, cf. Ps 119:1). With regard to the Land, Wisdom literature portrays a man who shares the human condition and who is deeply rooted in a very specific Land.

Wisdom literature stresses the universal rather than the particular. In contrast with the historical books that tell the particular and contingent history of Israel, Wisdom deals with human experience that is relevant always and everywhere. Land is, therefore, omnipresent, as it is in the saga of creation, because it is the very space for human existence. Even if the order of the biblical books is often variable here, the Book of Job is generally placed first among the Wisdom books in the Christian canon. Job has no genealogy and thus cannot be considered a son of Israel. His "land" is Uz (Jb 1:1) and not Israel, which confirms the tradition, both Jewish and Christian, that he is a Gentile. God in the Book of Job is the God of creation and the Law of God's creation is Wisdom rather than Torah. "Truly, the fear of the Lord, that is wisdom; and to depart from evil is understanding" (Jb 28:28). The universality underlined in the Book of Job, thus placed at the very beginning of the books of Wisdom, is an important indication regarding the place of the Land in wisdom literature. Even if it is mentioned in a few psalms that recall the history of the conquest, the specificity of the land of Israel is not the focus of Wisdom's concern. It would seem that in this part of the canon the Land (*aretz*) refers to the earth (*adamah*) as understood in the creation accounts at the beginning of the Torah where the particular gives way to the universal. What is at stake here is the convergence of human wisdom and divine will. This convergence is inscribed in the space offered by the whole of creation, beyond the restricted boundaries of the Land promised by God to Israel.

In the rich variety of Psalms there are references to the Land in its specificity. In Psalm 42, the psalmist, exiled in a distant country, expresses his nostalgia for the Land as a profound longing for intimacy with his God. Far from the Land, the psalmist is aware that God is his only permanent shelter. In Psalm 44, the psalmist laments the loss of the Land given by God. "You have made us like sheep for slaughter, and have scattered us among the nations" (Ps 44:11). He recalls the events recounted in the historical books. "You with your own hand drove out the nations, but them you planted; you afflicted the peoples, but them you set free" (Ps 44:2). However, this reminder is placed within the framework of God's covenant and of the people's corresponding debt toward God. "For not by their own sword did they win the Land, nor did their own arm give them victory, but your right hand and your arm, and the light of your countenance, for you delighted in them" (Ps 44:3). Here, the psalmist refuses to admit any guilt on his part and instead rouses God to action in order to end Israel's humiliation. "Rouse yourself, why do you asleep, oh Lord? Awake, do not cast us off for ever" (Ps 44:23). Other psalms also mention this national perspective, some celebrating the conquest of and entry into the Land (cf. Ps 68, 78, 83, 105, 108, 135, etc.), others lamenting the loss of the Land (cf. Ps 60, 74, 79, 80, 89, 106, 137), and still others joyfully proclaiming the triumphant return from exile. "When the Lord restored the fortunes of Zion, we were like those who dream. Then our mouth was filled with laughter, and our tongue with shouts of joy. Then it was said among the nations, 'The Lord has done great things for them'" (Ps 126:1–2).

But the dominant perspective in the Psalms is the universality of God's reign. Psalm 47 proclaims God's kingship over all creation, manifested through the election of Israel. The vocation of Jerusalem and her temple is to promote the universality of divine rule (Ps 48). More explicitly, Psalm 87 proclaims the universal significance of Israel's uniqueness in a hymn to Jerusalem. "Among those who know me, I mention Rahab and Babylon; Philistia too, and Tyre with Ethiopia, 'This one was born here,' they say. And of Zion it shall be said, 'This one and that one were born in it'" (Ps 87:4–5). In conclusion, the psalmist echoes the universality, proper to Wisdom literature: "All my springs are in you" (Ps 87:7).

Land of Dreams, Land of Violence

The rivers of Babylon—there we sat down and there we wept when we remembered Zion. On the willows there we hung up our harps.

For there our captors asked us for songs, and our tormentors asked us for mirth, saying, "Sing us one of the songs of Zion."

How could we sing the Lord's song in a foreign land? If I forget you, oh Jerusalem, let my right hand wither!

Let my tongue cling to the roof of my mouth if I do not remember you! If I do not set Jerusalem above my highest joy!

Remember, oh Lord, against the Edomites the day of Jerusalem's fall, how they said, "Tear it down. Down to its foundations!"

Oh daughter Babylon, you devastator, happy shall they be who pay you back what you have done to us! Happy shall they who take your little ones and dash them against the rock! (Ps 137)

Whereas tradition attributes the psalms to King David, four of the seven Wisdom books are attributed to King Solomon. This is not surprising, if one remembers the great wisdom for which Solomon is reputed (cf. 1 Kgs 3:12, 4:31, 5:7). In three of these works, written in Hebrew— Proverbs, Kohelet (Ecclesiastes), and Song of Songs—the Land plays no special role. None of these books deals with the particular history of Israel or the specificity of the Land. However, in the fourth work attributed to Solomon, the Wisdom of Solomon (written in Greek in the first century B.C.), the author reflects on the wisdom found in creation and in the history of salvation, particularly during the Exodus. The Land figures in this writing within the context of Wisdom's forceful rejection of idolatry. Although the principal wrongdoer in Wisdom is Egypt, the former inhabitants of the Land of Canaan are also mentioned. They are portrayed as unrepentant idolaters, punished by God. "Those who lived long ago in your holy Land, you hated for their detestable practices, their works of sorcery and unholy rites, their merciless slaughter of children and their sacrificial feasting on human flesh and blood. These initiates from the midst of a heathen cult, these parents who murder helpless lives, you willed to destroy by the hands of our ancestors, so that the Land most precious of all to you might receive a worthy colony of the servants of God" (Wis 12:3–7). These people must be vanquished by Israel, who have not succumbed to idolatry in any way. "For even if we sin we are yours, knowing your power; but we will not sin because we know that you acknowledge us as yours" (Wis 15:2, cf. 15:1–6). The author does not linger on the details of history, contenting himself with historical reflections in his attack on idolatry.

The book of Jesus ben Sirach (Ecclesiasticus), also a late wisdom writing, has a similar structure to the Book of Wisdom. Divided into three parts, it presents sayings about wisdom in general, wisdom in creation, and wisdom in history. The last part is a reflection on the history of Israel, praising the great men of Israel in generations past. It is interesting to note that references to the Land are made within a context of universality (Sir 36:17–22). The reflection takes up the themes in the first chapters of Genesis. The earth is full of the gifts of God (Sir 16:29). Man is taken from the earth (17:1, 33:10) and is expelled from the Garden in the Land because of his sin (17:23). The universal vocation of Abraham is stressed. "Therefore the Lord assured him with an oath that the nations would be blessed through his offspring; that he would make him as numerous as the dust on the earth, and exalt his offspring like the stars, and give them an inheritance from sea to sea and from the Euphrates to the ends of the earth" (44:21). The vastness of the Land is linked to the universality of the blessing that comes through Abraham. Likewise, the praise of Joshua and his victories against the Gentile nations in the Land are focused less on his having "cleansed" the Land of their presence than on his having made them aware that, by their deeds, they were behaving as enemies of God. The nations are defeated so that they "might know his armament, that he was fighting in the sight of the Lord" (Sir 46:6).

In the middle of this list of famous men, the author relates the destruction of the northern kingdom of Israel in terms that recall the historical books. "Despite all this the people did not repent nor did they forsake their sins, until they were carried off as plunder from their Land and were scattered over all the earth" (Sir 48:15). The author explains that the destruction of Jerusalem is a consequence of the sins of the kings, among whom only three are praised. "Except for David and Hezekiah and Josiah, all of them were great sinners, for they abandoned the Law of the Most High, the kings of Judah came to an end. They gave their power to others and their glory to a foreign nation, who set fire to the chosen city of the sanctuary and made its streets desolate" (Sir 49:4–6). This is the fulfillment of what had been prophesied by Jeremiah. "All who found them have devoured them, and their enemies have said, 'We are not guilty, because they have sinned against the Lord, the true pasture, the Lord, the hope of their ancestors!'" (Jer 50:7, cf. Sir 49:7). As in the historical books, the period of the exile is passed over in silence. However, the restoration and particularly the repair of the temple carried out by Simon the high priest are highly praised. As before, there is a shift in emphasis from a focus on the Land and political sovereignty to a focus on the temple and temple worship.

In conclusion, it may be noted that there is a double convergence in Wisdom literature. On the one hand, wisdom and Torah tend to come together: "All this is the book of the covenant of the Most High God, the Law that Moses commanded us" (Sir 24:23). On the other hand, the land of Israel exemplifies the entire surface of the earth. This is particularly clear in Ben Sirach 24. The land of Israel must become a model for the whole surface of the earth, in terms of human experience and search for God. "Over waves of the sea, over all the earth and over every people and nation I have held sway. Among all these I sought a resting place; in whose territory should I abide. Then the Creator of all things gave me a command, and my Creator chose the place for my tent. He said, 'Make your dwelling in Jacob, and in Israel receive your inheritance'" (Sir 24:6–8). And in conclusion: "Observe that I have not labored for myself alone, but for all who seek wisdom" (Sir 24:34).

THE LAND THREATENED, LOST, AND PROMISED AGAIN (ISAIAH THROUGH MALACHI)

In our canonical presentation of the Land in the Bible, there is yet another essential figure to discuss, namely, the prophet. The word *prophet* first appears in the Bible in connection with Abraham when God himself addresses Abimelech, king of Gerar, who had taken Sarah, Abraham's wife: "Now then return the man's wife; for he is a prophet and he will pray for you and you shall live" (Gn 20:7). This function of intercessor is repeatedly taken up in the Torah, particular when Moses intercedes before God for the people who have sinned. Moses, within the canon of the Old Testament, is presented as the prophet par excellence (Nm 12:7, Dt 34:10). He plays the role of an intermediary, defending the people before God and reminding the people of their obligations to God (particularly in the story of the golden calf (Ex 32)).

However, it is during the time of the kings that the prophets emerge as essential players in the history of Israel. From the moment that the people formulate their demand for an earthly king and are given one despite God's reservations (1 Sam 8:6–9), communication between God and the people becomes more and more difficult. In fact, the re-reading of the history of Israel has shown that the kings were more often kings who "did what was evil in the sight of the Lord" than exemplary kings who acted as protectors of God's law. Consequently, prophets appear on the scene to expose the sinfulness of the king and of the people and to publicly denounce the breaking of the covenant. The prophet speaks to God to defend the people and to the people to defend God. He (or she) guarantees open and ongoing communication, discerning present reality and future possibilities in the light of Israel's past sinful experience.

Prophets play an essential role in any discussion of the Land in the Bible. They are torn between bitter denunciation and dire warning, on the one hand, and consolation and encouragement on the other hand.[27] Prophets are men and women of the moment whose inspired insights transcend appearances. In sacred history, they discern three paradigmatic moments of God's manifestation to his people:

- the moment of *blessing* when the people received from God the law and the covenant
- the moment of *anger* when they were unfaithful and betrayed him
- the moment of *grace* when the promise of a future restoration is realized.

The Land constitutes the privileged space for these three moments.

BLESSING

In the beginning, blessing establishes the basis for the relationship between God and the believer, both as an individual and as a member of the community of Israel. The Land is the place where God is obeyed and where his love is experienced in the gifts of the Land. God provides for the people and the Land offers its fruits. These considerations regarding the original blessing are consistent with the basic insights of Torah and wisdom: a person lives life to the fullest when he/she accepts to obey the Creator who is also Father. This perspective is already present in the writings of the Prophet Amos, which are among the oldest of the Old Testament. The prophet presents the human person as the centerpiece of creation and as God's partner. "For lo the one who forms the mountains, creates the wind, reveals his thoughts to mortals, makes the morning darkness, and treads on the heights of the earth—the Lord, the God of Hosts is his name" (Am 4:13). In this context, human beings are called to a life of special intimacy with God, the experience of which the prophet is the model to be followed. "Surely the Lord God does nothing without revealing his secret to his servants the prophets" (Am 3:7). As God's close collaborator, he speaks for him, emphasizing God's original blessing. It is because of the people's abuse of this blessing that God unleashes his anger, and then, responding to the people's repentance or expressing his own fidelity and love, his grace and his pardon.

Justice (*Mishpat*) and Righteousness (*Tsedaka*) in the Land

The terms *mishpat* (justice) and *tsedaka* (righteousness) appear together about thirty times in the Bible. The first is derived from the verb *shafat*, meaning to judge or to govern. Often tied to a juridical activity, referring to the exercise of power, the term is also used to define the rights of an individual. *Tsedaka* refers to an action considered righteous, just and true. The term has a more subjective connotation than the first and is tied to a personal disposition that inspires the practice of the law. When expressed together, the two terms form a parallelism similar to those one finds in biblical poetry, each term close to the other and reinforcing one another. This association of terms is all the more potent when it is used to refer to the just and compassionate attitude of God toward his people. "I am the Lord, I act with steadfast love, justice and righteousness in the earth, for in these things I delight" (Jer 9:24). It is the Lord himself who "filled Zion with justice and righteousness" (Is 33:5, cf. Ps 99:2). Through this foundational attachment to the Lord, the God who liberates from slavery, justice and righteousness are no longer only an issue of human fairness and justice. They constitute a requirement inseparable from revelation. For those who are in power, then, be they king, priest, princes, or landowners, they constitute a domain where the social and the religious merge.

King David is the ruler who is seen to have best conformed to the requirements of God. "So David reigned over all Israel; and David administered justice and equity to all his people" (2 Sam 8:15).[28] The role of the prophets is to awaken the conscience of the powerful ones, installed on the Land but having forgotten the code of behavior that life in the Land obligates. Jeremiah recalls, in the name of God, the covenant with those who have received the Land. "Thus says the Lord: Act with justice and righteousness, and deliver from the hands of the oppressor anyone who has been robbed. And do no wrong or violence to the alien, the orphan and the widow, or shed innocent blood in this place" (Jer 22:3). Frequently, the prophet must denounce infidelity. "The way of peace they do not know, and there is no justice in their paths. Their roads they have made crooked, no one who walks in them knows peace. Therefore justice is far from us, and righteousness does not reach us; we wait for light and lo! there is darkness; and for brightness, but we walk in gloom. We grope like the blind along a wall, groping like those who have no eyes. . . . For our transgressions against you are many, and our sins testify against us. Our transgressions indeed are with us and we know our iniquities" (Is 59:8–12). Amos too accuses "the house of Israel" of turning "justice to wormwood" and bringing "righteousness to the ground" (Am 5:7, cf. Am 5:24).

Finally, justice and righteousness, as God expects them to be implemented, constitute a utopian objective out of reach of the human person. Only at the end of time will justice and righteousness be fully respected. "Until a spirit on high is poured out on us, and the wilderness becomes a fruitful field, and the fruitful field is deemed a forest. Then justice will dwell in the wilderness and righteousness abide in the fruitful field. The effect of righteousness will be peace and the result of righteousness, quietness and trust forever. My people will abide in a peaceful habitation, in secure dwellings and in quiet resting places" (Is 32:15–18).

THE ANGER OF GOD

In times of severe crisis, the prophet expresses the pain and anger of God over the sinfulness of Israel. The Land has become a place of sin. Therefore, instead of receiving the expected blessings, it becomes the arena of God's anger. The prophets thunderously denounce the transgression of the Torah. Several prophets focus on Israel's idolatry, whose roots are in the idolatry of the nations who lived in the Land before them. Others focus on the injustice that reigns in human relationships. Thus, Amos castigates Judah and Israel, the northern kingdom, for its sinfulness, which brings about divine punishment. "Thus says the Lord, "For three transgressions of Judah and for four, I will not revoke the punishment; because they have rejected the Law of the Lord, and have not kept his statutes, but they have been led astray by the same lies after which their ancestors walked. So I will send a fire on Judah and it shall devour the strongholds of Jerusalem." Thus says the Lord, 'For three transgressions of Israel and for four, I will not revoke the punishment; because they sell the righteous for silver, and the needy for a pair of sandals—they who trample the head of the poor into the dust of the earth, and push the afflicted out of the way; father and son go in to the same girl so that my holy name is profaned; they lay themselves down beside every altar on garments taken in pledge; and in the house of their God they drink wine bought with fines they have imposed'" (Am 2:4–8). This text underlines very well the convergence of sins that have a horizontal dimension (those committed against one's neighbor) and those that have a vertical one (those committed against God). A major function of the prophets is to clearly identify this sinfulness, of which the Land itself conserves an indelible trace in the blood spilt upon it. In the words of Ezekiel, God calls out to his unfaithful people. "Therefore say to them, thus says the Lord God: You eat flesh with the blood and lift up your eyes to your idols, and shed blood: shall you then possess the Land" (Ez 33:25, cf. 9:9).[29] In his definition of the upright man, Ezekiel points out three sinful entrapments: idolatry (which compromises one's relationship with God), sexual impurity (which compromises one's relationship with God as well as with one's fellow human beings), and socioeconomic injustice (which compromises one's relationship with others). The Land loses its fruitfulness and wholeness because of the sinfulness of the people who live on it. Other prophets emphasize that in ignoring the Sabbath, the vertical and horizontal dimensions come together, bringing disaster upon both the Land and the people (Jer 17:19–27, Am 8:4–6).

God's covenant with his people comprises obligations as well as consequences when these obligations are not respected. "You alone have I known of all the families of the earth; therefore I will punish you for all your iniquities" (Am 3:2). This threat resounds as loudly as the blessing in Deuteronomy that it evokes: "For you are a people holy to the Lord your God; the Lord your God has chosen you out of all the peoples on earth, his treasured possession" (Dt 7:6). Punishment is not far off if the covenant is not respected. "If you do forget the Lord your God and follow other gods to serve and worship them, I solemnly warn you today that you shall surely perish" (Dt 8:19). In the Torah, election makes Israel a source of blessing for all nations. In the prophetic texts, the sin of Israel transforms blessing into curse. The Land with all of its fruits becomes a Land of desolation. In a powerful text, the prophet Jeremiah uses the same words found in the first chapter of Genesis to describe the desolation affecting the Land itself (*tohu va-vohu*).[30] "I looked on the Land [*'aretz*], and lo, it was waste and void [*tohu va-vohu*]; and to the heavens and they had no light. I looked on the mountains and lo, they were quaking and all the hills moved to and fro. I looked and lo, there was no *adam* at all and all the birds of the air had fled. I looked and lo, the fruitful Land was a desert and all its cities were laid in ruins, before the Lord, before his fierce anger" (Jer 4:23–26). Thus, because of the people's sin and their rejection of the covenant, the cosmic order, particularly that of the Land of God, becomes undone and returns to primordial chaos.

THE LAND LOST

The cosmic consequences of the people's sinfulness are echoed in many prophetic texts that describe the moment of God's anger (*ira Dei*) when created order returns to primordial chaos (cf. Is 24:1, Hos 4:3, Jl 2:3–4, Zep 1:2–3). The perspective here is cosmic and does not focus on the particular borders of the land of Israel. Nevertheless, there is a link between the particular Land and the universal cosmos. When sin is committed in the Land by the people who should have been a blessing to the nations, it leads to a curse that affects the entire cosmos and endangers the created order. It was the sin of Israel that led to the people being exiled to Babylon (and Egypt), making them the laughingstock of the nations. "So my wrath and my anger were poured out and kindled in the towns of Judah and in the streets of Jerusalem; and they became a waste and a desolation, as they still are today. And now thus says the Lord God of Hosts, the God of Israel: 'Why are you doing such great harm to yourselves, to cut off man and woman, child and infant from the midst of Judah, leaving yourselves without a remnant? Why do you provoke me to anger with the work of your hands, making offerings to other gods in the land of Egypt where you have come to settle? Will you be cut off and become an object of cursing and ridicule among all the nations of the earth'" (Jer 44:6–8).

The prophetic writings explain why the Land that had been given was lost or was about to be lost. Isaiah, with whom the prophetic canon begins, explains the castigation of Judah and Jerusalem, likening them to Sodom and Gomorrah. "Your country lies desolate, your cities are burned with fire; in your very presence aliens devour your Land; it is desolate as overthrown by foreigners. And daughter Zion is left like a booth in a vineyard, like a shelter in a cucumber field, like a besieged city. If the Lord of hosts had not left us a few survivors we would have been like Sodom and become like Gomorrah. Hear the word of the Lord, you rulers of Sodom! Listen to the teaching of our God, you people of Gomorrah!" (Is 1:7–10). Jerusalem has become a harlot, a faithless and lawless city; she will have to bear the dire consequences. But no one is more eloquent in describing these nightmarish visions of the destruction of Jerusalem than Jeremiah. "Raise a standard toward Zion, flee for safety, do not delay, for I am bringing evil from the north and a great destruction. A lion has gone up from his thicket, a destroyer of nations has set out; he has gone out from his place to make your Land a waste" (Jer 4:6–7, cf. Hab 1:5–11).

Jeremiah, the Poet of the Land

In the Old Testament, Jeremiah is the poet of the Land par excellence. None was more visibly rooted in the old traditions of tribal Israel when land was held, after the manner of Naboth, with the vitality of gratitude and newness. None saw more clearly than he that Land cannot be held the way royal Israel tried to hold it. He knew unmistakably that Land would be lost. None treasured the Land more than he and none understood more clearly than he the flow of royal history toward exile.[31]

Jeremiah challenges the people to understand the meaning of what is happening. "I will make Jerusalem a heap of ruins, a lair of jackals; and I will make the towns of Judah a desolation without inhabitant. Who is wise enough to understand this? To whom has the mouth of the Lord spoken, so that they may declare it? Why is the Land ruined and laid waste like a wilderness, so that no one passes through?" (Jer 9:11–12). The prophet, speaking in God's name, does not leave his listeners in suspense. "And the Lord says: Because they have forsaken my law that I set before them, and have not obeyed my voice, or walked in accordance with it, but have stubbornly followed their own hearts and have gone after the Baals, as their ancestors taught them" (9:13–14).

It is not surprising that the Christian canon places the Book of Lamentations, attributed to Jeremiah, right after his own book of prophecy. It describes the abandoned city, laid waste by the invasion of Nebuchadnezzar's armies. "How lonely sits the city that once was full of people! How like a widow she has become, she that was great among the nations! She that was a princess among the provinces has become a vassal. She weeps bitterly in the night, with tears on her cheeks; among all her lovers she has no one to comfort her; all her friends have dealt treacherously with her, they have become her enemies" (Lm 1:1–2). Indeed, Israel's heritage has passed into the hands of others. "Our inheritance has been turned over to strangers, our homes to aliens" (Lm 5:2). The cry of Israel who does not understand what has happened echoes God's own cry as he looks for Adam in the Garden (Gn 3:9).[32]

In the consciousness of the prophets, the devastation of the Land is as much a manifestation of God's presence in Israel's midst as was the gift of the Land. It is God who is fighting against his people, just as he had previously fought on their behalf. According to Habakkuk, it is God who is stirring up the Chaldeans in their march toward Jerusalem, to conquer and destroy it. "For I am rousing the Chaldeans, that fierce and impetuous nation who march through the breadth of the earth to seize dwellings not their own. Dread and fearsome are they, their justice and dignity proceeds from themselves. Their horses are faster than leopards, more menacing than wolves at dusk; their horses charge. Their horsemen come from far away; they fly like an eagle swift to devour. They all come for violence, with faces pressing forward; they gather captives like sand" (Hab 1:6–9). The terrible image of a disappointed, wounded, and angry God reverses the image of God the Creator who gave the people the Land and bestowed blessings on them. Sin has eaten away at the people, corrupting them and turning the Land into a source of corruption. The God of blessing is now depicted as a God of anger. "Before him went pestilence, and plague followed close behind" (Hab 3:5). The last resort is the supplication of the prophet beseeching God: "in wrath may you remember mercy" (Hab 3:2).

GOD'S MERCY

Ezekiel represents a turning point in the consciousness of the people. They have experienced the destruction of Jerusalem, exile, and life in a foreign land. Ezekiel's visionary description of the departure of the glory of God from the temple and from Jerusalem (Ez 10–11) recalls the Book of Exodus. The people are about to move out of the Land, to follow the glory of God into exile. Everything seems to indicate that they are no longer a people because they have lost Land and temple, and that God has abandoned them to a bitter fate because of their sin. However, Ezekiel discovers that God still speaks to the people through him even though he is in a foreign land.

Although the prophets devote a lot of their energy to warning the people of the dire consequences of their sinfulness, this is only one dimension of their message. The other dimension is to reveal the true nature of God. He is a God whose love and mercy extend beyond his moment of anger and do not depend on the faithfulness of his people. "For a brief moment I abandoned you, but with great compassion I will gather you. In overflowing wrath, for a moment, I hid my face from you, but with everlasting love I will have compassion on you, says the Lord your Redeemer. This is like the days of Noah to me: just as I swore that the waters of Noah would never again go over the earth, so I have sworn that I will not be angry with you and will not rebuke you. For the mountains may depart and the hills be removed, but my steadfast love shall not depart from you and my covenant of peace shall not be removed, says the Lord who has compassion on you" (Is 54:7–10, cf.

Hos 11:9). Like the wilderness, the exile is a place where God and Israel can be reconciled, a place that allows for a new beginning, like a place of first love. "Therefore I will now allure her and bring her into the wilderness and speak tenderly to her" (Hos 2:16).

God so loves his people that he pursues them in order to give them new life and to liberate them from exile and death. Speaking in terms of resurrection, the prophet proclaims a return to the Land and the reconstruction of the temple. However, the ingathering and return to the Land is not to be accomplished through violence against other nations like at the time of Joshua. Ezekiel, in a series of texts, metaphorically describes the return of Israel from exile and the reconstruction of the Land (Ez 36:24–38), as a resurrection of dry bones (Ez 37:1–14). "Therefore prophesy and say to them, thus says the Lord God: I am going to open your graves, and bring you up from your graves, O my people; and I will bring you back to the Land of Israel" (Ez 37:12). Ultimately, the Lord will once again grant rest to his people on the Land. As a matter of fact, visions of restoration are found in almost all of the prophetic books. They focus on the Land and its recovered fruitfulness; and they reveal the true goodness and grace of God who is Creator, Redeemer, and ultimately Father. "For the Lord will comfort Zion; he will comfort all her waste places, and will make her wilderness like Eden, her desert like the garden of the Lord; joy and gladness will be found in her, thanksgiving and the voice of song" (Is 51:3).

Many of these visions of restoration also echo some of the particularity that is characteristic of the historical books. Israel re-experiences the privileges of election, whereas the nations are punished for their persecution of Israel. "In that day the mountains shall drip sweet wine, the hills shall flow with milk, and all the stream beds of Judah shall flow with water; a fountain shall come forth from the house of the Lord and water the Wadi Shittim. Egypt shall become a desolation and Edom a desolate wilderness, because of the violence done to the people of Judah, in whose Land they have shed innocent blood. But Judah shall be inhabited forever, and Jerusalem to all generations. I will avenge their blood and will not clear the guilty, for the Lord dwells in Zion" (Jl 4:18–21).

The oracles against Israel in times of anger are often followed by oracles against the nations in times of grace. Times of grace are also times of judgment: how does a person respond to God's gratuitous act of redemption? By all appearances, the nations are judged not because

God wants to avenge Israel but because they have failed to be a blessing for Israel, just as Israel had failed to be a blessing for them. "Sit in darkness and go into darkness, daughter Chaldea! For you shall no more be called the mistress of kingdoms. I was angry with my people, I had profaned my heritage; I gave them into your hand, you showed them no mercy; on the aged you made your yoke exceedingly heavy. You said, 'I shall be mistress forever,' so you did not lay these things to your heart or remember their end" (Is 47:4–7). Since Israel was called to be a source of blessing for the nations, could it be that the Lord expected the nations to intercede on Israel's behalf rather than rush to destroy it? Could it be that the Lord expected the nations to act as did Abraham who interceded for Sodom and Gomorrah, two cities he did not know? The salvation of the nations passes through Israel but Israel can not be saved without being a blessing for all of them.

It is toward the end of the book of Amos that we find one of the most exclusivist prophecies of restoration. "On that day I will raise up the booth of David that is fallen, and repair its breaches, and raise up its ruins, and rebuild it as in the days of old; in order that they may possess the remnant of Edom and all the nations who are called by my name, says the Lord who does it" (Am 9:11–12). In this passage, Amos promises a full restoration of the dynasty, the temple and the Land. It is fascinating to note, however, the rereading of these verses as they were translated into Greek and subsequently taken up into the New Testament. The rereading eliminates the nationalist overtones found in the Hebrew text: "they may possess the remnant of Edom and all the nations" (9:12) and it introduces a universal dimension. "So that all other peoples may seek the Lord—even all the Gentiles over whom my name has been called" (Greek Amos 9:12, Ac 15:17). In the words of Saint James at the Council of Jerusalem, this text serves as the justification for the inclusion of the Gentiles into the Church (Ac 15:16–18). In their New Testament context, these verses from Amos harmonize with the universal vision of the Land in Isaiah and Micah (Is 2:1–5, Mi 4:1–5), according to which Jerusalem becomes the center where the nations come together to learn the Torah. But this prophetic image of the nations converging on Jerusalem should not conceal the real heart of the message: the Torah flows out of Jerusalem toward the other nations, carrying in its wake all of the blessings promised them. As stated by Isaiah: "For my house shall be called a house of prayer for all peoples" (Is 56:7).

Isaiah points out that the blessings, originally attached to the Land, now extend far beyond its borders. "On that day Israel will be the third with Egypt and Assyria, a blessing in the midst of the earth, whom the Lord of Hosts has blessed, saying, 'Blessed be Egypt, my people, and Assyria, the work of my hands, and Israel my heritage' " (Is 19:24–25). Egypt and Assyria, traditional enemies of Israel, are now included in the inheritance of God and are called to salvation. The prophetic vision has merged with the call of Abraham, who was to be blessing in the Land for all nations.

The last three prophets in the Old Testament canon, Haggai, Zachariah, and Malachi, lived in the period following Israel's return to the Land from exile in Babylon. Their writings focus on Jerusalem, the city of Zion, rather than on the whole Land. Their message is concerned, as always, with living the Torah fully. "Thus says the Lord of Hosts: Render true judgments, show kindness and mercy to one another; do not oppress the widow, the orphan, the alien or the poor; and do not devise evil in your hearts against one another" (Za 7:9–10). According to Zachariah, Jerusalem must be a "faithful city" and a "holy mountain" (8:3). At this point, prophetic literature takes two different directions. The first follows the traditional line, which consists in warning the people of the dire consequences of not observing the Torah. The other, found in the second part of Zachariah and in Daniel, develops the prophetic style, which had its beginnings in Ezekiel and in chapters 25 to 27 of Isaiah. Here, the Land is not neglected but is treated differently. Already in the writings of Deutero-Isaiah, it is clear that, in the final restoration, God will transform the cosmos. Having become a wilderness after having been a Garden, overflowing with blessings for the earth as well as for humanity, the cosmos will become a Garden once again (cf. Is 41:18–20, 43:19–20, 45:8, Ez 34:25–31). The promises of restoration take on such cosmic proportions that the Land is no longer a limited geographical space to be rehabilitated but a truly new creation that will restore the original one. "I am coming to gather all nations and tongues; and they shall come and see my glory, and I will set a sign among them. From them I will send survivors to the nations, to Tarshish, Put and Lud, which draw the bow, to Tubal and Yavan, to the coastlands far away that have not heard of my fame or seen my glory; and they shall declare my glory among the nations. . . . For as the new heavens and the new earth which I will make shall remain before me, says the Lord; so shall your descendants and your name remain" (Is

66:18–24). The entire surface of the earth becomes privileged space where all of humanity can live in an intimate relationship with God.

It is in the Book of Daniel that this vision becomes programmatic for the apocalyptic end of time. "As I watched in the night visions, I saw one like a human being coming with the clouds of heaven. And he came to the Ancient One and was presented before him. To him was given dominion and glory and kingship, that all peoples, nations and languages should serve him. His dominion is an everlasting dominion that shall not pass away, and his kingship is one that shall never be destroyed" (7:13–14). There is an undeniable difference here between the small and problematic territorial entity that existed under the Persian, then Greek, and then Roman hegemony, and the renewed Land that, under the sovereignty of the mysterious son of man, will become an eternal empire extending over the entire face of the earth.

The canon of the prophets and of the Old Testament as a whole ends with the Book of Malachi. Though the people are now reinstalled in the Land after the exile, sin remains deeply embedded in the heart of the people. Malachi is not optimistic about the new beginnings and his prophecy ends with a renewed warning. "Remember the teaching of my servant Moses, the statutes and ordinances that I commanded him at Horeb for all Israel. Lo, I will send you the prophet Elijah before the great and terrible day of the Lord comes. He will turn the hearts of parents to their children and the hearts of children toward their parents, so that I will not come and strike the Land with a curse" (Mal 3:22–24 or 4:4–6). Thus the Old Testament ends with an enigma, an unresolved dilemma: is the Land a place of blessing or of curse?

THE LAND AS A PLACE OF REST

At the end of this reading of the Old Testament, a constant theme emerges from the great diversity of references to the Land, namely that in the Bible, the Land is not an absolute or an isolated gift. The Land is given to Israel for a distinct purpose: to provide a space in which it can embody faithfulness to the Torah. To live according to the Torah is to live in a place of rest. After having repeated the Torah in Deuteronomy, Moses reminds the people: "This is no trifling matter for you but rather your very life; through it you may live long in the Land that you are crossing over the Jordan to possess" (Dt 32:47). This refrain reverberates throughout the Old Testament, as in the psalm: "For he remembered his holy promise, and Abraham his servant. So he brought his people out with joy, his chosen ones with singing. He gave them the lands of the nations, and they took possession of the wealth of the peoples, that they might keep his statutes and observe his laws" (Ps 105:44–45).

The Changing Borders of the Land

One of the most confusing aspects of the Land in the Bible is its precise borders. In one place, God promises a Land to Abraham that stretches "from the river of Egypt to the great river, the river Euphrates" (Gn 15:18). This would include both Egypt and Mesopotamia, the two great centers of civilization in the ancient biblical world. However, in another text, the Land promised to Abraham is simply "all the land of Canaan" (Gn 17:8), referring only to historical Palestine.

This same confusion is introduced when the children of Israel are at the borders of the Land, about to enter it. God delineates the boundaries for Moses with enormous precision in Numbers 34:1–15, clearly marking the Mediterranean and the Jordan River as the western and eastern boundaries. This is the Land that Moses looks over from afar before he dies (Dt 34:1–4), hearing God's promise, yet again: "This is the Land of which I swore to Abraham, to Isaac and to Jacob, saying: I will give it to your descendants . . . (Dt 34:5). However, at the beginning of the Book of Joshua, a few verses after the text in Deuteronomy, God speaks to Joshua about borders that extend as far as the Euphrates again. "Every place that the sole of your feet will tread upon I have given to you, as I promised to Moses. From the Wilderness and the Lebanon as far as the Great River, the river Euphrates, all the land of the Hittites, to the Great Sea in the west shall be your territory" (Jos 1:3–4).

The borders of the Land in the biblical narrative have both a historical and an eschatological dimension. Although there are periods when the historical land of Israel is described as extending beyond the Jordan River (in the period of King David for example) the historical territory of the Land is often extremely limited, as is the case in the Persian period, when the small province of Judah included only a small part of the region around Jerusalem (Neh 11:25–35).

If the extended borders do not then correspond to an historical reality, what do they mean? It would seem that these are eschatological boundaries, as underlined by Isaiah: "On that day there will be a highway from Egypt to Assyria. . . . On that day, Israel will be the third with Egypt and Assyria, a blessing in the midst of the earth" (Is 19:23–24). The extended borders suggest that the entire surface of the earth has the vocation to be a promised land. It is this that is realized at the beginning of the Acts of the Apostles when the risen Jesus prepares his disciples to become apostles and "witnesses in Jerusalem, in all Judea and Samaria and to the ends of the earth" (Ac 1:8).

If God's Torah is not what determines the way life is lived on the Land the people received as a gift, then the Land is lost. When it is inhabited by a people that lives by the Torah, it is not only a heritage but also a place of rest and security. "You shall not act as we are acting here today, all of us according to our own desires, for you have not yet come into the rest and the possession that the Lord your God is giving to you. When you cross over the Jordan and live in the Land that the Lord your God is allotting to you, and when he gives you rest from his enemies all around so that you live in safety, then you shall bring everything that I command you to the place that I will choose" (Dt 12:8–10). Humanity is invited to live in harmony with God, with each other and with the entire cosmos. In the words of Isaiah, God proclaims his lordship over the heavens and the earth, as well as over human beings whom he loves, namely, "the humble and contrite in spirit who trembles at my word." "Thus says the Lord: Heaven is my throne and earth is my footstool; what is the house that you would build for me, and what is my resting place? All these things my hand has made, and so all these things are mine, says the Lord. But this is the one to whom I will look, to the humble and contrite in spirit who trembles at my word" (Is 66:1–2).

At important turning points in the history of Israel, God "gave rest" to his people (cf. Jos 21:44, 22.4, 23.1, 2 Sam 7:1, 1 Kgs 5:18, Ps 95:11, Jer 27:11). However, Israel rejected him and ultimately did not find rest in the Land of promise. When life is lived in disobedience to the Torah, the Land is a place of restlessness, characterized by violence and death. Consequently, the Land is lost and Israel goes into exile. Nonetheless, exile, even if not a place of rest, can become a place of repentance and of renewed faithfulness to the Torah.

The biblical dialectic is then one that moves from wilderness to Land and from Land to wilderness. It would be mistaken though to understand these two poles in strictly geographical terms. The Land can become wilderness and the wilderness Land. The definition of the Land as fertile and welcoming depends on it becoming a place of holy and righteous living. The definition of wilderness as barren and foreboding has less to do with its material characteristics than it does with the fact that it is a place of exile from God's presence. Whereas God intends the Land to be the people's ultimate resting place in the Old Testament (true for Adam and true for Israel too), the human person's tendency to choose sin and disobedience rather than holiness and righteousness makes the wilderness a repeated destination. Fertile Land is not treated as gift from God but rather as a right, gained through human prowess, home to myriad false gods created by human pride. Too often it seems that only in the wilderness of exile and despair does the human person turn again to God, crying out for redemption. In the barrenness of wilderness the human person is again reduced to total dependence on God and is led back to intimacy with him. Is this not the perversity of sin, revealed with utmost clarity in the Old Testament, that we are unable to receive gift in gratitude? Yet, beyond sin, the Old Testament reveals to us the ultimate fidelity of God, who seeks always to give us a Land of rest.

The insistence on Torah is consonant with the central message of the Old Testament. Obedience to the Torah is the key that opens the door to true life for the believer. Even when the Land is lost through infidelity to God and inhumanity to neighbor, there is still hope. God has the final word, he whose fidelity resists human infidelity and inhumanity. The Land will be restored in an outpouring of grace. But which Land? And under what circumstances? The dynamics involved in the gift, its loss and its return, ultimately concern not just Israel but all of humanity, of which Israel is the representative. The land of Israel typifies the entire face of the earth. Restoration of the Land then signifies the restoration of all of creation and the eradication of the traces of sin. All of humanity is called to sonship and all of the earth is the space given to live this filial relationship. "These all look to you to give them their food in due season; when you give it to them, they gather it up; when you open your hand, they are filled with good things. When you hide your face, they are dismayed; when you take away their breath, they die and return to their dust. When you send forth your breath, they are created; and you renew the face of the ground" (Ps 104:27–30).

2. The Land in the New Testament

Whereas the Old Testament, from beginning to end, devotes much time and attention to the theme of the Land, the New Testament, in contrast, seems, at first glance, to pay little attention to it. W. D. Davies, in his important study of the Land in the New Testament, shows that the Land is also present there. However, it takes on a different meaning and undergoes an important evolution and transformation, marked as it is, by the person of Jesus Christ.[1] This ambivalence manifests itself by means of a rich tension among three different perceptions of the Land. The first underlines an undeniable continuity with the Old Testament. The second adds, at the same time, a rejection of the territorial dimension and tends to spiritualize the concept. The third importantly transforms the concept of Land as seen through the person of Jesus Christ. In this chapter, we will not proceed as we did in the Old Testament, presenting each of the writings in succession. Rather, we will present each of these three perceptions in order to show that Land remains a fundamental category in the New Testament, molded and reworked by the person of Jesus in his life, death, and resurrection.

Continuity between the Old and the New Testaments is simply a matter of principle, true for all the important biblical themes: God, Torah, Spirit, etc. "Do not think that I have come to abolish the law or the prophets; I have come not abolish but to fulfill" (Mt 5:17). It remains to be seen, however, to what extent this is true for the Land because there are certain passages in the New Testament that reject the promise and gift of Land, as understood in the Old Testament. But it may be asked: is this rejection not the continuation of the clamorous prophetic discourse regarding the ingratitude of the people for God's gifts and the punishment that follows in its wake? In the New Testament, the rejection of Jesus by the Jewish authorities and people does have implications for the permanence of the promise of Land.[2] This rejection marks a significant shift, later greatly developed by the Fathers of the Church, toward a spiritualization of many aspects of the Old Testament. In some of their writings, this will lead to the disappearance of the territorial dimension, replaced by Jesus Christ or by the Church itself. The fulfillment of the promises in Jesus Christ, as told in the New Testament, implies a radical change concerning the place given to the Land in light of Jesus' life, death, and resurrection. The promise is no longer limited to one particular Land and to one specific people. Instead, it is addressed to the entire surface of the earth and to all of humanity, in a kind of return to the beginning of creation and the universal vocation of Abraham.

CONTINUITY

The New Testament is incomprehensible without the narrative and discourse of the Old. As the classic dictum says: "Vetus Testamentum patet in Novo, Novum Testamentum latet in Vetere" (The Old Testament is manifest in the New, the New Testament is hidden in the Old).[3] This is also true when it comes to the question of Land.

Undoubtedly, one of the most important elements in Jesus' teaching concerns the coming of the kingdom: "The time is fulfilled and the kingdom of God has come near; repent and believe in the good news" (Mk 1:15, cf. Mt 3:2, 4:17, Lk 8:1). It would be wrong to attribute only a spiritual meaning to this concept. The kingdom is to become a reality in this world by taking flesh in the social, economic, political, religious and spiritual values taught first in the Torah and then by Jesus himself. The continuity between the kingdom announced by the prophets and sung by the psalmists and the one preached by Jesus is palpable. This is a kingdom that radiates blessing to all the nations and whose divine raison d'être is not a nationalist selfishness but rather an opening to all the nations.

Although the "kingdom of God" and the borders of the Land are not synonymous, it is clear that Jesus' disciples, like all Jews rooted in the biblical traditions, thought that the kingdom would indeed correspond to the land of Israel. But what did Jesus himself think? Though answers vary from one evangelist to the other, the strongest references to the Old Testament are found in the Gospel of Matthew. There, Jesus orders his disciples not to leave the frontiers of the Land. "These twelve Jesus sent out with the following instructions, 'Go nowhere among the Gentiles and enter no town of the Samaritans, but go rather to the lost sheep of the house of Israel'" (Mt 10:5–6). Israel must be converted first and only then can Israel (represented by the twelve disciples) turn to the nations.

Nevertheless, Jesus did teach his disciples that the pagans could also be saved if they themselves turned to Israel. Praising the centurion whose servant he heals, Jesus says: "Truly, I tell you, in no one in Israel have I found such faith. I tell you, many will come from east and west and will eat with Abraham and Isaac and Jacob in the kingdom of heaven, while the heirs of the kingdom will be thrown into the outer darkness where there will be weeping and gnashing of teeth" (Mt 8:10–11, cf. Mk 7:24–30, Lk 13:28–29).

It is only after the resurrection that the borders of the Land are definitively transcended. "Go therefore and make disciples of all nations, baptizing them in the name of the Father and the Son and the Holy Spirit" (Mt 28:19). The resurrection of Jesus, totally unexpected from a human point of view, does not lead automatically to the conversion of all of Israel. Only a "remnant" of the Jewish people recognizes in Jesus the fulfillment of the Scriptures. The resurrection becomes the foundational event for the Jesus movement and the major stumbling block that, despite their similarities, distinguishes and opposes the Jesus movement and Judaism, as restructured by the rabbis after the Council of Yavneh (c. A.D. 80). On the other hand, for his followers, it is the risen Lord who inspires a rereading of the words and deeds of Jesus, giving rise to a radical transformation of the concept of the Land.

The apocalyptic sections of the Old Testament seem to be among Jesus' favorites. His teaching about the end times reflects this predilection. One particularly evocative passage from Luke (Lk 21:21–24) focuses on the city of Jerusalem "trampled on by the Gentiles." We find here a reminiscence of the time of the conquest of the Land by Joshua when it was the Israelites "who trampled" the Promised Land (Dt 1:36, 11:24, Jos 1:3, 14:9).[4] The reversal is clear: the Land, after having been trampled by the triumphant armies of Joshua, is trampled by the conquering pagan armies. This is the traditional prophetic teaching of Israel: if Israel is faithful to God, the whole world will follow Israel's example and Israel will be a blessing for the nations. However, if Israel follows the example of the nations and turns from the Torah, it will become the victim of these nations. In Jesus' apocalyptic teachings, the forthcoming destruction of Jerusalem is an important consequence of the people's rejection of his teaching (Lk 21:5–33, cf. Mk 13:3–32, Mt 24:1–36).

JESUS' ITINERARY IS ROOTED IN THE LAND

Even if one must admit that Jesus, in explicit terms, relates less often to the land of Israel than do most of the writers of the Old Testament, the Land, nevertheless, remains an essential part of his life and teaching. The reader of the gospel is quickly made aware of the fact that Jesus is a child of the land of Israel; he received his human and religious formation there and he never left the Land except in special circumstances and ever so briefly. He is born in the Davidic city of Bethlehem. It is at the Jordan, threshold of the Land, that he is proclaimed Son of God. From there he is led into the wilderness to be tempted for forty days. At the end of his life, Jesus will be crucified and buried in Jerusalem. He will appear there and nearby to his disciples in Jerusalem as well as in Galilee. The gospel writers present the life of Jesus within a basic geographic framework. He departs from Nazareth, the place of his childhood, toward Jerusalem, the place of his death. From the periphery of the Land, he goes to the center.

As an itinerant preacher, he traveled the length and breadth of this land in all seasons, and his teachings are peppered with references derived from the land of Israel. Jesus' teaching is often a meditation on the Land, with its agriculture and natural cycles, flora and fauna.[5] The sea, the high mountain, the wilderness, the way to Jerusalem are the backdrop to his ministry. These places are meant to resound within the context of the Old Testament's sacred geography of the Land. The fig tree and the vine, of which Jesus spoke as he entered Jerusalem (cf. Mk 11:12–14.21–22, 12:1–12, and parallels), evoke the gift of Land in the Torah (Dt 8:8) as well as the dire warnings of the prophets (Is 5:1–7, Jer 5:17, Jer 8:13, Hos 1:12) and the outpouring of God's grace (Hos 14:8, Jl 2:22, Am 9:13–14). Jesus' parables, so central to his public ministry and consistent with the ancient prophetic traditions, are fully comprehensible only within the concrete context of the Land, its cultures, customs, and social life. This is what makes them intelligible to his listeners, who share with him the same culture, history, faith, and sense of belonging to the land of Israel.

Nazareth

Within the basic geographic framework of Jesus' life, each gospel writer has his own particular way of describing the sacred geography in which Jesus moves about. Mark's sacred geography is the simplest. Jesus moves from Nazareth to the Jordan, comes back to Galilee and finally goes up to Jerusalem. The mention of Nazareth at the beginning of his gospel marks a break with sacred geography insofar as this town is never mentioned in the Old Testament. In view of all the symbolism surrounding the biblical places in the Old Testament, Nazareth thus appears as a marginal town, a strange place for a future Messiah to hail from. John's gospel echoes this in Nathanael's reaction: "Can anything good come out of Nazareth?" (Jn 1:46). Matthew explains that Jesus and his family settled in Nazareth as a result of the threats against the life of the child from the political authorities in Jerusalem. In Matthew's account, Nazareth is mentioned only after the hasty departure from Bethlehem and the sojourn in Egypt.

Luke's gospel is the only one that presents Nazareth as an important place in Jesus' life. It is in Nazareth that the Annunciation to Mary takes place. "In the sixth month, the angel Gabriel was sent by God to a town in Galilee called Nazareth" (Lk 1:26). For Luke, Nazareth is also the place where Jesus begins his public ministry by preaching in the synagogue. After a reading from the prophet Isaiah (Is 61:1–2), he proclaims: "Today this scripture has been fulfilled in your hearing" (Lk 4:21). However, the announcement of the birth of John the Baptist in Jerusalem precedes the Annunciation in Nazareth and Jesus will ultimately be born in Bethlehem. The obvious discomfort with Jesus' Nazarene origins clearly illustrates how much the Old Testament idea of the Land and its sacred contours remains a basic reference in the life of Jesus.

However, in Luke's gospel, it is noteworthy that Jesus' roots in the land of Israel are in tension with this gospel's insistence elsewhere on the continuity with the Old Testament. Nazareth and the entire region of Galilee, where Jesus begins and develops his teaching, have been entirely marginal in the history of salvation up to this point. Nevertheless, Nazareth (like the figure of Mary, a young peasant girl) represents an important break, an unexpected shift in this history of salvation. Unlike Mark and Matthew, Luke has Jesus' public ministry begin in Nazareth, an insignificant location when compared to Jerusalem, the spiritual center of the faith. After his rejection in Nazareth, Jesus preaches in the towns and villages of Galilee. Luke then goes on to describe the journey of Jesus as a dramatic going up from Galilee to Jerusalem (9:51–19:45). From the moment Jesus "set his face to go to Jerusalem" (Lk 9:51), the narrative unfolds as the dramatic narrative of a prophet's ascent to his destiny in Jerusalem, continually punctuated by the refrain that Jesus is drawing near to the city (13:22, 17:11, 19:11).

Bethlehem

Both Matthew and Luke place Jesus' birth not in Nazareth but in the town of Bethlehem. Whereas Nazareth is unknown on the geographical map of the Old Testament, Bethlehem is renowned. Mentioned more than forty times in the Old Testament, it is the place of origin of David, the exemplary king and prototype of the ideal Messiah (anointed one) and his father, Jesse (1 Sam 17:1.18). Consequently, it is not surprising that the prophet Micah, in his messianic oracles, refers explicitly to Bethlehem. "But you, O Bethlehem of Ephrathah, who are one of the little clans of Judah, from you shall come forth for me one who is to rule in Israel" (Mi 5:2, cf. Mt 2:6). Matthew, particularly attentive to the fulfillment of Old Testament prophecies in the life of Jesus, specifies that Jesus' origins follow the pattern established by the people of Israel. He is not only born in the city of David, but also goes down to Egypt and returns to the Land, fulfilling the prophetic oracle: "Out of Egypt I called my son" (Hos 11:1, cf. Mt 2:15). Matthew presents the birth and infancy of Jesus as the fulfillment of the Scriptures, mentioning three places linked to salvation history: Bethlehem, Egypt, and Nazareth, with no identifiable quotation from the Old Testament justifying the inclusion of Nazareth.[6]

The Jordan River

In Mark's gospel, Jesus appears for the first time as an adult and makes his entry at the Jordan River. In all four gospels, Jesus' baptism is a key moment in his life, not only from the point of view of the event itself but also from that of the spot where it took place. In the Old Testament, the Jordan is the threshold marking the people's passage from the wilderness to the Land. Here, Jesus is linked both to Moses and to Joshua son of Nun, whose name ("God saves") he bears.[7] On the banks of the Jordan, Moses spoke to the people for the last time, leaving his place to Joshua (Jesus), who will lead and settle the people in the Land. Just as the waters of the Sea of Reeds parted at the beginning of their voyage, so too did the waters of the Jordan open up and allow the chosen people to enter the Land. The people followed Joshua into the Land in order to establish the kingdom of God. They embarked on a campaign to "purify" the Land of the idolatrous peoples living there. Later on, the Jordan will also witness the departure of Elijah, ascending into heaven in a fiery chariot and leaving behind his disciple Elisha to carry on his work. At the end of time, this same Elijah will return in order to prepare for the end of days (Ml 3:23). This backdrop clarifies the significance of the man Jesus, who is being baptized at this particular place. It is here that Jesus inaugurates his mission to drive out the demons from the Land and to prepare the way for the coming of the kingdom of God. For Mark, Jesus, enters his public life on the banks of the Jordan as a new Joshua.

The Wilderness

After his baptism, Jesus is led into the wilderness to be tempted by the devil. The wilderness in the Old Testament is the place of exile, far from the Garden. Instead of fruit from "every tree that is pleasant to the sight and good for food" (Gn 2:9), there are but "thorns and thistles" (Gn 3:18). This is part of God's judgment after Adam had sinned. It is also the place of punishment after Israel had refused to enter the Land out of fear of its inhabitants. "But as for you, your dead bodies shall fall in this wilderness. And your children shall be shepherds in the wilderness for forty years and shall suffer for your faithlessness, until the last of your dead bodies lies in the wilderness" (Nm 14:32–33). The wilderness, however, is also a place of preparation, where God educates the people, guiding them from childhood to adulthood. "Remember the long way that the Lord your God has led you these forty years in the wilderness, in order to humble you, testing you to know what was in your heart, whether or not you would keep his commandments. He humbled you by letting you hunger, then by feeding you with manna, with which neither you nor your ancestors were acquainted in order to make you understand that one does not live by bread alone but by every word that comes from the mouth of the Lord" (Dt 8:2–3).

In the wilderness, Jesus, triumphant in the face of the devil's temptations, reverses the disobedience of both Adam and Israel. He is the obedient son, nourished by the Torah, which is light for his path. In the gospels of Matthew and Luke, it is with citations from Deuteronomy that Jesus responds, thus vanquishing Satan. The Land once cursed and turned into wilderness because of Adam's disobedience (Gn 3:17), now regains its original harmony and fruitfulness. Mark, with his customary conciseness, paints an idyllic picture of the situation that follows the temptation: "He was with the wild beasts and the angels waited on him" (Mk 1:13). This evokes the promise made by the prophets of a time of peace and harmony extending even to relations between man and beast (cf. Is 9:6–9). Luke develops a similar perspective by inserting the genealogy of Jesus that shows his descent from Adam between the baptism and the temptation. It is in the wilderness that Jesus, unlike "Adam, son of God" (Lk 4:22), reveals himself to be truly the obedient son of God.

On the Shores of the Sea of Galilee

On the shores of the Sea of Galilee, Jesus calls his first disciples, teaches in the synagogues, and performs his first miracles. The sea (actually a large lake) plays an important role in the gospels. For Israel, more land oriented than seafaring, the Sea of Galilee is often thought to be a real sea, which, in stormy weather, can become a symbol of violence and death like the waters in the Old Testament. This is the case, when Jesus calms the raging storm on the sea (Mk 4) and, master of the waters, expels the unclean spirit from the possessed man (Mk 5). It is on the shores of the Sea of Galilee that the people, amazed at his authority, begin to flock to him.

In Mark's gospel, the sea is also the border that separates the land of the Jews from the land of the Gentiles. Jesus' dramatic crossing of the sea in Mark 4 prefigures the passing of his message to the Gentiles and the universal opening of his mission. In Mark's gospel, the first crossing of the sea calls to mind the person of Jonah, the reluctant apostle of repentance to the pagan nations. Jesus, like Jonah, sleeps through the storm on the sea, but unlike Jonah, Jesus willingly preaches his gospel to the possessed pagan on the other side. During his time in Galilee, Jesus, in Mark's gospel, crosses the sea back and forth, preaching to Jews on one side and to Gentiles on the other. This is already a geography of salvation that foreshadows the breaking out of the borders of the Land.

Jesus is outside the Land when he meets the Syro-Phoenician woman, who recognizes Jesus' lordship (Mk 7:24–30). Whether he is in the Land or outside of it, what is important seems to be Jesus' own person and his ability to go beyond the borders of Israel. In Matthew's account, this woman is a Canaanite (Mt 15:21–28). Were there still Canaanites in the time of Jesus? This is not really the issue for Matthew. The fact is that the Canaanites had once inhabited the Land. Did Matthew, by means of this anachronism, seek to obscure the fact that Jesus had crossed the borders of the Land? In fact, in Matthew, Jesus teaches his disciples not to leave the Land (Mt 10:5–6). According to Matthew, it is only after the death and resurrection of Jesus, when all things have been fulfilled, that Jesus sends his disciples beyond the borders of the Land.

The Mountain

At the center of Mark's gospel is the recognition of Christ by Peter, the denial of the Passion and the event of the Transfiguration (Mk 8:27–9:13). The vision of the transfigured Jesus, in conversation with Moses and Elijah, on the high mountain is also in keeping with the sacred geography of the Old Testament. It is on a high mountain (Sinai/Horeb) that both Moses and Elijah met with God. In Matthew's gospel, Jesus is clearly presented as a new Moses. The theme of the mountain is introduced with the very first of Jesus' major teachings, when he ascends the mountain (Mt 5:1). However, there is a perceptible tension between a desire to tie the message to a given sacred place like Sinai in the Old Testament, and an effort to distance it from any geographical location. Where the reader might have liked to find references to precise locations, Matthew (and the other synoptic gospels) deliberately remains vague (cf. Mt 5:1, 14:23, 15:29, 17:1). Nevertheless, the link with Moses is explicit: on the mountain, Jesus teaches his disciples the Torah that fulfills the Mosaic Torah.

Jerusalem

John's gospel devotes much more space to Jerusalem than the other gospels. Here Jesus spends more time and returns more often. However, without a doubt, Jerusalem is at the center of the geography of all four gospels. It is here that Jesus fulfills his mission. This too is in continuity with the sacred geography of the Old Testament, particularly with the reforms of King Josiah (621), who centralized worship in Jerusalem (2 Kgs 22–23). In Mark, Jesus enters Jerusalem for the first time a few days before his arrest and crucifixion. The reader is soon made aware that everything that has preceded these events in Jerusalem has been in preparation for this moment. It is in Jerusalem that Jesus' life takes on its ultimate meaning. Matthew follows Mark in this. Even though Jesus is born in the vicinity of Jerusalem, he does not enter the holy city until the end of his earthly life. His entry into Jerusalem is a royal one, acclaimed by the people. Palpable here is the ambivalence of this kingship, rooted in the biblical tradition and tacitly accepted by Jesus, but falling short of the popular expectation of a triumphant and glorious king.

Luke maintains a certain independence with regard to Matthew and Mark. This is particularly evident for the cities of Nazareth and Jerusalem. Luke's gospel begins in Jerusalem, with the annunciation to Zechariah, one of the priests in the temple. From there, with the Annunciation to Mary, the narrative moves to a house in the town of Nazareth. Jerusalem and the priest Zechariah both signify continuity with the Old Testament and with its center, Jerusalem, as well as with the temple, the very heart of the holy city. At the very beginning of Luke's gospel, Jesus is introduced into the precincts of Jerusalem and the temple. Even if his origins are elsewhere, the Child Jesus manifests an astonishing familiarity with salvation history.

THE RESURRECTION

For all four gospel writers, the empty tomb in Jerusalem is the sign of the resurrection. In Matthew, the resurrected Jesus appears in Jerusalem only to the women who are instructed to tell the disciples that they must go back to Galilee to meet him and receive his last instructions. Thus Jesus, at the end of his life, returns to the marginal milieu from which he came. Here, once again, Luke has a different approach. For him, the gospel ends where it began, in Jerusalem. Jesus appears to his disciples and then takes leave of them, from Jerusalem he ascends to his Father. In John's gospel, Jesus appears both in Jerusalem and in Galilee.

The question posed by the disciples to Jesus at the beginning of Acts shows that they see themselves in continuity with the Old Testament, still dreaming of an earthly kingdom in the land of Israel. "Lord, is this the time when you will restore the kingdom to Israel?" (Ac 1:6). Even if in Acts the significance of the person of Jesus and the outpouring of the Spirit give the Land a different meaning than it had in the Old Testament, it remains true that Jerusalem occupies a central position with regard to the journeys undertaken by the apostles and to the organization of the life of the early community.

Stephen, in his summary of the history of salvation, refers to the centrality of the Land for his hearers, evoking the story of Abraham. "God had him move from there to this country, in which you are now living" (Ac 7:4). At the end of his speech, however, he opens more universal and spiritual perspectives. "Yet the Most High does not dwell in houses made with human hands, as the prophet says: Heaven is my throne and earth is my footstool. What kind of house will you build for me, says the Lord, or what is the place of my rest? Did not my hand make all these things" (Ac 7:48–49). Likewise, Paul, in his sermon in the synagogue at Antioch of Pisidia, evokes the gift of the Land. "After he had destroyed seven nations in the land of Canaan, he gave them their Land as an inheritance" (13:19).

Though additional references can be found to illustrate continuity between the Old and New Testaments, an important fact intervenes leaving an indelible mark on the experiences of the early Christian community and its writings, particularly those of Saint Paul. This is the death and resurrection of Jesus, in the light of which his Jewish background and teaching are reinterpreted, thereby irrevocably altering the relationship to the Land.

REJECTION AND SPIRITUALIZATION

The temptations of Jesus in the wilderness, as narrated by Matthew and Luke at the threshold of his public life, evoke the temptations faced by Israel in the Land. Where Israel had failed by transforming the Land that had been given into a Land of idolatry and oppression, Jesus reveals himself to be the obedient son nourished by the word of God.

Behind the dramatic presentation of the temptations, one can discern an opposition between the kingdom that Jesus announced and the one the Jewish people including Jesus' own disciples had been dreaming of. Many exegetes consider the scene of the temptations as a synthesis of the various temptations Jesus met with throughout his public ministry. They echo, in a very pedagogical manner, the opposition between him and his contemporaries regarding the notion of kingdom. We have already drawn attention to the fact that the kingdom not only implies a spiritual reality but also supposes an earthly tract of land with borders, a king, and subjects. It was at the time of the establishment of the monarchy in Israel that there developed a theology of kingdom, particularly in the Psalms.

Within an overall context of continuity, the preaching of Jesus, nevertheless, breaks with the past. Face to face with Nathanael, "an Israelite in whom there is no deceit," Jesus does not protest when Nathanael proclaims that he is "the Son of God . . . the king of Israel" (Jn 1:49). However, Jesus withdraws to the mountain when he has the premonition that the Jews wish to make him king (Jn 6:15). In doing so, he is letting it be known that his kingdom does not correspond to the expectations of his contemporaries. However, when he makes his entry into Jerusalem, mounted on a donkey, he does not reject the acclamations of the crowds who cry out, "Hosanna, blessed is the one who comes in the name of the Lord, the King of Israel" (Jn 12:13). After all, it was in Jerusalem that the messianic king was expected. Jesus enters as a peaceful king. But one must wait for the Passion to discover the distinctiveness of his kingdom. In the Gospel of John, it is only when Jesus appears before Pilate that he reveals the exact nature of his kingdom and the true identity of its king.

WHAT KINGDOM AND WHAT KING?

When Pilate interrogates Jesus about his kingdom, Jesus responds ambiguously with the words "you say that I am a king" (Jn 18:37). In so doing, he distances himself from all earthly notions of kingship but, at the same time, refuses to deny that he is a king. The narrative that follows then specifies the kind of kingship he is laying claim to, and thus the type of kingdom he seeks to establish. To express the distinctive nature of his kingdom, Jesus stresses that "my kingdom is not from this world" (Jn 18:36), an unequivocal distancing from the earthly kingdom awaited by the Jewish people. An earthly kingdom can be recognized according by the size of its territory, the breadth of its borders, the strength of its armies, the accumulation of its wealth, the number of its subjects, the scope of its conquests and the regal majesty of its king. Jesus draws a clear line between this earthly notion and his own view: "If my kingdom were from this world, my followers would be fighting to keep me from being handed over to the Jews" (18:36).

To explain his royalty and his kingdom, Jesus uses expressions and images that, at first hearing, seem incompatible with the world of royal power. His kingdom is a reality *not of this world.* Jesus has come into the world *to testify to the truth.* Whoever belongs to the truth *listens to his voice* (cf. Jn 18:37). Here, it is important to note that the qualifying term "of the Jews" has disappeared. He simply says "I am a king," which gives a far more universal dimension to the title of king. His kingship comes from somewhere else, from there where "he was born" and from whence "he came," he the one who "preexisted" before all things. This kingship is not established by a force that imposes itself but by a Word that reveals itself. In this passage, John distances himself from the synoptic writers who envisaged the king as "son of David." The kingship of Jesus calls to mind that of God in the Old Testament where kingship is recognized by the fidelity of the people to the covenant. Those who welcome him become subjects of the kingdom, not only at the end of time but in the here and now. His subjects are those who "belong to the truth," that is to say those who listen to the Word.

Verse 18:37 is a Christological peak, marking the culmination of a slowly unfolding revelation that began at the beginning of the gospel. Jesus presents himself to Pilate and to the readers as one coming from elsewhere in order to *testify*, in other words to publicly and solemnly proclaim that which he has seen and come to know. He has come to testify to the Truth about God his Father, that is to say, his consistency, his authenticity, his faithfulness, and in the final analysis, all that constitutes his identity. Witness to the truth, he is the very way that leads to the truth. At a deeper level, accessible only to the believer, truth becomes identified with the person of Jesus. He is the real judge in this strange legal proceeding where both the accusers and the judge are put on trial by the one who presented himself as "the way and the truth and the life" (Jn 14:6). In order to understand the depth of this truth, one must become part of it: "Everyone who belongs to the truth listens to my voice" (Jn 18:37).

The synoptic gospels dwell more on the ethical dimension of Jesus' kingdom. It is a kingdom for the poor (Lk 6:20), the poor in spirit (Mt 5:3), the humble, those who are persecuted for the sake of righteousness (Mt 5:10), and children (Mt 19:14, Mk 10:14, Lk 18:16). The formulation of the Beatitudes in Matthew's gospel begins and ends with the reality of the kingdom: "Blessed are the poor in spirit, for theirs is the kingdom of heaven. . . . Blessed are those who are persecuted for righteousness' sake, for theirs is the kingdom of heaven" (Mt 5:3.10).

Blessed are the meek, for they shall inherit the Land (Mt 5:5)

To be fully understood, this beatitude must be seen in the context of the Old Testament and particularly of Psalm 37, where the expression "inherit the Land" is repeated five times and where the conditions for inheriting the Land are also specified. "Trust in the Lord and do good, so you will live in the Land and enjoy security (37:3). . . . For the wicked shall be cut off, but those who wait for the Lord shall inherit the Land. Yet a little while and the wicked shall be no more; though you look diligently for their place, they will not be there. But the meek shall inherit the Land, and delight themselves in abundant prosperity" (37:9–11). Following the Greek Septuagint version of Psalm 37, Matthew uses the term "meek" to translate the Hebrew *anawim*, thereby suggesting that the "meek" are the poor, those who rely on the Lord and fear him. The Psalm harks back to the liberation of the Hebrews after they had been freed from slavery in Egypt and had entered into the rest of the Land promised to their ancestors. Alas! This entry into the Land, far from being the culmination of a spiritual adventure was the point of departure for a long series of disillusionments. It begot injustices, particularly toward the poorest among the people. The dream of a kingdom of justice and peace for everyone was shattered. The impious prospered and crushed the poor. The Land of the covenant became the Land of oppression and injustice.

The thinking of the psalmist ties in with that of the prophets who put the people on guard against the dangers of forgetting the covenant and of settling down in this land without providing justice for all. The sins involved here have less to do with offenses committed against God, the giver of the Land, than with injustices inflicted on the poor, those dispossessed of the very Land that had been promised them. Jesus' teaching, in keeping with that of the prophets, proclaims a kingdom which is both "already here" and "not yet here" and in which the poor will have the first places. In the overall context of the gospel, this land promised to the poor prefigures the kingdom inaugurated by Jesus that will come about at the end of time. But this kingdom is no longer linked to a particular land. It begins and develops anywhere in the world wherever the disciples of Jesus live by this beatitude.

Neither Here Nor in Jerusalem

There is a place in the gospel where Jesus sums up the consequences of his revelation for the kingdom, its territory, and borders. In his dialogue with the Samaritan woman (Jn 4), he substantially relativizes the Land. Asked by the woman to choose between Gerizim, the holy place of the Samaritans, and Jerusalem, the Jewish center of faith, Jesus proclaims: "Woman, believe me, the hour is coming when you will worship the Father neither on this mountain nor in Jerusalem. You worship what you do not know; we worship what we know, for salvation is from the Jews. But the hour is coming and is now here, when the true worshippers will worship the Father in spirit and truth, for the father seeks such as these to worship him. God is spirit and those who worship him must worship in spirit and truth" (Jn 4:21–24). Jesus is challenging here the normative albeit restrictive character of a specific space to worship God. If God is indeed Spirit, the heart of all believers who are inspired by the Spirit becomes a permanent interior space of adoration. Jesus is questioning the need for a particular territory in order to maintain a relationship with God.

However, by stressing that "salvation is from the Jews" (Jn 4:22), he recognizes that in order for this spiritual worship to become a reality, there had been a need for this land, well-defined in its particularity and sanctified throughout the long centuries of salvation history. Thus, Jesus stresses once again the idea of the continuity with the religious heritage of Israel: the salvation that comes from the Jews has been transmitted throughout history, in this land made holy through the mediation of the Jewish people. In the final analysis, the kingdom preached by Jesus is no longer rooted in a particular land within specified borders but rather in the person of Jesus, in his life and teaching.

In all four gospel accounts, Jesus' kingship culminates on the cross. All the accounts note the title that is inscribed on the cross, indicating, according to Roman custom, the reason for his condemnation. However, it is John who gives the inscription an exceptional importance having Pilate himself write the words in three languages, Hebrew (probably Aramaic), the language used by the Jews; Latin, the language of the Roman occupiers; and Greek, the language of the empire. In addition, the inscription is the subject of a discussion between Pilate and the Jews. Pilate, who, until this point, has given in to all the Jewish demands, shows himself to be intransigent regarding the wording of the inscription. "What I have written I have written" (Jn 19:22). In a sense, he, who had capitulated to the Jews and to Jesus, becomes obstinate and closes the debate with a clear affirmation, what is written is written. Since then, this inscription, recorded in the Book, announces the advent of the messianic kingship of Jesus, surrounded here by his first subjects, particularly his mother and the disciple he loved. "What is written is written" also means that this kingship, inscribed in the three universal languages known to the Evangelist, embraces all cultures and peoples. It depends neither on a particular period of history nor on a specific place. The inscription is addressed to all readers of all times and all lands.

The resurrection of Jesus is what allows the kingdom to escape becoming a pure utopia. The resurrected Jesus ushers in a different type of kingdom that has no geographical limits and is present wherever there are disciples of his. This kingdom is still incomplete, destined for completion only when Jesus Christ returns in glory. Until then, his disciples live the kingdom as a hidden reality, all the while living within the city among believers and non-believers alike.

The Kingdom in the Letter to the Hebrews

The Letter to the Hebrews is the New Testament writing that perhaps best develops the new approach to the Land. Chapters 3 and 4 introduce the topic of the Land by speaking of Joshua and Jesus (who have identical names in Greek). The Land is the ultimate resting-place in salvation history. Moses leads the people out of Egypt toward the Land of promise but "they were unable to enter because of unbelief" (3:19).

Pursuing the parallel with the Pentateuch and the historical books, the Letter continues: "The promise of entering his rest is still open" (4:1). At this point, the author uses the two most important expressions to denote rest in the Old Testament: the Land, a place of rest, and the Sabbath, a time for rest. The two moments of missed opportunity for full rest are evoked alongside one another. The first was when God rested on the seventh day after having created the world. Adam, instead of resting with God in the fullness of creation, introduced humanity into disobedience, sin and death. The second moment was at the time of Moses and Joshua. Under Moses, the people were to be led to their rest but instead chose disobedience in the wilderness where they experienced death rather than rest. "Since therefore it remains open for some to enter it, and those who formerly received the good news failed to enter because of disobedience, again he sets a certain day—'today'—saying through David much later, in the words already quoted: Today if you hear his voice do not harden your hearts" (Heb 4:6–7).

The failure to gain rest is not limited to the saga in the wilderness but includes all of the history of Israel from the moment it entered the Land until the moment it lost it at the time of exile. "For if Joshua had given them rest, God would not speak later about another day" (4:8).

In the Letter to the Hebrews, the failure is the result of disobedience, prefiguring what would happen when Jesus' blood was poured out on the cross. The author suggests that the rest prefigured in the Old Testament's Land and Sabbath, is gained in Christ: "Since the Law has only a shadow of the good things to come and not the true form of these realities" (Heb 10:1). The Land, the Sabbath, and ultimately the entire ritual system of the Old Testament are destined to disappear in the fulfillment of all things in Christ.

In the magnificent hymn to the exemplary faith of our ancestors, there are several references to the Land. "By faith, Abraham obeyed when he was called to set out for a place that he was to receive as an inheritance and he set out not knowing where he was going" (11:8). Here, the author of Hebrews introduces an unexpected element into the Abraham saga. "By faith he stayed for a time in the Land he had been promised as in a foreign land, living in tents as did Isaac and Jacob, who were heirs with him of the same promise" (11:9). The Land was not Abraham's ultimate destination. "For he looked forward to the city that has foundations, whose architect and builder is God" (11:10). Thus Abraham, as a "foreigner," is the exemplar of all those who live in faith. "All of these died in faith without having received the promises, but from a distance they saw and greeted them. They confessed that they were strangers and foreigners on the earth, for people who speak in this way make it clear that they are seeking a homeland. If they had been thinking of the Land that they had left behind, they would have had opportunity to return. But, as it is, they desire a better country, that is a heavenly one. Therefore, God is not ashamed to be called their God, indeed he has prepared a city for them" (11:13–16). That same destiny awaits Jesus' disciples who, by refusing any earthly city, manifest their faithfulness to the crucified Lord. "Therefore, Jesus also suffered outside the gate in order to sanctify the people by his own blood. Let us then go to him outside the camp and bear the abuse he endured. For here we have no lasting city, but we are looking for the city that is to come" (13:12–14).

Although the Letter to the Hebrews is the most explicit in its spiritualization of the Land and its rejection of sacred territory, other New Testament writing also moves in this direction albeit more discretely. In his spiritual experience on the way to Damascus, Paul received a revelation that illuminated his entire teaching: in Christ, creation has come to a new stage and the borders established by religious systems have collapsed. "There is no longer Jew or Greek, there is no longer slave or free, there is no longer male and female, for all of you are one in Christ Jesus" (Ga 3:28). In his list of divine gifts to Israel, eternally valid according to the plan of God, Paul makes no mention of the Land, despite it being a promised gift in the Old Testament. "They are Israelites, and to them belong the adoption, the glory, the covenants, the giving of the law, the worship and the promises, to them belong the patriarchs and from them, according to the flesh, comes the Messiah, who is over all, God blessed forever. Amen" (Rm 9:4–5).

The spiritualization of the Land, often implied in the New Testament and quite explicit in the Letter to the Hebrews, leads to a change: the person of Jesus Christ takes the place of the Land. Nowhere is this more powerfully expressed than in the sacrament of the Eucharist. In the Old Testament, the Land gives its fruits to nourish the people. Gifts from God, these fruits manifest his loving care for the people, who, lest they forget, must show their gratitude each year by thanking him for his generosity. "So now I bring the first of the fruit of the ground that you, O Lord, have given me. You shall set it down before the Lord your God and bow down before the Lord your God" (Dt 26:10, cf. Dt 26:1–11). The body of Christ replaces the Land as the source of food that nourishes and gives life (cf. 1 Cor 10–11). John, in the discourse on the bread of life, develops this metaphor. Jesus is the bread that comes down from heaven, given for eternal life. "Jesus said to them: I am the bread of life. Whoever comes to me will never be hungry and whoever believes in me will never be thirsty" (Jn 6:35).

TRANSFORMATION

How much has Jesus Christ transformed the Old Testament? This question has always been one of the most sensitive in understanding the relationship between the Old and the New Testaments. Concerning the Land, there is indeed, in Jesus' time, a break with the past, but the break occurs within a context of continuity with the message of Israel's Scriptures, particularly with that of the prophets.

In this final section, we intend to demonstrate how the concept of Messiah, as expressed in the life, death, and resurrection of Jesus of Nazareth directly correlates with a transformation of the concept of Land. It is true that during his lifetime, Jesus hardly ever ventured beyond the borders of the land of Israel. However, after his death and resurrection, his disciples did not remain very long in Jerusalem but went throughout the world preaching the good news. As promised in the Old Testament, the Land became a source of blessing that had to be spread over the entire surface of the earth. The subtle yet radical transformation of the understanding of Land is most evident in the Acts of the Apostles and in Saint John's Book of Revelation. Acts describes the origin (*arkhe*) of the Church, the body that prolongs in time the presence of Jesus in the world, while the Book of Revelation describes its end (*telos*).

THE ACTS OF THE APOSTLES

In the book of Acts, which tells the story of the early Church, the return of Jesus to his Father ushers in a new geography of the history of salvation. The mission given by the resurrected Jesus is to reach out beyond the land of Israel to the entire surface of the earth. "You will receive power when the Holy Spirit has come upon you; and you will be my witnesses in Jerusalem, in all Judea and Samaria and to the ends of the earth" (Ac 1:8). In the canonical structure of the New Testament, the Book of Acts can be compared to the historical books in the Old Testament. Just as these books chartered the way Israel lived the Torah, so Acts describes how the early community of disciples embodied the message and the acts of Jesus who had physically departed from this world.

With Acts, the center of history is changed from Jerusalem to the ends of the earth. Jesus' life and teaching have altered the concept of the Land. The passage is not an easy one. When Jesus is about to depart, at the beginning of Acts, his disciples ask him, "Lord, is this the time when you will restore the kingdom to Israel?" (Ac 1:6). Formed by the glorious, earthly representations of the kingdom, the disciples understandably expect the restoration of Israel's kingdom and want to know when it will come about. However, Jesus invites them to renounce this feverish anticipation of the end times and calls on them to receive the kingdom and proclaim it. "He replied, 'It is not for you to know the times or periods that the Father has set by his own authority'" (Ac 1:7). The Spirit that is promised them will not help them reestablish the kingdom of Israel but rather to be witnesses "to the ends of the earth" (Ac 1:8).

THE EXPANSION

Jerusalem is the setting for the first seven chapters of Acts in which Peter occupies a central place. The first to receive the Good News are the inhabitants of Jerusalem. It is only after the martyrdom of Stephen that journeys are undertaken outside of the city and that Philip goes to preach in Samaria to the north and on the road to Gaza to the south (Acts 8). Chapter 9 introduces Saul, the one who will carry the gospel far and wide, beyond the land of Israel. Then Peter reappears, going first to Lydda and then to Jaffa (further and further from Jerusalem). In Caesarea (even further to the north), in the episode with Cornelius, he becomes conscious of the call of the pagans to salvation. A new outpouring of the Spirit takes place, confirming the Church as a body made up of Jews and Gentiles and demonstrating what is said in the Epistle to the Ephesians about the role of Jesus in the community. "For he is our peace; in his flesh he has made both groups into one and has broken down the dividing wall that is the hostility between us" (Eph 2:14). Paul would also say in his Epistle to the Romans, "For I am not ashamed of the gospel; it is the power of God for salvation to everyone who has faith, to the Jew first and also to the Greek" (Rm 1:16). From chapter 13 until the end of Acts Paul becomes the driving force behind a missionary activity that seeks to find a modus vivendi for a community made up of both Jews and Gentiles. Even if difficulties and resistance arise from time to time, the decisions of the meeting in Jerusalem (Acts 15) allow for a compromise.

Peter, who never sets foot outside of the land of Israel in Acts, progressively disappears as the word increasingly spreads beyond the borders of the Land. Antioch slowly becomes the center of a model community made up of Jews and Gentiles, developing together the universal dimension of their identity in Christ (11:19). This community's location beyond the borders of the land of Israel is significant. Paul is called to Antioch to lead this assembly and organize missionary expansion. The city then becomes the center of intense missionary activity to the charted world at the time.

Just as Stephen's death served as the driving force behind the missionary expansion beyond Jerusalem, so the innovative leadership of James at the so-called "Council of Jerusalem" paves the way for a new understanding of the restoration of "the dwelling of David which has fallen" (Am 9:11 cited in Ac 15:17). But the context in which Amos is quoted radically changes the meaning intended by the prophet. In Amos, the issue was the conquest of Edom and its neighboring territories by a revitalized Davidic monarchy, whereas in Acts it is the need to bring salvation to "all other peoples . . . even all the Gentiles over whom my name has been called" (Ac 15:17).

With this legitimacy accorded to Paul's mission, we now follow him on his missionary journeys through Asia and into Europe (16:9) and finally to Rome. The rest of Acts is taken up with the account of the exemplary missionary activities of Paul, who always addressed his preaching first to Jews and then to Gentiles. Jerusalem remains a point of reference, even for Paul, as the gospel takes root in other cities. However, Jerusalem and the Holy Land cease to be considered as exclusive centers. The gatherings of believers are no longer turned toward Jerusalem but are focused on the resurrected Christ wherever Jesus' disciples are to be found. The world of Christian faith no longer has one geographical center but rather many centers. The land of Israel has not disappeared. It remains the place where Christianity was founded. But henceforth, communities spread out more and more over vast expanses of land. The borders of the "kingdom of God" preached by the apostles of Jesus transcend those of the land of Israel and extend to "the ends of the earth" (Ac 1:8).

THE BOOK OF REVELATION

The Book of Revelation is part of the literature that was both very popular among the early Christians yet regarded with suspicion by the au-

thorities. It was its prophetic dimension as well as the central place it
gave to Jesus that ensured this extravagantly imaginative writing a
place in the Christian canon of the New Testament. This book raises
and partially explains a particularly painful issue for the early Church:
how to deal with the enormous discrepancy between the kingdom that
is already within our midst following Jesus' resurrection, and the painful situation of the Church confronted by persecution? This is the
book's principal raison d'être. Jesus Christ is already enthroned in the
heavens as victor over the powers of evil. However, the earth is still
subject to the powers of darkness that have already been vanquished in
heaven. In order to comfort the believers, the visionary, with his eagle-
eyed perspective, anticipates that which has not yet happened. "The
kingdom of the world has become the kingdom of our Lord and of his
Christ, and he shall reign for ever and ever" (Rv 11:15). Though Jesus'
victory over the kingdom of evil and death is an undeniable reality, it
will become fully manifest only at the end of time when he returns in
glory.

In heaven, a divine liturgy unfolds in harmonious order, recalling
creation as well as the perfect worship in the temple. On earth, however, battle wages between the forces of evil and the forces of good
provoking the impatience of the righteous: "Until when, o holy and
true Lord, will you refrain from judging and avenging our blood on
those who dwell on the earth" (6:10). Finally, chapter 12 opens on a
hopeful note. In this violent combat, the immolated Lamb will be vic-
torious. Interestingly, it is on Mount Zion that the Lamb assembles his
armies (14:1). Between heaven and earth, Jerusalem remains the crossroad. Confronting her, Babylon rises up and is the place where the
counter-forces of evil gather together (17:5). A great voice in heaven
proclaims the ultimate victory of the Lamb (19:1) over death and the
forces of evil. The last two chapters of Revelation, which bring to an
end the entire Christian Bible, proclaim the restoration of creation.
"Then I saw a new heaven and a new earth" (21:1). Here, the prophecy
of Isaiah is finally realized. "For I am about to create new heavens and
new earth, the former things shall not be remembered or come to
mind" (Is 65:17).

In the beginning of Genesis, the Land meant the whole surface of
the earth, a place for human beings to live in harmony and intimacy
with God the Creator. After relations were broken off as a result of
Adam's sin, God promised and gave Israel a piece of land where a filial

relationship between him and the people might develop. The purpose in marking the boundaries of the land of Israel as a Land of promise was to restore the sanctity, the promise and blessings that were intended for the entire surface of the earth. In the long history of covenants offered and often refused, Jesus, son of Israel, fulfills the people's vocation through his filial obedience and restores to perfection an intimate relationship with the Father. "This is my Son, the Beloved, in whom I am well pleased" (Mt 3:17). From this moment on, it is the surface of the earth that is impacted by this restored relationship.

Like in Isaiah, the new creation is presented in Revelation as a new Jerusalem. "I saw the holy city, the new Jerusalem, coming down out of heaven from God, prepared as a bride, adorned for her husband" (21:2). However, the new Jerusalem has no temple in its midst. There is no need for a particular place of worship. "I saw no temple in the city, for its temple is the Lord God the Almighty and the Lamb" (21:22). In contemplating the heavenly city descending to earth, the reader realizes that its contours do not resemble those of the earthly Jerusalem that the people of the Old Testament and Jesus himself had frequented. It evokes rather the first chapters of Genesis and the return to the Garden, lost because of Adam's disobedience. The city is watered by a river like in Eden (cf. Gn 2:10). On its banks is the tree of life. The fruits of this tree are now offered to all humanity and its leaves cure the sickness of the nations (22:2). The originality of the Garden of Eden and of the heavenly Jerusalem-come-down-to-earth is in their being a place where the relations between God and the children of Adam have been restored. Christ's victory over the forces of darkness, sin, and death has made it possible for human beings to return to the Father. As in the beginning, creation has once again become a place of life with God.

Whereas with Abraham, God chose a particular individual and his descendants and gave them a well-circumscribed Land as their heritage, in Jesus the election is open to all and the heritage is creation itself. All of humanity is called to participate in the divine life, no longer in the closed space of the land of Israel, but everywhere on the face of the earth. This is a new creation. Human beings are restored to the divine image. The place where this restoration comes about is the body of Jesus Christ, the Church. Assembled there, in his body, foreshadowing the coming of the kingdom over the entire face of the earth, are those who follow the way of Jesus of Nazareth.

The Land and Christ

"The witness of the New Testament is therefore twofold: it transcends the land, Jerusalem, the temple. Yes: but its History and Theology demand a concern with these realities also. Is there a reconciling principle between these apparently contradictory attitudes? There is. By implication, it has already been suggested, the New Testament finds holy space wherever Christ is or has been: it personalizes 'holy space' in Christ, who, as a figure of History, is rooted in the land; he cleansed the temple and died in Jerusalem, and lends his glory to these and to the places where he was, but, as Living Lord, he is also free to move wherever he wills. To do justice to the personalism of the New Testament, that is to its Christo-centricity, is to find the clue to the various strata of tradition that we have traced and to the attitudes they reveal: to their freedom from space and their attachment to spaces. . . . In sum, for the holiness of place, Christianity has fundamentally though not consistently, substituted the holiness of the Person: it is Christified holy space."[8]

—W. D. Davies, *The Gospel and the Land*

Part II
The Land in Christian Tradition

3. Visiting the Land

A reading of the Christian Bible from Genesis to the Book of Revelation underscores that, from one end of the Bible to the other, the Land occupies a central place. Before we discuss the important shifts in interpretation brought about by modern biblical criticism, especially regarding the historicity of certain events and the circumstances under which these narratives were written, it is fitting to draw attention to the richness as well as to the complexity of the various interpretations of the Land in history. This diversity of interpretation is related to the foundational experience at Sinai, to the spiritual evolution of Israel through the centuries and to the historical concrete circumstances of this small people. However, psychological, cultural, and religious factors shared by the original authors and their first readers, but not necessarily by later readers, must also be taken into account. These include numerous assertions about God, about the way he manifests himself in the world and about the way he intervenes in the course of history and in the life of the people of Israel. Unlike the biblical text, which is fixed for all time in written form, these factors can vary according to the experiences of the readers who find themselves in different contexts and which lead to different readings and interpretations. Here, we examine various Christian interpretations of the Land both in Christian tradition as it developed through the centuries as well as in our own times.

We have already seen how the meaning of the Land changed each time Israel was called to live a new experience: the entry into the Land of Canaan; the inauguration of the kingdom with its dreams, crises, and disillusions; the shock of the exile and the loss of traditional points of reference; the return and refoundation in the middle of the sixth century, followed by the successive occupations by Persians, Greeks, and Romans; the brief period of independence gained by the Maccabees; the two wars against the Romans; and finally the dispersion of the Jewish people by Hadrian after the Second Jewish War (132–135). It is clear that the interpretation of the Land underwent a succession of transformations in the light of the vicissitudes of history.

This was also true of the "Jesus Movement." Seeing itself as heir, together with the Jewish people, of the promises of the Old Testament, the disciples of Jesus reread the history of salvation through the prism of the resurrection of Jesus. This constituted for them the basis upon which they reread and reinterpreted the Scriptures. From that moment on, the teaching, the acts, and, most of all, the event of the Resurrection of Jesus determined the attitude of early Christians toward the Holy Land. However, the historical circumstances of the expansion of Christianity in the world also played a part. Among the historical constraints, the First Jewish War (66–73) and the fall of Jerusalem (70) followed by the Second Jewish War against Rome led to the expulsion not only of Jews from Jerusalem and the country at large, but also of the followers of Jesus, who were not yet considered non-Jews. The parting of the ways between Jews and Christians, difficult to date accurately, certainly came much later.

In the first part of our presentation of the Land, we sought, as much as possible, to present the biblical texts according to their order in the Christian biblical canon. Although the biblical interpretations of the Land were not homogeneous, a number of major considerations emerged, highlighting the particularity of the Land that was given to a people so that it might establish there a covenant with God and live in harmony with each other, respecting each other's rights, and practicing justice. From the beginning of the Scriptures, Land, people, and covenant are interrelated: a Land promised then given by God to a people called to live a covenant; a Land lost through infidelity to a commitment undertaken; a Land dreamed of and desired, always promised, so that the first and original covenant might be lived once again. It may be said that the Jewish prayer that implores God to bring about the return to Jerusalem "next year" reverberates throughout the entire history of the Jewish people. This prayer remained utopian until historical circumstances shifted and allowed for the Jews to come to the Land they conceived of as that of their biblical ancestors.

As we continue our journey, our interest will focus on texts produced by Christians and intended for Christians. It is not our intention to present extensive texts explaining the Jewish perspective because, as mentioned earlier, our purpose here is to explore the way in which the Land was viewed by the Christian tradition. Throughout, however, we will touch upon the relation between the Jews and the Land, not directly as seen by Jews but as in a mirror held up by Christians, as we discuss the interpretation given by Christians to the theme of the Land, from the time of the Church Fathers until the present day.

We seek to show, with the help of a few examples, how the early Church put into practice the changes that Christ himself and, after his resurrection, his disciples, introduced regarding the Land. The places sanctified by the passage of Jesus on earth did eventually become objects of veneration. Though the gospel accounts took place within a geographical context made sacred by centuries of salvation history, they, nevertheless, do not reveal any particular insistence on these places. Thus, and it is striking, the gospel writers do not try to specify where certain events took place. The Transfiguration, for example, took place on "a high mountain" (Mk 9:2). Jesus enters "a synagogue" (Mk 3:1) or withdraws to "the lakeside" (Mk 3:7). This detachment from precisely named and identified locations reflects the situation of the evangelists and of the communities they were writing for, living outside of Palestine. It is also constitutive of the liturgical use that was made of these texts; a practice that tended to obscure whatever was too closely linked to a specific time or place in order to underscore the universal dimension that is applicable to readers of all times and all places. The basic theological perspectives of the gospels and their desire to be universally open to everyone led to a relativization of the specifically topographical details of Jesus' life. Yet, this detachment should not be taken as indifference to the foundational sites in the history of salvation. Archaeological digs have uncovered the extent of Jewish-Christian veneration for certain important places like Nazareth, Capernaum, and specific areas in the city of Jerusalem. It is not impossible that some New Testament texts originated within the context of liturgical pilgrimages to the places sanctified by the presence of Jesus. This is one of the exegetical hypotheses used to explain the visit of the women to the tomb in Mark's Gospel (16:1–9).

Only the most fragmentary information concerning the years that directly followed the death and ascension of Jesus exists. "We know of almost no certain case of a cultic veneration of the holy places in the second and third centuries."[1] It is unlikely though that Christian memory was wholly constructed later from purely imaginary elements. There must have been, among the inhabitants of Jerusalem who survived the torments of the two wars with Rome, some disciples of Jesus who remained in the city. Surely, they would have preserved some distinct reminders of the places sanctified by the presence of Jesus. Eusebius of Caesarea (265–340) relates that in the middle of the second century a certain Melito of Sardis (d. c. 190),[2] coming from Asia Minor, visited the places "where the Scriptures had been preached and fulfilled."[3] Origen (d. 254), traveling from Alexandria, also came "to look for the traces of Jesus, his disciples and the prophets."[4]

Pilgrimage in the Bible

In the Vulgate, one of the Latin versions of the Bible, Saint Jerome translates the common Hebrew term *ger* (resident alien) with the Latin word *peregrinus*, meaning traveler. Likewise, Jesus becomes a *peregrinus* in the exclamation of Cleopas: "You must be the only sojourner in Jerusalem who does not know" (Lk 24:18). In Christian vocabulary, the term *pilgrim* came to mean the one who embarked on a voyage with a religious purpose. The practice of pilgrimage is one of the most universal dimensions of religion. Holy places, venerated because of some extraordinary event (a cosmic phenomenon, the manifestation of a divinity, the memory of a charismatic personality), attract travelers eager to be empowered by the energy and power linked to these high places. Within the Bible itself, the practice of pilgrimage is attested to very early in the history of the Hebrew people. Like other believers, Elkana and his two wives, Pnina and Hannah, make the yearly pilgrimage to Shiloh (1 Sam 1). The prophet Elijah is one of the first who returns to the origins of the primitive faith, traveling to Mount Horeb, where God revealed himself to Moses. Depressed by failures and threats against his life, Elijah goes to the holy place of Horeb (1 Kgs 19:8–15) in order to be reinvigorated. Naaman, the head of the army of the King of Aram, must make a pilgrimage to the waters of the Jordan in order to be cured of his leprosy (2 Kgs 5). After the reform of King Josiah, the pilgrimage three times a year to Jerusalem becomes a religious obligation for all the faithful (Dt 16:16).

The exile that leads to the dispersion of the Jews from their land gives birth to a loving nostalgia for Jerusalem and motivates some to return for the occasional festive celebration. Tobit, however, makes us understand that there were not many who undertook the journey: "Often I was quite alone in making the pilgrimage to Jerusalem, fulfilling the law that binds all Israel perpetually" (Tb 1:6). The Gospel of John emphasizes that Jesus himself also abides by this obligation to go on pilgrimage to Jerusalem (2:13, 7:10, 12:12). When Philip meets the Ethiopian eunuch on the road to Gaza, he is returning from a pilgrimage to Jerusalem (Ac 8:27).

In modern times, Pope John Paul II published a letter on pilgrimage, in 1999.[5]

The first community professing belief in Jesus Christ was born and lived for a time in Jerusalem. The memory of certain precise locations connected with the important events in the life of Jesus, particularly the event of the resurrection, must surely have survived and been transmitted from generation to generation. Those who argue that the only credible Christian traces date from the epoch of Constantine (d. 337) must be reminded of the importance of the tradition that venerated memories before they became shrines. In about 150, the apologist Justin Martyr (d. c. 165) declared that Jesus had been born in a cave not far from Bethlehem. The second-century Palestinian historian Hegesippius knew of the stele and tomb of James, brother of the Lord, "close to the Temple." "Even if few in number, these traditions existed and one can see how they were carefully drawn upon at the beginning of the fourth century in order to form a list of theological holy places. Eusebius of Caesarea refers to them frequently in his *Onomasticon.*"[6]

CONSTANTINE AND THE RETURN OF THE CHRISTIANS TO JERUSALEM

In terms of the Land, Byzantine emperor Constantine's edict of 313, which granted religious freedom to Christians, brought about two important transformations. The first was the establishment of official Christian communities in Jerusalem. The second was the development of Christian pilgrimages to the holy places. We have already mentioned that after the Second Jewish War (132–135), Emperor Hadrian destroyed the city of Jerusalem, subsequently transforming it into a new Roman city called Aelia Capitolina. Constructed on the model of the ancient Roman towns, it comprised a central road (Cardo) as well as a transversal one (Decumanus), a forum and a temple dedicated to the Capitoline triad of Jupiter, Mercury, and Venus. With the rise of Constantine, the original name of the city was restored and it became known as Jerusalem once again. From as early as the first half of the fourth century, sanctuaries began to be erected on the principal sites sanctified by the presence of Jesus. However, was this not a step backward with regard to the teaching of Jesus, who interiorized religion to the point of considering all space capable of becoming holy through the presence of "saints" dispersed throughout the world?

It is useful to recall at this point some of the texts that illustrate the way in which certain Church authorities dealt with the tension between the transformation Jesus had wrought and the blossoming construction of shrines which attracted pilgrims.

SAINT JEROME (331–419)

Although Jerome himself chose to take up permanent residence in Bethlehem in a life consecrated to the study of Scripture, he was careful not to attribute an exaggerated importance to residing in the holy places. In a letter, written in about 395, to Paulinus of Nola (355–431), who was planning to go on pilgrimage to the holy places, he relativized the importance of the place, faithful to the perspective introduced by Jesus:

> What is praiseworthy is not to have been to Jerusalem but to have lived a good life while there. The city we are to praise and to seek is not that which has slain the prophets and shed the blood of Christ but that which is made glad by the streams of the river, which is set upon a mountain and so cannot be hid, which the apostle declares to be the mother of the saints and in which he rejoices to have his citizenship with the righteous. In speaking thus I am not laying myself open to a charge of inconsistency or condemning the course I myself have taken. It is not, I believe, for nothing that I, like Abraham, have left my home and people. But, I do not presume to limit God's omnipotence or to restrict to a narrow strip of earth Him whom the heaven cannot contain. Each believer is judged not by his residence in this place or in that but according to the desserts of his faith. "The true worshipers worship the Father neither at Jerusalem nor on Mount Geri-

zim; for God is a spirit and they that worship Him must worship Him in spirit and truth (Jn 4:24)." . . . Therefore, the spots which witnessed the crucifixion and the resurrection profit those only who bear their several crosses, who, day by day, rise again with Christ and who show themselves worthy of an abode so holy. Those who say: "The temple of the Lord, the temple of the Lord" (Jer 7:4) should give ear to the words of the apostle: "We are the temple of the Lord" (2 Cor 6:16) and "the Holy Spirit dwelleth in you" (Rm 8:11).[7]

After mentioning both the Holy Sepulcher, profaned by the figure of Jupiter and the statue of Venus, and Bethlehem desecrated in like manner, Jerome concludes:

"Access to the courts of heaven is as easy from Britain as it is from Jerusalem, for 'the kingdom of God is within you' (Lk 17:21). . . . To assure you that nothing is lacking to your faith, although you have not seen Jerusalem and that I am none the better living where I do."[8]

ATHANASIUS: ADVICE FOR VIRGINS RETURNING FROM A PILGRIMAGE TO JERUSALEM

In about 350, Athanasius, bishop of Alexandria from 328 to 373, wrote a letter containing a wealth of information about both the significance of the foundational places for believers as well as about their relative importance. He was addressing "certain virgins who, having gone to pray in Jerusalem, had returned." Athanasius underlined that the promises of the Old Testament and their fulfillment in Jesus Christ give these holy places their fundamental meaning. He further concedes that distancing oneself from these holy places might indeed be a source of pain:

"We have commiserated with you, servants of Christ, because, when you departed from the holy places, you shed rivers of bitter tears. As you walked on, distancing yourselves from the grotto of the Lord, you cried. . . . Leaving these pearls, you were cast into despair."[9]

After a detailed introduction, stressing the symbolic richness of the grotto of Bethlehem, of the tomb left empty by the resurrection, of Golgotha and of the Mount of Olives, the bishop transcends understandable emotions in order to explain what the holy places should represent for Christians:

"Console yourselves and do not be sad because you are never far from the holy places. There where Christ resides is holiness, there where Christ is present, is also the abundance of the joys of holiness. For he lives in our temples if we preserve holiness at all times without stain."[10]

For these virgins, their having walked in the footsteps of Jesus only had meaning if it was followed up by a true conversion, as in the case of Jesus' very first companions.

> Especially you who have gone to the holy places! Peter saw our Lord Jesus Christ and he left his nets to follow him (Mt 4:20); Zaccheus the publican saw him and he rejected all profit from fraud and received the savior (Lk 21:3–8). The sinner woman saw him and with her tears and hair she washed and dried his feet (Lk 7:37–38). Mary saw him and never left his feet (Lk 10:39). You too visit these holy places, and in these places of salvation see Christ walking. Reject the nets of this world, that is worldly attachments and attach yourselves to Christ, rejecting them, just like Zaccheus, and thus ransoming your life. Love greatly the Lord like that woman, shedding tears in your prayers, handing over to him the growth of your head of hair. Sit yourselves down at the feet of Jesus. Choose for yourselves the better part (Lk 10:42) and do not distance yourselves from the hearing of divine speech. Do not withdraw from Jerusalem but await the promise of the Father (Ac 1:4). You have seen the place of the nativity, let your souls be reborn. You have seen the place of the cross, let the world be crucified for you and you for the world (Ga 6:14). You have seen the place of the ascension, lift up your spirits on high. Let your bodies be on earth but your spirits in heaven, your residence with your father but your life with your Father in heaven.[11]

OBJECTIONS OF GREGORY OF NYSSA

The reactions of Jerome and Athanasius converge with another debate provoked by a letter of Gregory of Nyssa (331–394), one of the three Cappadocian theologians (together with his brother Basil of Caesarea and their common friend Gregory of Nazianzus). This debate was revived at the time of the Reformation as part of a polemic between Catholics and Protestants concerning the value of pilgrimages. The question debated is similar to the one found in the letter of Saint Jerome but more intensely polemical. The letter of Gregory of Nyssa dates from the time that he was bishop, at the end of the fourth century, a period in which he played a leading role in the East. After a visit to Arabia, Gregory paid a visit to Jerusalem, convoked there by certain "heads of the holy churches of Jerusalem" and not by Cyril of Jerusalem, bishop of Jerusalem (d. 386). The second letter, which interests us here, was written to the superior of a group of monks, trying to help him solve problems that had arisen in monastic life. One of the questions addressed concerns whether going on pilgrimage to Jerusalem has value for monks and nuns.

> As it seems that there are among those who have chosen the solitary life of withdrawal some who believe that it is a pious duty to see the places of Jerusalem in which one can see the traces of the sojourn of the Lord in the flesh, it would be praiseworthy to examine the rule. Do the commandments indeed demand this, commanding the fulfillment of this action as a prescription ordered by the Lord? However, if it is foreign to the commandments of the master, I do not know what it can mean to seek to fulfill a prescription that has been formulated for oneself only as a praiseworthy norm.[12]

Having formulated the problem in this fashion, the solution for Gregory is clear. "When the Lord calls the chosen ones to inherit the kingdom of heaven, he did not list the journey to Jerusalem among the good acts. When he enunciates the Beatitudes, he did not include any such activity."[13] Gregory then denounces the danger of immorality for monks and especially for nuns because of rampant promiscuity occasioned by lodging in pilgrim hospices along the way. Then, going to the heart of the matter, he affirms:

"In any case, what does the one who goes to these places have over and above everyone else? It is not as if the Lord lives in these places bodily even until today and that he is absent from our own parts. It is not as if the Holy Spirit were given in abundance to the residents of Jerusalem and that it is impossible for the same Spirit to come to us where we are."[14]

After emphasizing the fact that, unlike Cappadocia, Jerusalem is far from being exemplary, it being rather a place "where evil seems quite at home to such an extent that nowhere else does one seem have the same propensity to murder,"[15] Gregory offers some important advice:

You, then, who fear the Lord, praise him in those places where you are. Changing place does not in any way bring you closer to God. Rather, God will come to you there where you are, if the habitation of your soul is found to be such that the Lord might dwell in you and move about there. However, if your "interior man" is full of evil thoughts, even if you are on Golgotha itself, if you are on the Mount of Olives, even if you are in the tomb of the Anastasis [Greek for *resurrection*], you are as far from receiving Christ within yourself as those who have never even confessed faith in him.[16]

The Holy Spirit and the Holy Places

"Advise the brothers to leave their bodies in order to go toward the Lord rather than to leave Cappadocia in order to go toward Palestine. If anyone quotes the word of the Lord, who urges his disciples not to depart from Jerusalem, let him understand the meaning of this declaration. It was because the grace of the Holy Spirit had not yet come to be distributed to the apostles that the Lord told them to stay in the same place until they were clothed with power from on high. Certainly, if that which had happened at the beginning were to be reproduced today—that the Holy Spirit in the form of a fire, distributed his gifts to each one—it would be necessary that each one be at the place where this distribution of grace takes place. However, because 'the Spirit blows where it will' the believers here are also participants in grace according to the measure of their faith and not because of any travel to Jerusalem."[17]

—Gregory of Nyssa

CHURCHES IN JERUSALEM

Between 330 and 540 sanctuaries sprung up in Jerusalem. They were constructed in order to memorialize places that had been particularly sanctified by the presence of Jesus. The place of the death and resurrection of Jesus was the first to become a monument. Helen, mother of Emperor Constantine, having come to Jerusalem, had identified the place of the Holy Sepulcher. Around 325, Constantine sent his architect, Zenobius, to construct an edifice over these foundational places of Christianity. The structure was to commemorate both Calvary and the

Tomb within the same sacred space. This became known as the "Anastasis" (resurrection), the founding place of the "Jesus movement." Other construction projects followed: the Eleona, at the summit of the Mount of Olives, commemorating the final teachings of Jesus to his disciples; the Basilica of the Agony (c. 380); and the Ascension Church (c. 390) and Holy Sion in memory of the descent of the Holy Spirit on the apostles (413). Saint Mary of the Probatica (beginning of the fifth century) was first connected to the cure of the paralytic (Jn 5), but, from an early period, was venerated as the birthplace of the Virgin Mary. Churches consecrated to Saint John the Baptist (c. 450) and Saint Stephen (c. 460), located at the traditional place of the stoning of Stephen, were also dedicated. At the end of the fifth century other churches were added, that of Siloam, near the pool mentioned in Jn 9, and Saint Peter in Gallicantu (the cockcrow), commemorating the tears of Peter, not far from the palace of Caiphas. Finally, mention must be made of one of the most prestigious of these churches, the great "Nea" (new) church of Mary Mother of God constructed during the reign of Justinian and consecrated in 543.

Christians sought to construct memorials at the important places marked by the life of Jesus, where they could then come on pilgrimage. They did not come to stay at these places but rather they came to be touched by the events that had taken place there and then to move on to other places that had also become holy, where the presence of Jesus was no less palpable than in the places where everything began.

In the list of holy places that developed in Jerusalem, one might indeed be surprised by the lack of any mention of a memorial or monument in the vast area where the magnificent temple of the Lord had once stood. How might one explain that the most sacred space in Jewish history, where Jesus had left his mark both because of his prophetic acts and his teaching, was ignored by Jesus' disciples? One explanation might be that dead stones, present or absent, speak louder than words. In the fourth century, when the Church took possession of Jerusalem, she considered Judaism as no longer endowed with any of the ancient promises. Christians had now become the "new Israel," and, in that role, they were the sole depositories of the heritage of biblical history. According to the striking formula of the Jewish philosopher Yeshayahu Leibowitz, Christians, who presented themselves as the heirs of the Jews, were implying that, for Christians, Judaism had died; indeed, one can only inherit from the dead:

From the Christian point of view, the legitimate existence of a Judaism outside Christianity ceased long ago and that community which has continued nominally to exist for more than 1900 years in the form of a Jewish people that is not Christian is not a genuine religious community but a ghost, a mirage, or an act of Satan intended to mock Christianity and enrage it.[18]

A CONVENT OF WOMEN AT THE HEART OF THE CITY OF DAVID

A recent archaeological discovery might nuance the idea of a Christianity that had deliberately forgotten its Jewish origins. From 1968 until 1978, the Israeli archaeologist Benjamin Mazar supervised digs in the southern sector of the Esplanade that had once housed the Temple, in an area where the City of David had once been. One of his most astounding discoveries was the remains of what he described as a convent of consecrated virgins, constructed over the ruins of a Herodian structure. Mazar died in 1995 without having published the results of his finds; however, his granddaughter, Eilat Mazar, undertook to complete the publication of her grandfather's work.[19] The convent, built on an area of 18 m², might have been encircled by a hospice for pilgrims. This discovery seems to harmonize with a text written by the pilgrim Theodosius, who visited Jerusalem at the beginning of the sixth century: "Down below the Pinnacle of the temple is a monastery of virgins, and whenever one of them passes from this life, she is buried there inside the monastery. Throughout their lives they never go out of the door by which they entered this place. The door is opened only for a nun or penitent who wishes to join the monastery."[20]

The Land and the Rabbinic Tradition

In this discussion of the Land as seen by Christian authors, we can only briefly evoke the complex attitude of the rabbis, who formulated Jewish teaching on the Land in the Talmudic and post-Talmudic periods. The rabbis taught that the exile was God's punishment but they insisted that God would eventually bring about a return of his people to the Land that had been promised to the patriarchs. In the Jewish tradition, one "goes up" (*aliyah*) to the Land and "goes down" (*yeridah*) from there to any other place in the world. Here, we present three texts that show the complexity of rabbinic teaching.

A first text is from the Babylonian Talmud, foundational compendium of Rabbinic Judaism (which achieved its final form in the fifth century A.D.), and explains the privileged position of the land of Israel.

"Our Rabbis taught: One should always live in the land of Israel, even in a town most of whose inhabitants are idolaters, but let no one live outside the Land, even in a town most of whose inhabitants are Israelites; for whoever lives in the land of Israel may be considered to have a God, but whoever lives outside the Land may be regarded as one who has no God. For it is said in Scripture, 'to give you the Land of Canaan, to be your God' (Lv 25:38). Has he, then, who does not live in the Land, no God? But [this is what the text intended] to tell you, that whoever lives outside the Land may be regarded as one who worships idols. Similarly it was said in Scripture in [the story of] David, 'for they have driven me out this day that I should not cleave to the inheritance of the Lord, saying: Go, serve other gods' (1 Sam 26:19). Now, whoever said to David, 'Serve other gods'? But [the text intended] to tell you that whoever lives outside the Land may be regarded as one who worships idols" (Babylonian Talmud, Ketubot 111a).

However, in typical dialectic fashion, the Talmud goes on to discuss why it is forbidden for a Jew to leave the Diaspora in order to go up to the land of Israel before the time that God has fixed for the redemption of Israel.

"R. Zera was evading Rab Judah because he desired to go up to the Land of Israel while Rab Judah had expressed [the following view:] 'Whoever goes up from Babylon to the Land of Israel transgresses a positive commandment, for it is said in Scripture, They shall be carried to Babylon, and there shall they be, until the day that I remember them, says the Lord' (Jer 27:22). And R. Zera?—That text refers to the vessels of ministry (cf. Jer 27:19 ff). And Rab Judah?—Another text also is available: 'I adjure you, O daughters of Jerusalem, by the gazelles, and by the hinds of the field, [that ye awaken not, nor stir up love, until it please]' (Cant 2:7). And R. Zera?—That implies that Israel shall not go up [all together as if surrounded] by a wall. And Rab Judah?—Another 'I adjure you' (Cant 3:5) is written in Scripture. And R. Zera?—That text is required for [an exposition] like that of R. Jose son of R. Hanina who said: 'What was the purpose of those three adjurations?—One, that Israel shall not go up [all together as if surrounded] by a wall; the second, that whereby the Holy One, blessed be He, adjured Israel that they shall not rebel against the nations of the world; and the third is that whereby the Holy One, blessed be He, adjured the idolaters that they shall not oppress Israel too much.'" (Babylonian Talmud, Ketubot 111a–b).

Finally, a tendency toward the spiritualization of the Land can also be found in the Jewish tradition, as expressed, for example, by Rabbi Menachem ben Solomon HaMeiri (1249–1316) in his commentary on the above cited Talmudic text: "Any place where wisdom and fear of sin are present has the normative status of the land of Israel" (Commentary on Ketubot 111a).

For Orthodox Jews throughout the centuries, a return to the Land was only possible once the messianic age had dawned. For this reason, many Orthodox Jews strongly opposed modern Zionism, arguing that it was a rebellion against God's plan for the Jewish people.[21]

PILGRIMAGE AND THE CONQUEST OF THE CRUSADES

It is impossible to speak of the Christian relationship to the Land without evoking the episode of the Crusades, so influential for the image of Christians as perceived by both Muslims and Jews. Various factors motivated these expeditions of knights to the Holy Land and to the other lands of the East: the growing awareness of Europe as it faced the Islamic world; the imperial heritage of Byzantium; and the desire to complete the project of Charles Martel, who had been stopped by the Arabs at Poitiers in 732. The arrival of the Arabs in the Holy Land in 638 had not brought to a stop the flow of pilgrims even if the movement did slow down considerably. Despite some rather brief periods of intolerance, Islam, on the whole, showed itself relatively hospitable to Christian pilgrims. One testimony can be found in the account of the pilgrimage of Arculf, a French bishop, who arrived in the Holy Land in about 700, shortly after the arrival of the Arabs, written by Adamnan, abbot of Iona. This account greatly influenced the Anglo-Saxons, becoming a basic reference and intensified their desire to go on pilgrimage to the Holy Land. With the rise of the Seljuk Turks, the West was troubled by the growing intolerance shown to Christians; however, taken in isolation, this factor alone cannot explain the launching of the Crusades at the end of the eleventh century.

Numerous other hypotheses have been formulated in order to account for the launching of the Crusades at this precise moment. Was it a desire to respond to the appeals for help coming from the Byzantine emperor in Constantinople, threatened by the arrival of the Turks? Was it a dream to reconstitute a lost unity between the churches of the East and those of the West? Was the West overpopulated and seeking new territories? Or was it a desire for adventure on the part of young nobles deprived of land? These factors do not, however, fully account for the enthusiastic response given to the call made by Pope Urban II at the Council of Clermont in 1095. He asked the knights of France and of all Europe to take up arms and go off to reconquer Jerusalem and in particular the Tomb of Christ, which had fallen into the hands of Muslims: "They have seized possession of the holy city, illustrious for the passion and resurrection of Christ, reducing her and her churches to intolerable servitude."[22] The knights crossed themselves, shouting "Deus lo volt! Deus lo volt!" (God wills it). A war broke out that took on all the aspects of a "holy war," prolonging the reconquest of Spain and the defense of Europe against Islam.

In addition to these political factors, there was also an undeniable messianic dimension. While the Crusades can be seen as a continuation of the flow of pilgrims to the Holy Land, their aim was quite different from that of former pilgrims, for they sought to establish the kingdom of Christ by conquering the Land and restoring it to Christian rule, a sentiment expressed in Latin as *de recuperatione terrae sanctae*.

The War for God

From 1146 onward Saint Bernard of Clairvaux (1090–1153) was heavily involved in promoting the Second Crusade (1147–49) through his preaching. Through his family ties, he was very close to many of the knights who had gone off to conquer the Holy Land. Because of these links (Hugues du Payns, founder of the Order of the Templars, was a cousin) and especially because of his great love for the Land of God, he was troubled by the news of the great difficulties encountered by the Crusaders upon their arrival in the Land. In his *In praise of the New Chivalry*, he expressed his passion for the Holy City, "you who are sanctified by the Most High to be his tabernacle" (Ps 45:5) and for the Land of promise where "milk and honey had once flowed" (Ex 3:6) and for its inhabitants. His apologetics for a holy war cannot but evoke contemporary discourse about *jihad* in some extremist Muslim circles. "The knights of Christ carry out the battles of their Lord with confidence, without having to doubt in the least that they are committing a sin in killing the enemies or facing the danger of being killed themselves. In fact, death for Christ, whether it is undergone or inflicted, carries no guilt but rather is worthy of great glory. On the one hand it is for Christ that one gains this glory and on the other hand it is Christ himself who is gained. He surely accepts willingly, we do not doubt it, the death of an enemy who must be punished and who gives himself even more willingly to the knight in order to console him. Thus, and I repeat, the knight of Christ inflicts death with complete security and undergoes death with even more assurance. . . . If he dies it is for his own good and if he kills it is for Christ."[23]

In concluding this presentation of the transformation of the significance of the Land initiated by the first disciples of Jesus, we note that holy places had been sanctified both by the history of Israel and events in the life of Jesus. They retain their symbolic importance with the development of Christianity. From the very beginning and to the present day, the Mother Church of Jerusalem has maintained a presence in the Land, a local church that has played the role of "custodian" of the Christian memory. The living stones, the Christian men and women who make up this local church of Jerusalem, have been confronted with many trials throughout the centuries and still today they struggle to survive. The particular status of these holy places, which bear witness to the memory of the people of Israel, to that of the life of Jesus, and finally to the mysterious "night journey" of Muhammad, is disputed in the name of different religious experiences that are sometimes in conflict. Thus, one may speak of a triple "geo-theology," Jewish, Christian, and Muslim, with all the dangers that are involved when the same space is claimed by different and even opposing religious institutions and traditions. The Church of Jerusalem has the singular and grave responsibility of being rooted in the places sanctified by Christ. It is thus unlike any other church. Since the time of Constantine, the "Holy Places" (Constantine was the first to explicitly use the term) have continued to exercise a powerful attraction on the Christian imagination. From all over, pilgrims have flowed toward the Land, first as isolated individuals and then in group pilgrimages, in order to discover the places where their faith was born. The anonymous pilgrim of Bordeaux (333–34) and, later, the mysterious Egeria (c. 380), were the first to recount in writing their experiences and discoveries. They sought not only to share what they had seen but also to encourage others to follow in their footsteps. They would have many successors, whose subsequent travel accounts are a precious source of information for studying the history of this much-tormented Land.

The rise of Islam did not interrupt the flow. Pilgrims continued to come and share their experiences, whether orally or in writing. Listeners and readers were thus also able to share in the fascination that these places, sanctified by the events in the life of Jesus, exercised. The period of the Crusades shows how much this fascination with the Holy Land stirred the Christian imagination as well as how pilgrimage could be transformed into military expeditions in order to conquer the Land by force of arms.

The Land and the Muslim Tradition

The language, imagery, and many of the characters in the Quran, the holy writ of Muslims, resonate with the biblical narrative of the Old and the New Testaments. In fact, at first Muhammad, founding prophet of the religion of the Quran, Islam, directed his disciples to pray facing Jerusalem and only later changed the direction of prayer to Mecca, in the Arabian peninsular. The Quran echoes the accounts of the promise of the Land to the people Moses led out of Egypt:

"Moses said to his people: Oh my people, remember the favor of God to you, when he made prophets among you, made you kings and gave you what he had not given to any other people. Oh my people enter the holy land (*al-ard al-muqaddasah*) which God has assigned to you and turn not back ignominiously, for then you will be overthrown to your own ruin" (Quran, Surat al-Maida 5, 20–21).

The narratives, as retold in the Quran, give a special place to the Land and thus it is not surprising that Muhammad is depicted as having come on a mystical journey from the Arabian peninsular to the Land that was home to the prophets that preceded him:

"Glory [to God] who did take his servant for a journey by night from the Sacred Mosque (*masjid al-haram*, understood as Mecca) to the Farthest Mosque (*masjid al-aqsa*, understood as Jerusalem), whose precincts we did bless—in order that we might show him some of our signs: for he is the all-seeing and the all-hearing" (Quran, Surat al-Isra' 17.1).

The Prophet's night journey to Jerusalem, commemorated by Muslims each year on the night of *al-isra' wa-l'mi'raj* (the journey and the ascent) became emblematic for mystical experience in Islam. This was developed by many later writers, the best known among them being the Andalusian-born mystic Ibn al-Arabi (d. 1240) in his *Cosmic Tree*. Jerusalem was ruled by various Muslim governments from the conquest of Umar (in 638) until the end of the Ottoman period (1917), except for the time of the Crusades, and the city remains marked by the magnificent shrines that were constructed there, particularly the two mosques, Al-Aqsa Mosque and the Dome of the Rock, on the mount that had once been the place of the Temple. Muslim tradition strengthened the Muslim link to the city of Jerusalem, making it a privileged place of pilgrimage, second in importance only to the shrines in Mecca and Medina. As a Muslim from Jerusalem wrote in the tenth century:

"Verily Mecca and Medinah have their superiority by reason of the Qa'a-bah (sacred black stone) and the Prophet—the blessing of Allah be upon him and his family—but, in truth, on the Day of Judgment both cities will come to Jerusalem and the excellencies of them all will then be united. And as to Jerusalem being the most spacious of cities, why, since all created things are to assemble there, what place on earth can be more extensive than this."[24]

The spiritual journey of Saint Francis of Assisi (1182–1226) stands in stark contrast to the violence of the Crusades. Francis was especially motivated by the desire for martyrdom, which prompted him to seek out encounters with Islam, first in Spain and then in Morocco. It was his journey to the East, at a difficult period in his life with regard to the spiritual and lay movement that he had founded, that allowed him to discover the reality of Islam. In 1219, at Damietta in Egypt, he doubted whether the small army of the Crusaders would be able to vanquish the armies of the Sultan. Francis was a critic not so much of the Crusader idea as of the blindness that it could foster. Without arms or an escort, he paid a visit to the Sultan in the hope of converting him to the Christian faith in order to prevent the spilling of more blood. Later, having returned to Italy, he distanced himself even from this tactic of direct preaching, preferring to promote a presence and respect that are expressed in the First Rule of 1221:

The brothers, who so desire, may live spiritually among the Saracens (medieval term for Muslim) in two different ways. One way is not to engage in dispute or quarrel, but rather to be submissive to every human creature because of God and to confess the Christian faith. The other manner is, when one sees it is possible and pleasing to the Lord, to proclaim the Word of God so that the infidels might believe in God Almighty, Father, Son and Holy Spirit, in the creator of all things and in the Son, redeemer and savior so that they might be baptized and become Christian. The

one who is not reborn of water and spirit cannot enter the kingdom of God.[25]

Franciscans would maintain a privileged relationship with the Holy
Land. They were forced to leave after the fall of Saint John of Acre (in
May 1291) but, during a period based in Cyprus, the provincial minister
preserved the title of "Minister of the Holy Land." In 1333, the Franciscans were given charge of four Holy Places, in Bethlehem and Jerusalem. That year saw the birth of the Custody of the Holy Land, with
its seat in Jerusalem. From the pope, it received the mission to maintain
a living Christian presence in the Holy Places.

   In order to counterbalance the violence of the Crusades, we mention
here the name of another Franciscan, Raymond Lull (1236–1316). This
native of Majorca, a great figure among the early humanists and theologians of the late Middle Ages, after having completed his studies in the
great universities of Europe, spent close to sixty years as a missionary
in Muslim lands. With him, another page was turned in the relationship
with Muslims and Islam, one diametrically opposed to the one written
by the Crusaders. He wrote:

"I believe that this conquest must not be carried out in any way other
than that shown by you and your apostles, Lord. This is the way of
love, prayer and the shedding of tears. Thus, the holy knights of religion
should set out, arming themselves with the sign of the cross, being filled
with the Holy Spirit and let them preach to the infidels the truths of the
Passion."[26]

4. A Christian Reading of the Land until Vatican II

With the expansion of Christianity, thanks to the official status granted it by Emperor Constantine making it the official religion of the Empire in the fourth century, the relationship between Christians and Jews entered a new stage exemplified by the latter's forced submission to the former. Pinchas Lapide, a noted Jewish historian of Catholic-Jewish relations, commented: "Since the third century, the behavior of Christians toward Jews is characterized by a strange ambivalence: on the one hand a Platonic love for an abstract Israel, which, for good or for bad, remains 'the people of the Bible' or of 'the Old Covenant,' and on the other hand a rising hostility toward the Jews, who were traitors according to the narrative of Matthew concerning Judas or murderers according to the Gospel of John. It is with this mixture of hate and love that eighteen centuries of Jewish history were written."[1]

As of the fourth century, a language of Christian domination with regard to the Jews developed. Christians saw themselves as the new Israel, which had "replaced" the first Israel, and therefore had become the heirs of Israel's privileges. According to the brutal formula of John Chrysostom: "Do you wish me to bring forward against you other prophets who clearly state the same fact, namely that your religion will come to an end, that ours will flourish and spread the message of Christ to every corner of the world, that a different kind of sacrifice will be introduced which will put an end to yours."[2]

As a result of this vision, Jews were supposed to submit themselves to the Christian interpretation of history, including the assessment of their own role in the history of salvation. The continued existence of a Jewish community despite the coming of Christ was understood either as an anomaly, brought about by the stubbornness of Israel and which could only be explained in Christian theological terms, or as a permanent sign of contradiction ultimately demonstrating the truth of Christianity. Without in any way justifying the anti-Judaism that was prevalent in Christian theology, Gavin Langmuir points out that these attitudes also constituted a defense mechanism against a perceived threat. "For Christians, the ability of Jews to maintain their own identity was not only annoying or hateful in the way ethnic differences so often are, it was an intimate and enduring threat to their sense of identity, a challenge built into their own religion."[3]

The dispersion of the Jews throughout the world, although predating Christianity by many centuries and largely the result of historical circumstances, received a new and normative interpretation, based upon a certain reading of the gospels. In this chapter we will not document the various types of treatment, often humiliating, meted out to Jews especially after the Constantinian era (fourth century). Well documented also is how the Fathers of the Church and Christian tradition contributed to the development of negative and humiliating attitudes, discourse, and behavior directed toward the Jews (and termed "a teaching of contempt" by the Jewish historian Jules Isaac).[4] Likewise, we will not deal here with the thorny question of the degree to which the gospels contributed to this process. It is evident that the gospels, and especially the Gospel of John, often use the term "the Jews" with growing hostility (so that the reader might forget that the gospel writers were themselves Jews) and this perhaps already contains the seeds that would subsequently produce the bad fruit of anti-Jewish teaching century after century. According to Daniel Marguerat, the gospels impose on those called "the Jews" "the role of the bad guy."[5] These texts as they were read by generations of Christians undoubtedly inspired negative attitudes toward the members of the Jewish community. With historical hindsight, and particularly after the unimaginable tragedy of the Holocaust with its six million Jewish dead, one can understand today the historical blindness of the Church, whose attitude toward the Jews paved the way for the Nazi genocide. It is hoped that, today, Christians have become more aware of the dangers of certain anti-Jewish literalist interpretations of the Bible. The Second Vatican Council (1962–1965) marked a liberating turning point in the interpretation and understanding of the Jewish reality for all Catholics.

This study of Christian discourse concerning the relationship of the Jews to the Land of their ancestors will first examine the writings coming from the early centuries of the Church (especially those of the Church Fathers), then, in the next chapter, the declarations of the Church in the period after Vatican II.

THE JEWS ACCORDING TO TERTULLIAN

In the face of the unjust accusations made against Christians and the persecutions that followed these accusations, Tertullian (155–222) decided to write a well-formulated defense of Christianity that was addressed to the magistrates of the Roman Empire at the end of the second century. "Let the truth reach your ears by the private and quiet avenue of literature."[6] After having shown "the great antiquity" of the writings of the Jewish people, he points to the emergence of the Christians and their identity within a hostile context. "The origin of this religion . . . dates from the time of Tiberius. Truth and hatred come into existence simultaneously. As soon as the former appeared, the latter began its enmity. It has as many foes as there are outsiders, particularly among the Jews because of their jealousy, among the soldiers because of their blackmailing and even among the very members of our own household because of corrupt human nature."[7]

One can sense here the state of relations with the Jews at the end of the second century. Tertullian develops what is almost a caricature of the history of Israel, opposing the justice, faith, and merits of the patriarchs with the innumerable sins of the Jews in his own time. The current state of the Jews is nothing other than the consequence of their sinfulness according to Tertullian:

> At all times the Jews enjoyed favor with God and there also were
> outstanding justice and faith on the part of their original founders.
> As a result, their race multiplied and their kingdom rose to exalted power. Such good fortune was theirs that by the words of
> God, whereby they were taught, they were forewarned about
> serving God and not offending Him. To what extent they failed,

being so filled with presumptuous confidence in their ancestors as to stray from their teaching into the manners of the world—even if they did not acknowledge it themselves—the unhappy lot that today is theirs would indicate. Scattered, wandering about, deprived of land and sky of their own, they roam the earth without man or God as king, a race to whom there is not accorded the right granted to foreigners to set foot upon and greet one land as home.[8]

This text reproduces a number of the most important anti-Jewish motifs that are taken up time and again in Christian literature:

(1) The Jews have been unfaithful to the faith of their fathers.
(2) The Jews rejected "the truth" as soon as it appeared. They have become enemies and even a deicide people (killers of God).
(3) The subsequent punishment (in italic below) is described in an impersonal and passive form, implying that it is God himself who is responsible for the sanctions mentioned.
(4) At the center of the punishment is the relationship with the Land that God had given to their forefathers. Now the Jews are "*scattered, wandering about, deprived of land and sky of their own,*" undeniable proof of the punishment for their lack of faithfulness.

This text is important because it contains an interpretation of history that will be repeated, more or less brutally, by successive generations. It provides Christians with the justification for the presence of the Jews in their midst and for their exile from the Land. This theological reading of history ignores the fact that the dispersion of the Jews is much more complex and that it preceded the birth of Christianity by many centuries. Jewish migration from the Land had generally followed wars and natural disasters leading to the forcible transfer or migration of populations. Furthermore, from a Christian point of view, this dispersion was far from being a negative phenomenon because the Jewish communities of the Diaspora laid the groundwork for the preaching of the first Christian missionaries as retold in the Book of Acts.

Christian Reading of the Old Testament

"Christianity . . . grew out of Judaism amidst a conflict with non-Christian Jews, and that birth trauma was enshrined in Christian revelation and central to Christian theology. The Christian acceptance of Jewish scripture and the

Christian claim to be the true Israel meant that, for Christians, Jews were a central element of God's providential plan. Moreover, the continued existence of Judaism after Jesus was the physical embodiment of doubt about the validity of Christianity. Unlike pagan anti-Judaism, Christian anti-Judaism was a central and essential element of the Christian system of beliefs. The elaboration of anti-Judaic doctrine and polemics and the effort to prove that Christianity was foreshadowed in the Old Testament would be a theological enterprise for centuries."[9]

"When pressed for evidence of the supernatural origins of Christianity, the second-century Church sought an answer principally in the fulfillment by Jesus of Old Testament prophecy and the universal diffusion of the faith. Indeed for many centuries, the exposition of prophecy continued to form the prime content of the instruction given to catechumens when they were taught about the person of Christ. But there also had to be an explanation of why Jews did not interpret the same scripture, their scripture, as Christians did. Consequently, virtually every major Christian writer of the first five centuries either composed a treatise in opposition to Judaism or made this issue a dominant theme in a treatise devoted to some other subject. Central to these polemics were arguments that Jews misinterpreted the meaning of passages in Hebrew Scripture. As Justin Martyr put it in the second century, when talking to a Jew, they are "your Scriptures, or rather not yours but ours for we believe and obey them, whereas you, though you read them, do not grasp their spirit" (Dialogue with Trypho)."[10]

"The practice among Christians that has historically dominated the Church is to read the 'Old' Testament as a collection of promises. The glorious hopes of the Hebrew Scriptures find fulfillment in the 'New' Testament in the person of Jesus Christ. The Church Fathers consistently mined the Hebrew Scriptures in search of texts that prophesied the coming of Christ and they found 'evidence' wherever they looked. . . . In its struggle to establish its own legitimacy, the early Church developed a polemical attitude toward the Jewish people. The Church characterized the Jews as blind to the truth of their own Scriptures. Some Christians maintained that the Jews did recognize the spiritual treasure within their Scriptures but refused to accept it because they were in league with the devil. The process of laying claim to the Bible either dispossessed Jews of their Scriptures by writing them out of their own story or it demonized them as adversaries of biblical truth."[11]

—A. Pessah, K. Meyers, and C. Leighton,
"How Do Jews and Christians Read the Bible?"

ORIGEN: "MOSES, THE SERVANT OF GOD, IS DEAD"

Origen's commentary on the Book of Joshua has come down to us only in the Latin translation by Rufinus. Specialists, however, attribute a great degree of reliability to this translation with regard to the lost original. This work, written at the time of the persecutions of Christians under Emperor Decius (249–250), is one of Origen's last biblical commentaries. It represents a fine example of an allegorical reading of the biblical narrative. It demonstrates the power of the allegorical interpretation in playing down the omnipresent violence of the narratives of the Israelite conquest of the Land and in emphasizing the present relevance of the book: "It is for us, who come at the end of the centuries, that this book has been written." Each reader is invited to "cross the Jordan with haste."[12]

The giving of the Land, as told in the Book of Joshua, is at the center of these homilies. However, Origen proposes a Christian reading of this story which is allegorical, both Christological and spiritual. For example, he sees in the original inhabitants of the Land demons that dwell within each one of us. "Within us are all those breeds of vices that continually and incessantly attack the soul."[13] For Origen, the Promised Land is to be found in the person of Jesus Christ. "If, therefore, you receive this second circumcision of the vices cut off every defect of wrath, pride, jealousy, lust, greed, partiality and other such things from yourself, then the reproaches of Egypt are wiped away from you and, transported to the Land of promise, you will receive the inheritance of the kingdom of heaven through the true Jesus, Christ, our Lord and Savior."[14]

It is in the person of Jesus that the promises of the Land are fulfilled, as laid out in the New Testament.

In Origen's writings we do not find the vengeful tones that will later be found in the writings of John Chrysostom. However, for Origen also, Judaism has served its purpose and can now disappear, as is illustrated by this commentary on the death of Moses.

If, then, you should observe that Jerusalem is destroyed, the altar forsaken, that there are no sacrifices, victims or libations, nowhere priests, nowhere high priests, nowhere service of the Levites—when you see all these things cease, then say: "Moses, my servant, is dead." If you see no one "coming three times a year into the presence of the Lord" (Ex 23:17), neither to offer gifts in the temple, nor to slaughter the Paschal lamb, nor to eat unleavened bread, nor to offer the first fruits, nor to dedicate the first born—when you see none of these things celebrated, then say: "Moses, the servant of God, is dead." When, indeed, you see the nations entering into the faith, churches raised up, altars sprinkled not with the flowing blood of beasts but consecrated with "the precious blood of Christ" (1P 1:19); when you see priests and Levites ministering not "the blood of bulls and goats" (Heb 9:13) but the Word of God through the grace of the Holy Spirit, then say that Jesus received and retained the leadership after Moses, not Jesus the son of Nun but Jesus the son of God.[15]

For a Jew, humanly speaking, the Land has been lost forever. What remains for the Jew is to overcome this loss by searching for the true Land.

If, therefore, o Jew, coming to the earthly city of Jerusalem, you find it overthrown and reduced to ashes and embers, do not weep as you do now "as if with the mind of a child" (1 Cor 14:20), do not lament; but search for a heavenly city instead of an earthly one. Look above! And there you will discover "the heavenly Jerusalem that is mother of all" (Ga 4:26). If you see the altar forsaken, do not be sad; if you do not find the high priest, do not despair. There is an altar in heaven and there stands a high priest "of good things to come, according to the order of Melchisedek" (Heb 5:10), one chosen by God. Thus, therefore, the earthly inheritance has been demolished for you, although with the tenderness and compassion of God, so that you may seek in inheritance in heaven.[16]

The True Land

"The Lord said to Jesus, the son of Nun, the assistant of Moses: 'Moses, my servant, is dead. Now, therefore, rising up, cross over this Jordan, you and all this people, into the Land that I am giving you' (Jos 1:1–2). Perhaps you seek to know in what way our Lord Jesus, the son of God, could also be the assistant of Moses? It is because, "when the fullness of time had come God sent his own son made of a woman, made under the Law" (Ga 4:4). Through this, therefore, that he was "made under the Law" he became the assistant of Moses. God tells them to cross over into the Land, not the Land Moses gave, but "that which I am giving you." Therefore, you see that God gives the Land to the people through Jesus after Moses was dead. What Land? Doubtless, the Land about which the Lord says: "Blessed are the meek, who will possess the Land as their inheritance."[17]

JOHN CHRYSOSTOM: THE JEWS EXILED FOR ETERNITY

The discourse of John Chrysostom (354–407) against the Jews is particularly virulent. Enclosed in a very tightly woven argumentation, he represents an important Church interpretation of the "theological" status of the Jews in the fourth century. *The Eight Discourses against the Jews* aim to turn Christians away from Jews, especially at the time of Jewish feasts, when Christians were attracted by the synagogue. John Chrysostom begins with concrete facts of community life and elaborates a particularly severe and even starkly negative reading of Judaism. His interpretation of the exile follows the traditional lines already established but he also goes much further. In order to turn Christians away from the contemporary synagogue, he equates the Jews of his day with those who crucified Jesus: "Is it not foolish then to show such readiness to flee from those who have sinned against a man but to enter into fellowship with those who have committed outrages against God himself? Is it not strange that those who worship the crucified keep common festival with those who crucified him? Is it not a sign of folly and the worst madness?"[18]

Through his resurrection, Jesus showed his power, which continues to have effects on the Jews today: "What does the Jew say? 'The man who said this is my foe. I crucified him, so how am I to accept his testimony?' But this is the marvel of it. You Jews did crucify him. But after he died on the cross, he then destroyed your city; it was then that he dispersed your people; it was then that he scattered your nation over the face of the earth. . . . Because you were not willing to recognize his power through his benefactions, he taught you by his punishment and vengeance that no one can struggle with or prevail against his might and strength."[19]

With regard to the dispersion of the Jews, John Chrysostom, using certain prophetic texts with great liberty, seeks to show that the Jews had to undergo four captivities: the Egyptian, that of Nebuchadnezzar, that of Antiochus Ephiphanus, and finally that of the Flavian emperors after the Second Jewish War. For the first three, "God saw that each captivity was prophesied. He carefully foretold the place, the duration, the kind, the form of their misfortune, the return from slavery and everything else."[20] However, the fourth captivity, which begins with the period of the Church and which is now in force, will have no end:

> When you hear Daniel say: "Until the end of time," what else is left for you Jews to look forward to? . . . What is there for me to say to you now that has not already been said? When the prophets predicted the other captivities, they spoke not only of the captivity, but also of the length of time it was appointed for each bondage to last; for this present captivity, however, they set no time, but, to the contrary, said that the desolation would endure until then end.[21]

Chrysostom's discourses on the Jews already contain most of the clichés that would be repeated over the centuries:

(1) The Jews have always been an "impudent and obstinate nation" (*Fifth Discourse*).

(2) Their supreme infidelity was to have become "the murderers of God himself."

(3) God, strong and invincible, punishes them and wreaks vengeance.

(4) A list of these punishments include: "wandering, exiled, destitute, subject to Roman domination, passing from one place to another without have an ensured residence in any city, in any house."[22]

(5) According to the Scriptures, this exile, unlike the others, would last for all eternity.

A question remains unanswered: how should one react to such a reading of the Bible? Needless to say, it reflects a particular context, whose underlying assumptions and gross limitations have been highlighted by critical biblical analysis. It might be added that the particularly vehement tone of Chrysostom's discourses probably bears witness to the fact that there was a Jewish community in Antioch that was dynamic, vigorous, and attractive in Chrysostom's time. To deter Christians from joining this community, John Chrysostom had recourse to arguments that, with hindsight, amounted to an unacceptably literalist reading of the Scriptures.

The interpretation of the exile as divine punishment is indeed present in the Bible, especially in the prophetic texts. Why then, when

Chrysostom makes use of this biblical ploy, does it seem so intolerable? Some reasons can be suggested. The Bible does attribute historical events that are understood as being punishment to God. However, this occurs within the confessional context of the awareness of the people punished. Israel, in exile, confesses her sin to God, admitting the justice of his punitive acts. This is neither historical analysis nor accusation by an outsider but rather the expression of profound remorse. Furthermore, the prophetic biblical discourse that thundered against the sins of Israel was directed by spokespeople from within the Jewish people in a condemnation of their own failings. The prophet, in criticizing his own people, is always one of them, an insider, wrenched apart by his role of announcing God's anger. He must be the voice of God denouncing the sins of Israel and calling Israel to repent, but he is also the voice of the people, defending them before God. In stark contrast, the angry discourse of John Chrysostom comes from the outside and, in the name of the gospel and the Church, interprets, judges, and condemns.

AUGUSTINE: THE JEWS DISPERSED IN ORDER TO BEAR WITNESS

Like many of his theologian predecessors in the first centuries of the Christian era, Augustine (354–430) often refers to the place of the Jews in salvation history. This is particularly true in his polemical writings *Adversus Judaeos* (against the Jews), where he contrasts his understanding of Scripture with that of the Jews.[23] The role occupied by the Jews in the apologetic and theological writings of the first Fathers shows how important the Jews were for Christian self-understanding. Far from being marginal, the Jews were successful in attracting pagans and Christians alike to the synagogue. Without justifying the vociferous anti-Judaism in the writings of the Fathers, recognizing Judaism's vitality might help understand the vigorous tone used by the Fathers when talking about the Jews. Augustine is, however, usually respectful of his adversaries, not failing to recognize a certain degree of affinity with them. "Whether the Jews receive these divine testimonies with joy or with indignation, nevertheless let us proclaim them with great love for the Jews. Let us not proudly glory against the broken branches; let us rather reflect by whose grace it is, and by much mercy, and on what root we have been ingrafted. Then, not savoring of pride but with a deep sense of humility, not insulting with presumption but rejoicing with trembling, let us say: 'Come ye. . . .' "[24]

Recalling "the Babylon wherein we are captives and the Jerusalem for a return to which we are sighing,"[25] Augustine points out: "The former Jerusalem indeed, by the Jews is not now inhabited, for after the crucifixion of the Lord, vengeance was taken upon them with a great scourge, and being rooted up from that place where with impious licentiousness, being infuriated, they had madly raged against their Physician, they have been dispersed throughout all nations, and that land hath been given to Christians; and there is fulfilled what the Lord had said to them: 'Therefore the Kingdom will be taken away from you and it shall be given to a nation doing justice.'"[26]

In his commentary on Psalm 108, Augustine sees Judas as a symbol of the Jewish people with all the consequences that follow from such a characterization. "So Judas doth represent those Jews who were enemies of Christ, who both, then, hated Christ and now in their line of succession, this species of wickedness continuing, hate him."[27]

In the *City of God*, Augustine describes the behavior of the Jews face to face with Jesus and the consequences that followed: "But the Jews who rejected him and slew him, according to the needfulness of his death and resurrection, after that were miserably spoiled by the Romans, chased all into the slavery of strangers, and dispersed then over the face of the whole earth. For they are in all places with their Testament, to show that we have not forged those prophecies of Christ. . . . That suffices us that we have from the books of our enemies, which we acknowledge in that they preserve it for us against their wills, themselves and their books being dispersed as far as God's Church is extended and spread."[28]

The generalization is already seemingly present in the Gospel of John: the *Jews* were the ones who put Jesus to death. Historically, as we are now all too aware, the wording is imprecise. In reality, *some* Jews living in Jerusalem in the first century collaborated with the Roman authorities at the time in the execution of Jesus. Again, like in the writings of his predecessors, the consequences of the Jews' actions are formulated in the passive voice: "chased . . . dispersed." Implicitly, God is the author of this dispersion. The dispersion, however, has a particular function: the Jews witness to Christianity in spite of themselves. Augustine, frequently, separates the unique value of the Book from the quality of those carrying it, qualifying the latter as enemies. The dispersion of the Jews permits the entire world to become familiar with the Scriptures. But, this testimony is not derived from any particular activ-

ity on their part. It is due rather to the fact that the Scriptures are preserved within the Jewish community. Augustine comes back time and
again to this motif. For example, he uses the announcement God made
to Rebecca (Gn 25:23), suffering because of the conflict of the two twin
brothers in her womb, to comment: Maior minori serviet (the elder will
serve the younger). In this way, he justifies the subordinate role the
Jews must play in their relations with Christians. "The Jews serve us,
they are as our satchellers,[29] we studying, they carry our books."[30]

Augustine is a towering figure in the Christian tradition. His influence was felt in the writings of many later theologians like Caesar of
Arles (d. 542), Cassiodorus (d. 580) and others. We might conclude
here with a brief citation from the *Glossa ordinaria,* a popular biblical
commentary of the second half of the twelfth century, which provides
evidence of Augustine's heritage:

"Blessed is the God of Israel (Aug). The Jews are our satchellers
[*capsarii*] who carry our books, we who are Israel. Otherwise, the pagans might have supposed that what is said of the Christ and the Church
is simply fable, but they are won over by the testimony of our enemies
[the Jews]."[31]

BOSSUET AND PASCAL AND THE JEWS

We have emphasized the coherence of the presentation of the Jews by
the Fathers of the Church, who believed that they were defending Christian identity in the face of vibrant and well-organized Jewish communities. Their formulations, totally unacceptable by modern standards,
must, nevertheless, be placed within their context, which was one of
relatively peaceful coexistence between Jews and Christians. Furthermore, our selective treatment of the attitude of the Fathers toward the
Jews should not make us forget the enormous richness of their teaching
and the important contribution they made to the tradition of the Church,
particularly regarding the Christian reading and interpretation of the
biblical texts. However, we can discern in the writings of later theologians the full extent of the negative influence the Fathers had on them
with regard to the Jews. The catastrophic consequences of this trend in
Christian thinking must, today, be apparent to all. In order to illustrate
the influence on future generations of the writings of the Church
Fathers concerning the Jews, we present here two French Christian

thinkers from the seventeenth century, Jacques Bossuet (1627–1704) and Blaise Pascal (1623–1662).

Bossuet, Roman Catholic bishop of Meaux in France, was an avid reader of the Church Fathers. A celebrated preacher, he was also a committed polemicist, sometimes allowing himself to express "the regrettable excesses of an old man's anger."[32] This might indeed be the case in a homily on the goodness and sternness of God:

> It was this hardening of heart that set the Jews so stubbornly against the Romans, against the plague, against famine, against God, who waged war against them so openly. This hardening of the heart, I say, made them so obstinate that, after so many disasters, their city had to be taken by force, this being the last outburst of anger against it. If they had decided in favor of capitulation many Jews would have been saved. Titus himself only watched them perish with great regret. Yet, divine justice necessitated an infinite number of victims, eleven thousand men lay in the square in the aftermath of the siege of one single city. And after that, pursuing the remnants of this unfaithful nation, he dispersed them all over the face of the earth. For what reason? Like magistrates, having had some wrongdoers flayed, they order that they be exposed in different places along the important byways, their body parts drawn and quartered in order to terrify other scoundrels. This comparison horrifies you, yet God acts in an almost like fashion. *After having executed the death sentence against the Jews, which their own prophets, so long ago, had announced to them, he scattered them here and there throughout the world, carrying everywhere as a sign imprinted on them the mark of his vengeance. A monstrous people without hearth or home, without land and from every land; once the happiest people in the world and now the ridicule and hateful disdain of the whole world. Miserable, without being pitied by anyone, having become in its misery, through a particular curse, the laughingstock of even the most restrained.* Do not think for a moment that my intention is to insult them because of their misfortune. No, rather God would not want me to forget even now the gravity of this flesh![33]

Pascal composed an apology of the Christian religion, which was finally published incomplete, only after his death. Even in its unfinished form, it is a powerful document, radiating the mystery of revelation.

God both hides and reveals himself in his Scriptures. According to Pascal, this is what explains why the Jews have not understood the spiritual meaning of the Scriptures, fulfilled in Jesus Christ. Although Judaism often appears in a positive light in the writings of Pascal, it remains subordinate to Christianity. Without a polemical bent, Pascal takes up many of the themes found in the Church Fathers concerning the punishment of the Jewish people. "It is amazing and peculiarly remarkable to see the Jewish people survive for so many years and see them always wretched, but it is necessary as a proof of Christ that they should survive to prove him and be wretched, since they crucified him. And although it is contradictory to be wretched and to survive, they still survive, despite their wretchedness."[34]

It would seem, and yet perhaps unconsciously, that Pascal too takes up the discourse found in John Chrysostom with regard to the eternity of the exile of the Jewish people. "It was no real captivity when there was the certainty of being delivered in seventy years, but now they are captive and without hope. God promised them that though he scattered them to the ends of the earth, yet if they remained faithful to his law, he would gather them in again. They remain most faithful to it, but still oppressed."[35]

The Myth of the Wandering Jew

The myth of the wandering Jew has very ancient roots in the religious history of the West. It seems to have its origins in the narrative about the high priest's servant who struck Jesus in John's gospel (18:20–22). One can find an early outline of the myth in the reflection of Prudentius, a writer in the Iberian peninsula who lived in the fourth century. "The Jew wanders here and there, a vagabond, unfailingly chased into new exiles, from the time that, uprooted from his own land, he expiates by his torment the murder that he committed, from the time that he undergoes the punishment for his contract, for the blood of the Christ he denied has gushed out over him."[36] Throughout the Middle Ages and up until the nineteenth century, the figure of the wandering Jew was well known in Europe, recognized in different forms. At its origin, one finds a legend linked to the Passion of Jesus. Stumbling toward the hill of Golgotha, place of the crucifixion, Jesus, worn out, calls out to Ahasuerus, a Jewish tailor, asking to rest a while next to his shop. However, the hardhearted tailor refuses to accord Jesus this kindness and rebuffs him, sending him on his way to the cross. It is then that Jesus passes judgment on the Jew, condemning him to wander the earth until Jesus' return. This nomadic wandering, whereas positive when it comes to Christian knights in search of the Holy Grail, is negative here. There is a clear inversion of values—the knight is a symbol of devoted self-sacrifice, wandering the earth in search of the holy treasure, whereas the Jew wanders as a just punishment for his callousness. Although promised eternal life, the enforced wandering of the Jew became a symbol of Jewish lack of roots and untrustworthiness. This figure appeared in folktale and literature and made "apparitions" throughout Europe. Both the German poet Goethe and the English poet Shelley took up this theme in their writings.

At the end of this highly selective survey, a certain number of elements emerge that shed light on the theme of the Land. It seems clear that from the beginning of the Jesus movement, a growing hostility pitted that small group of disciples that would eventually give birth to Christianity against the dominant Judaism of the time. After the destruction of the Second Temple, toward the end of the first century, Judaism would slowly reconstitute itself as rabbinic Judaism, focused on the study of Torah. Today, exegetes admit that many New Testament texts, and most prominently the Gospel of John, bear the scars of a time when Judaism, plural in its forms and doctrinally flexible, included different schools, some of them sharply opposed to each other. Disagreements among the schools, expressed on the basis of a common faith and practice, concerned the representation of the Messiah, the relationship to the Torah, the role of the religious institutions, etc. The community of Qumran, for example, although having broken with the Temple, saw itself as the community of the end of times and the true Israel. The Pharisees constitute another group, with their own rules and regulations, their particular gatherings, their interpretations and commentaries on the Law, and their vision of the end of time. The Jesus movement manifested its own originality without this leading immediately to a rupture with the Judaism of the time. It is clear in the New Testament that the disciples of Jesus continued to frequent the Temple after his death and perhaps until its destruction.

With the adoption of Christianity as the official religion of the Empire, these divergences, perfectly legitimate in a heterogeneous society, stirred up by new religious questions, were perceived in a radically different fashion. Placed in their original cultural and religious context, the polemics between Christians and Jews did not have the disastrous effect that they would have later. By and large, Jews and Christians co-existed peacefully and harmoniously. Unfortunately however, over time, these divergences of opinion led to an often violent rejection of Judaism, reduced to being simply a tool in the service of the truth as presented by the dominant interpretation of the Church. This had a direct bearing on the way in which the loss of the Land and the exile of the Jews after the two wars with the Romans were interpreted. It could be argued that this Christian perspective was nothing more than a throwback to the discourses of the prophets of the Old Testament, in which they tried to warn the people of the risks they ran if they were unfaithful. The Land was given on condition of faithfulness to the covenant. To refuse the covenant was tantamount to opening the door to the punishment of God and, consequently, to the expulsion from the Land. However, the break between Jews and Christians created completely new conditions. Whereas the biblical prophets spoke from within the community with which they were in total solidarity, the Church developed an accusatory discourse that was exterior to the community in question, namely the Jews. Thus the Church, in the name of its God, judged and justified, as if from on high, the wretched fate often inflicted by Christians themselves on the Jews. The texts we have chosen show a relative degree of constancy in anti-Judaic discourse in the interpretation of the Land in Christian tradition.

In the nineteenth and twentieth centuries, new conditions were created as Church and civil society slowly evolved. In the biblical field, a critical revolution took place despite resistance from the churches. One of the consequences of this new critical reading of the Bible was that a literal reading of it became more and more difficult to defend in the face of modern science and study. The understanding of the texts about the Land was profoundly affected by this change. In addition, Christian anti-Judaism, which became even more entrenched in the nineteenth century, reached unimaginable dimensions in the twentieth century, culminating in the Holocaust, the organized genocide of six million Jews. As a result, eventually the Church would radically revise its understanding of the Jewish people in history. The Second Vatican Council would draw the necessary conclusions, opening the way for new readings of the Land, the Jewish people, and their destiny. However, another element, often overlooked, would make the task of developing a contemporary Christian discourse about the Land even more complicated—the existence in the Land not only of Jews but also of an indigenous Palestinian Arab population, consisting of both Muslims and Christians. They too have embarked on a struggle for the Land they received from their ancestors, defending their right to continue living there.

5. Shaking Up a Familiar Landscape

The Second Vatican Council (1962–65) inaugurated a new epoch in the history of the Catholic Church. Amidst many innovations and changes that redefined the Church's attitudes to the modern world, a new perspective on Judaism and the Jewish people also emerged. The Church recognized that it had not only ignored its own Jewish origins but had also acted with contempt toward those who witnessed to these origins, the Jewish people. It was during the Council that the Church first officially called to mind the disastrous consequences of its own "teaching of contempt" with regard to the Jews over the long centuries of history. Vatican II thus represents the inauguration of a new age in the Church's attempts to build a positive relationship with the Jewish people within the context of the attitude to the world at large and to all non-Catholics and non-Christians. Undoubtedly one of the major factors in this innovative new beginning was the reflection on what had happened during the Holocaust in Europe and the Church's own part in responsibility for these catastrophic events. Here, we would like to present some of the important factors that motivated the change in the Church's attitude and which would impact the Church's position with regard to the Land.

Tragedies and Mutations

The mass murder of six million Jews by the Nazis during the Second World War, men, women, and children put to death for the simple reason that they were Jews, is at the center of the Church's struggle to come to terms with its own role in the propagation of anti-Jewish attitudes and behaviors. How was it possible for such an evil to take place in countries that were identified as Christian? What part in the responsibility for these events must be borne by Christians, not only as these events were taking place but also in the centuries that preceded these same events? How can one ensure that such events never take place again? For the Church, born within the matrix of Judaism, the Holocaust (or Shoah) is an open wound, obliging a profound and constant account of conscience and necessitating a change in attitudes toward Jews and Judaism. For centuries Christians had imposed the unbearable responsibility for the crucifixion of Jesus Christ on the Jews, who continued to refuse to accept Christ as their savior. Because of this accusation of "deicide," the Church had justified the unjustifiable: the harassment of Jews that increased and intensified at different periods, sometimes leading to persecution, violence, and even massacres. Despite the French Revolution (1789) and the consequent progressive loss of Church influence, the suspicion and even hatred of Jews remained widespread in Europe, often coming to the forefront in Christian discourse and slowly transforming into modern, secular anti-Semitism.

The important Vatican document "We Remember" (1998) seeks to examine the role of Christians in contributing to the climate that led up to the Shoah. The document states: "Sentiments of anti-Judaism in some Christian quarters, and the gap which existed between the Church and the Jewish people, led to a generalized discrimination, which ended at times in expulsions or attempts at forced conversions."[1]

The document goes even further, asking "whether the Nazi persecution of the Jews was not made easier by the anti-Jewish prejudices imbedded in some Christian minds and hearts. Did anti-Jewish sentiment among Christians make them less sensitive, or even indifferent, to the persecutions launched against the Jews by National Socialism when it reached power?"[2] The document concludes: "Finally, we invite all men and women of good will to reflect deeply on the significance of the *Shoah.* The victims from their graves, and the survivors through the vivid testimony of what they have suffered, have become a loud voice calling the attention of all of humanity. To remember this terrible experience is to become fully conscious of the salutary warning it entails: the spoiled seeds of anti-Judaism and anti-Semitism must never again be allowed to take root in any human heart."[3]

ZIONISM AND THE CREATION OF THE STATE OF ISRAEL

The birth of Jewish political Zionism in the nineteenth century and the creation of the State of Israel in 1948 also ultimately led to an important shift in Church attitudes toward the Jews and the Land they claimed as their homeland. Jewish Zionism emerged among European Jews amidst a general European nationalist awakening in the nineteenth century.[4] European nationalism and entry into modernity awakened among many European Jews dreams of renewal that found expression in religious and cultural reform movements. Undoubtedly, the emergence of strong currents of anti-Semitism in various European nationalist circles led some Jews to formulate their own version of a Jewish national movement that sought a return to "the land of our ancestors."[5] A Jewish reaction to anti-Semitism was coupled with the struggle to preserve a specific Jewish identity in the face of a strong pull toward assimilation within European society.

Judaism, Zionism, and the State of Israel

Modern Zionism was born in the context of nineteenth-century Europe, the rise of European national movements, and the formation of modern anti-Semitism. One of the founders of modern political Zionism was the Austro-Hungarian Jewish publicist Theodor Herzl (1860–1904), who wrote in his manifesto, *The Jewish State*, published in 1896: "Palestine is our unforgettable historic homeland. The very name would be a marvelously effective rallying cry. . . . We should there form a part of a wall of defense for Europe in Asia, an outpost of civilization against barbarism."[6]

The contribution of Rabbi Abraham Isaac Kook (1865–1935) was fundamental in giving a Jewish religious coloration to Herzl's secular vision: "*Eretz Israel* is not something apart from the soul of the Jewish people; it is no mere national possession, serving as a means of unifying our people and buttressing its material, or even its spiritual, survival. *Eretz Israel* is part of the very essence of our nationhood; it is bound organically to its very life and inner being. Human reason, even at its most sublime, cannot begin to understand the unique holiness of *Eretz Israel*; it cannot stir the depths of love for the land that are dormant within our people."[7]

Many religious Jews were much more wary of modern Zionism though, fearing that it was simply a copy of secular European nationalism and that it contained dangerous and false messianic pretensions that would be disastrous for the Jewish people. One of the leaders of Orthodox Judaism in Eastern Europe, Rabbi Shulem Schneerson, the Lubavitcher Rebbe, wrote in 1903 to warn Jews of Zionist manipulation of biblical texts to legitimate their ideology: "They [the Zionists] also study the Bible through commentaries which they compile out of their imaginations in order to clothe the verses with nationalist nuances. In their speeches they make use of treacherous interpretations. All this was commended by Herzl. . . . This method is the basis of their propaganda which is directed at the one aim of removing the heart of the people from the Torah and the holy beliefs that are in the heart of Israel and of implanting instead nationalism as Judaism."[8]

In addition, some Jews were troubled when they discovered that the Land they dreamt of was not an empty wasteland waiting for their return but inhabited by another people, Palestinian Arabs. Martin Buber (1878–1965), the great German Jewish philosopher, formulated a form of Zionism that tried to take into account the existence of the Palestinians, too. In 1939 he wrote to Mahatma Gandhi: "I belong to a group of people who from the time Britain conquered Palestine have not ceased to strive for the concluding of a genuine peace between Jew and Arab. . . . We consider it a fundamental point that in this case two vital claims are opposed to each other, two claims of a different nature and a different origin which cannot objectively be pitted against one another and between which no objective decision can be made as to which is just and which is unjust. We considered and still consider it our duty to understand and to honor the claim which is opposed to ours and to endeavor to reconcile both claims."[9]

The Declaration of Independence of the State of Israel, promulgated on May 15, 1948, insisted on the Jewish link to the Land: "*Eretz Israel* was the birthplace of the Jewish people. Here their spiritual, religious and political identity was shaped. Here they first attained to statehood, created cultural values of national and universal significance and gave to the world the eternal Book of Books. After being forcibly expelled from their land, the people kept faith with it throughout their Dispersion and never ceased to pray and hope for their return to it and for the restoration in it of their political freedom."

Zionism predicated a return to Jewish biblical sources and emphasized the passionate love Jews had preserved for Zion, another name for the city of Jerusalem, throughout the ages. After the destruction of the Temple and their expulsion by the Romans, Jews continued throughout the centuries to remember Zion in their prayers. Jewish liturgy constantly consoled Jews that at some point in the future God would bring them back to Zion and that they would reconstruct the Temple in Jerusalem. Reminding Jews that Zion was not just an otherworldly and eschatological reality, the early Zionists began to work toward establishing a foothold in Palestine and arousing international support for Jewish settlement there. Zionism was particularly successful in the Jewish communities of Eastern Europe where anti-Jewish sentiment led to a succession of pogroms in the late nineteenth and early twentieth centuries. The first large wave of Jewish emigration to Palestine began in 1882, after the attacks on the Jewish population in Russia in the wake of the assassination of Emperor Alexander II.

At first, most of the Jewish traditional leadership rejected Zionism. Many Rabbinic authorities accused Zionism of being a false messianism; the return to Zion had to be initiated by the Messiah who was yet to appear. Other Orthodox Jews feared that Zionism was a mass movement of assimilation, Jews seeking to become a nation like all other nations.[10] Many secular Jews feared that Zionism would ultimately pose a danger to Jewish life in the Diaspora, undermining the struggle for full Jewish equality and integration in the countries of their residence. However, in the aftermath of the Shoah, Zionism became the mass movement of many Jews all over the world, deemed a necessity for the survival of the Jewish people in a world that had rejected them. The creation of the State of Israel in May 1948 with the support of the international community and the increasing immigration of Jews to Israel showed that Zionism as a political ideology had indeed prevailed among Jews.

The powerful image of Jews "returning" to "the ancestral homeland" after emerging from the death camps of Europe attracted the attention of many Christians, sensitive to the biblical visions evoked. It seemed to many Christians and Jews that the prophetic words contained in visions of return in Isaiah, in Ezekiel, and elsewhere had come alive. Abraham Joshua Heschel, the great Jewish-American theologian and social activist, summed this up shortly after the 1967 war, a great military victory for the State of Israel: "The land presents a perception which seeks an identity in us. Suddenly we sense coherence in history, a bridge that spans the ages. Israel reborn is an explicit rendering of an ineffable mystery. The Presence is cloudy, but the challenge is unmistakable. This is part of our exultation: to witness the resurrection of the land of the Bible; *a land that was dead* for nearly two thousand years is now a land that sings."[11]

Zionism and the Biblical Heritage

"The Zionist enterprise defined itself in the language of biblical expression as 'the return to Zion' (Ps 126:1) and saw the resurrection of the Bible—that is to say: the establishment of the study of the Bible at the center of the Hebrew school curriculum—as an integral part of the resurrection of the Jewish people, its land, and language. The return to the Land of Zion and to Jerusalem—to the national independence of the days of the First Temple, to working the land, to the bravery of battle, and to speaking and creating in the language of Amos and Isaiah—took on a quasi-religious inspiration from the Bible, which came to represent the aim and vision of this generation: "the renewal of our days as of old." Leaders, writers, and educators believed that, on the one hand, the Bible bestowed legitimacy on Zionism, as it testified to the people of Israel's ownership of the land called by its name, predicting the return of the children to their borders, the building up of the land, and the ingathering of exiles. On the other hand, they believed that Zionism added luster to the Book of Books, by actualizing its prophecies and thus certifying its eternal truth. Thus the Bible became an exalted commentary on the present, just as the present became a commentary that brought alive the Bible. The clear relevance of the biblical saga—at the beginning of which was the immigration of individuals who heard the command 'Go from your country' (Gn 12:1), then the exodus of masses from the house of slavery, followed by the sluggishness of the 'Wilderness generation' and the determination of the 'conquerors of Canaan,' and at whose peak were the defensive battles of the Judges and the establishment of the monarchy—bestowed on the present past glory. Just as biblical history gave the young Zionist movement roots in the depths of time, so too biblical geography, with its sites laden with memory, gave it a sense of belonging to place, and biblical archaeology gave the recently arrived immigrants and their children after them palpable proofs that they were natives in this old-new land."[12]

—U. Simon, *Seek Peace and Pursue It*

THE TRAGEDY OF THE PALESTINIAN PEOPLE

Was the Land dead though? "A land without a people for a people without a land" was a widespread slogan among those rejoicing in the Jewish settlement of Palestine.[13] However, Palestine was a land inhabited by an indigenous population composed of a majority of Muslims and a minority of Christians and some indigenous Jews. Edward Said, eloquent Palestinian spokesman in the West, explained that the struggle between Palestinians and Zionism was "a struggle between a presence and an interpretation, the former constantly appearing to be overpowered and eradicated by the latter."[14] Palestine had become a predominantly Muslim and Arabic-speaking country in the last centuries of the first millennium. The Arab and predominantly Muslim identity of the Land was strengthened after the departure of the Crusaders (at the end of the thirteenth century). Although the indigenous population did not enjoy political sovereignty, ruled by foreign empires in succession, Muslims, Christians, and Jews had lived side by side in this land for centuries. It was to this land that the European Jewish immigrants flowed beginning in the 1880s and increasing in numbers throughout the first decades of the twentieth century. The Palestinians, faced with the Jewish newcomers to the Land, tended to see them as European colonial settlers rather than as a people returning to their biblical homeland. The Jews, most of whom were culturally European, often looked at the Palestinian Arabs as primitive natives who should welcome the civilization and progress they brought. The clash between the two populations, each one claiming the Land, grew in intensity throughout the twentieth century and has found no resolution despite the loss of lives on both sides.

Palestine, Palestinian Arabs, and Palestinian Nationalism

The Palestinian national movement was born in the context of the struggle against European colonialism in the late nineteenth and twentieth centuries. Most of the local indigenous population in Palestine (composed of both Muslims and Christians) opposed Zionist claims to the Land. In the aftermath of 1948, the Palestinian national movement took on the form of a resistance movement that used political, military, diplomatic, and popular (*intifada*) means to oppose the State of Israel and reassert the national rights of the Palestinians to their lost lands. This struggle has known different expressions, including guerrilla attacks that have killed civilians, too.

The Palestine National Charter of the Palestine Liberation Organization, promulgated in 1964, opens with definite claims on the Land of Palestine: "Article 1. Palestine is an Arab homeland bound by strong national ties to the rest of the Arab countries and which together form the large Arab homeland.

Article 3. The Palestinian Arab people has the legitimate right to its homeland. . . ." (The Palestine National Charter, 1964).

In more recent times, and as a result of the beginning of the negotiations between Israelis and Palestinians, the PLO has recognized the State of Israel. However, the Palestinian people continues to demand its right to freedom, despite ongoing suffering. Palestinian anthropologist Ali Qleibo (b. 1953) has written of Palestinian identity and the Land: "Palestinian society has been the primary victim of the Israeli state since the 1948 catastrophe. The majority of the Palestinians have been coerced out of their homeland and dispersed all over the earth. . . . Strangers abroad and threatened with alienation in their homeland, the Palestinians' existence is enveloped by feelings of melancholic nostalgia. A deep sense of loss and grief permeates everyday existence, for all that is related to our sense of identity."[15]

Palestinian thinker Edward Said (1935–2003), from his exile in the United States, wrote: "The proof of whatever small success we have had is not that we have regained a homeland, or acquired a new one; rather, it is that some Israelis have admitted the possibility of sharing a common space with us, in Palestine. The proposed modes of such a sharing are adventurous and utopian in the present context of hostility between Arabs and Jews but on the intellectual level they are actual, and to some of us—on both sides—they make sense."[16]

By the time of the creation of the State of Israel the Jewish population in Palestine had grown from 24,000 (about 5 percent of the total population) in 1882 to 650,000 (about 35 percent of the total population) in May 1948. After the Shoah, many of the Jewish survivors sought refuge in Palestine. Faced with the claims of the two peoples, Jews and Palestinian Arabs, and the changed demographic character of the country, the United Nations proposed a partition of the land between Jews and Arabs, each with their own state. This was voted on by a majority of the member states in November 1947, accepted by the Jews, who rejoiced in the international legitimacy that this accorded their cause, and rejected by the Arabs, who still dreamed of a full liberation from those perceived as colonial settlers. During the war that followed the partition decision and heralded the creation of the state, the majority of Muslim and Christian Palestinians became refugees (some fled and some were forcibly evicted). After the war, they were prevented from returning to their homes. Due to the exit of the refugees and the great influx of Jewish immigrants following the establishment of the State of Israel, the Jews now made up almost 90 percent of the population of the new state, whereas the Arabs (Muslims and Christians) were reduced to just over 10 percent by 1949. Israel controlled almost 78 percent of historical Palestine. In 1967, Israel, in the wake of a war on all fronts, occupied the rest of historical Palestine (the remaining 22 percent, the West Bank and the Gaza Strip). This time there was no massive population migration from these territories (which already housed a large refugee population from the 1948 War).

For the Church, the Palestinian reality is a very sensitive one because most indigenous Christians in the Land today are Palestinian Christians. Many of the local intellectuals who first became conscious of the threat from Zionist settlement and began to formulate counter Palestinian nationalist claims on the Land were Christians. In 1948, many of the local Christians lost their homes and became refugees alongside their Muslim compatriots. Palestinian Christians have remained prominent in the Palestinian national movement that seeks to address the fundamental injustice that emerged in 1948 with the displacement of the Palestinians from their ancestral homeland. In a 1998 pastoral letter, Michel Sabbah, Roman Catholic Patriarch of Jerusalem, the highest-ranking Catholic dignitary in the Holy Land, wrote: "Since 1948, the Jewish people have enjoyed their own state with its sovereignty and freedom. In contrast, the Palestinian people are still under Israeli military occupation on the little land which remains theirs. . . . [T]hey still demand their security, their freedom, the right to self-determination and complete independence in their own state."[17]

As we will see in the next chapter, the Church is challenged to reject any trace of anti-Judaism, which marks its history and is still current among the enemies of the Jewish people. At the same time, the Church is challenged to take a position regarding the rights of the Palestinians, transformed into a people of refugees, reeling under military occupation, and still in search of a just resolution to their plight.

THE SCIENTIFIC CRITIQUE OF THE BIBLE

The new sociopolitical and religious landscape that emerged in the twentieth century, within its context of violence and complexity, led to important changes and new questions with regard to the Christian attitude toward the Land. These changes in attitude are even more significant when we take into account the development of the historical-critical study of the biblical text and the important archaeological discoveries that have come to light in the sands of Israel and Palestine.

For centuries, both the Jewish people and the Church understood the history in the biblical text literally. This was true too of the five books of the Pentateuch that speak repeatedly of the promise of the Land, made to Abraham, Isaac, and Jacob. According to Christian tradition, the Bible is *the Word of God* because God is the true author of the Scriptures. This affirmation, which has its origins in the New Testament,[18] is repeatedly found in the writings of the Church Fathers and is taken up time and again in the official declarations of the Catholic Church right up until the documents of the Second Vatican Council. There are important consequences that result from this affirmation that influence the interpretation of the Bible and its application to the lives of the faithful. Coming from God himself, the Scriptures must be absolute truth in all domains, including the domains of history, geography, and natural sciences. Because the Bible is the Word of God it cannot contain any errors. Consequently, it is characterized as "inerrant" (without error). In a letter to Saint Jerome, quoted in Pope Leo XIII's encyclical *Providentissimus Deus* (1893), Saint Augustine describes the relationship between the faithful reader of the Bible and the truth that is found in the Bible: "On my part I confess to your charity that it is only to those Books of Scripture which are now called canonical that I have learned to pay such honor and reverence as to believe most firmly that none of their writers has fallen into any error. And if in these Books I meet anything that seems contrary to truth, I shall not hesitate to conclude either that the text is faulty, or that the translator has not expressed the meaning of the passage, or that I myself do not understand."[19]

During the nineteenth and twentieth centuries, this kind of Christian reading of the Bible underwent radical criticism and was largely deconstructed. The modernist crisis, reaching a head at the beginning of the twentieth century, set in motion a critical reflection within the Church that had revolutionary consequences for the understanding of the Word of God. For figures like Dominican exegete Father Marie-Joseph Lagrange (1855–1938), founder of the French École biblique (Bible School) in Jerusalem and an important actor in the drama, the reading of the Bible must necessarily pass through modern criticism even if this is a harrowing experience. He wrote to a friend, "Only scientific criticism can cure the disease caused by scientific criticism."[20] In a letter that he believed to be his last will and testament, written to his favorite disciple, Father Vincent, he dreamed, in the midst of the anti-modernist repression, then in full swing, that "intelligence would again assume its rights and that finally the Church would provide an answer to the biblical questions that have been raised."[21] This is indeed what happened throughout the twentieth century.

Multiple discoveries of ancient Near Eastern texts in the nineteenth and twentieth centuries enabled the important work of placing the Bible within the cultural, historical, and literary context in which it had been composed during the second and first millennia before Jesus Christ. Modern Christians were thus slowly able to admit that the Bible, without ceasing to be the Word of God, was also a human undertaking, sharing the characteristics of other ancient writings and including their historical dimension. There was a growing realization that the meaning of the biblical texts is only fully accessible through a study of the ancient languages in which they were written, the archaeology of the ancient world, the history of religions at the time, comparative literature, and other fields that, although related to biblical studies, are also autonomous and have their own rules and methods. With regard to the study of the biblical text, it was recognized that there were obligatory steps that had to be passed through in ascertaining the text's meaning, including textual criticism, the history of the translations and versions, research into the sources of the text, the definition of literary genres, the history of tradition as well as of the redaction (editing) of the text, and its canonical status. The ethos of the historical-critical method that developed was to allow the contemporary reader to take into account the historical dimension of revelation in order to arrive at a better and deeper understanding of texts clearly written in other times for other readers yet still read today and applied to our times.

In 1993, the Roman Catholic Pontifical Biblical Commission published an important document, *The Interpretation of the Bible in the Church*. It affirms that the historical-critical method is an obligatory stage in a modern reading of the Bible. "The historical-critical method is the indispensable method for the scientific study of the meaning of ancient texts. Holy Scripture, inasmuch as it is 'the Word of God in human language,' has been composed by human authors in all its various parts and in all the sources that lie behind them. Because of this, its proper understanding not only admits the use of this method but actually requires it."[22]

Yet, face to face with the biblical text, clearly marked by the perspectives of its original author and readers, one cannot ignore the long history of two thousand years of the reading of these texts by generations of Jewish, Christian, and other readers. All these readers received the biblical texts, yet because of their often widely varying perspectives, interpreted the texts quite differently.

Today, with some distance from the original debates and revolutions in the development of the historical-critical approach, we can identify a certain number of achievements concerning the interpretation of the Land as it is presented in the Bible.

(1) It is quite certain now that the Bible, and especially the Pentateuch, was constituted at a relatively late date, probably after the Babylonian exile. Modern biblical criticism focuses on two great theological schools brought together in this literary activity: the Deuteronomist school and the Priestly school. At the time of the exile and in its aftermath, these two schools produced a rereading of salvation history up to that point. The period of the exile was astonishingly productive, bringing into being the Judaism that would be dominant until the coming of Jesus. This rereading was in fact a reconstruction of Israel's history and so thorough that it is almost impossible to reconstitute the events that had really taken place in the centuries before the exile. This is true, first and foremost, for the narratives of the Patriarchs in Genesis, pivotal texts with regard to the promise of the Land.

(2) We no longer have direct access to the "real events" of history. Today, many exegetes believe that the Deuteronomist and Priestly compositions, written during and after the exile, sought to root the territorial frontiers of David and Solomon in the origins of the people, thus also creating a divine legitimization of these frontiers. It is thus likely that it was at this time (sixth and fifth centuries B.C.) that the theme of the promise of the Land was rewritten and endowed with its breadth, its solemnity, and its power. This amplification of the theme would give the returning exiles solid foundations rooted in a sacred history.

This is clearly discernible when we approach the biblical text with the tools offered by the critical method. The coherent and harmonious presentation of the tradition of interpretation is shattered. Origins are generally obscure and whoever looks into the question of the promises and the giving of the Land cannot escape this general rule. We will never know how this theme made its way into Israel's consciousness. The sacralization (and simplification) of this theme in the Bible have completely effaced its labored and obscure origins. Without being too daring, we might well imagine that the first steps of Israel in the Land were no different than those of many other peoples who conquered or settled a particular territory. Here, the comments of the exegete W. D. Davies are particularly helpful:

> Interest in Israel in strictly historical origins, if it ever existed as such, was submerged as the tradition developed, and became insignificant and irrelevant. For the understanding of our proper task what is important is not the rediscovery of the origins of the promise to Abraham, but the recognition that that promise was so reinterpreted from age to age that it became a living power in the life of the people of Israel. Not the mode of its origin matters, but its operation as a formative, dynamic, seminal force in the history of Israel. The legend of the promise entered so deeply into the experience of the Jews that it acquired its own reality. What Jews believe to have happened in the Middle East has been no less formative in world history than that which is known to have occurred.[23]

ARCHAEOLOGY AND HISTORY

After the particularly moving rediscovery of and digs at Pompei (1790), followed by those of Schliemann (1873) that brought back to life the legendary city of Troy, the Holy Land became the object of systematic explorations in the nineteenth century. At that time, archaeology was a nascent science that was fast developing because of the passion and enthusiasm of its founding fathers. The archaeologists dreamed of resurrecting ancient buried cities, hidden under mounds of dirt and soil, which were known as *tels* (Arabic for hill). These discoveries would, in the opinion of the first generation of archaeologists, confirm the "truth" of the biblical narratives. One telling title of a German archaeological manual describing digs in the Holy Land said it all: *The Bible is right after all.*[24] At that time, the common term was "biblical archaeology," contested by many today who prefer to speak of Syro-Phoenician or Palestinian archaeology.

One of the foundational moments for the rediscovery of the land of the Bible was the work of the great pioneer Edward Robinson, who, aided by Eli Smith, crisscrossed the Land, Bible in hand, seeking out the ancient Arab names for towns and villages in order to identify them according to the biblical texts. From 1850 onward, the survey of the surface of the Land continued alongside the first systematic archaeological excavations. Felicien de Saulcy believed that he had discovered the site of Sodom and Gomorrah. In Jerusalem, archaeologists, at this same period, believed they had discovered the tombs of the ancient kings, in fact later shown to be Herodian burial grounds. In 1865 the Palestine Exploration Fund was established, the first of a number of associations that had as their aim the raising of funds and materials for the promotion of the excavation of Palestine. The statutes of this fund define objective research founded on hard facts as its aim. Jerusalem was, of course, one of the most important centers of archaeological activity; the archaeologists hoped to uncover the secrets of the holy city. At the end of the nineteenth century, two English military officers, employed by the Palestine Exploration Fund produced a topographical survey of the places that would later become important excavation sites. Special attention was paid to the numerous "tels" spread all over the country. These, it was believed, would recount for those who knew how to decipher them, layer after layer, the entire history of the town buried beneath them. The wind of optimism was palpable. The names of the places, often preserved in their Arabic form, corresponded to the buried realities that offered up their treasures in the form of concrete artifacts, jars, jewels, bones, and even writings.

After the First World War, the exploration of sites like Beit Shean, Megiddo, Bethel, Lachish, and Jerusalem contributed to uncovering biblical Israel's past. The Bible had discovered in archaeology a docile, respectful, and useful servant. W. F. Albright, a master who formed a generation of archaeologists in the first decades of the twentieth century, could write with great optimism: "Seen against the background of the ancient Near East, innumerable obscurities become clear and we begin to comprehend the organic development of Hebrew society and culture. However, the uniqueness of the Bible, both as a masterpiece of literature and as a religious document has not been lessened, and nothing tending to disturb the religious faith of Jew or Christian has been discovered."[25]

THE QUESTIONS RAISED BY ARCHAEOLOGY

Seventy years later, it would be almost impossible to find an archaeologist who would agree to such an optimistic manifesto. Archaeology has evolved greatly. Its methods have become more rigorous, thanks, in particular, to the scientific use of information derived from pottery found during the excavations. Having matured into adulthood, archaeology no longer accepts being the docile servant of the Bible. In the 1960s, a radical change both in spirit and in methodology appeared, particularly among Israeli and European archaeologists, dubbed the "new archaeology." Scientific research, demanding a nonconfessional approach, studies the human past, working on extended areas and taking into account a whole array of finds (bones, animal remains [that reveal dietary habits], grain, oil, wine, production of stones, tombs, habitation) along with its relationship to the natural environment (deforestation, irrigation, terracing of land, ecology) as well as elements of the human environment (economic life, artistic production, psychology, and religious belief, etc.).

Furthermore, the political tensions between Israelis and Palestinians, who both claim the same land, have had inevitable repercussions on the orientations and options of the archaeologists. In the debates among Israelis and Palestinians, archaeology is a particularly sensitive area. Recent events have even seen the criminal marketing of objects, clandestinely dug up or, even worse, produced in workshops that specialize in fabricating fake artifacts. This was the case with a black stone tablet, written in the first person, in ancient Hebrew script, attributed to King Yehoash (ninth century B.C.), describing the repairs carried out in the Temple, conforming to the descriptions in 2 Kings 12. The optimists among the archaeologists "presumed that the inscription constituted the first authentic testimony, perhaps composed by King Yehoash himself, confirming the biblical description."[26]

To simplify a complex and disputed area of research, one can say that there are two schools that are in conflict. The first, named "maximalist," has the tendency to look for what confirms the Bible in archaeology, especially with regard to the installation of the Hebrews in Palestine. The other, dubbed "minimalist," seeks neutrality at all times, refusing to slide into biblical apologetics. Not without illusions, the latter proclaims itself scientific and objective, but is often accused of being too willing to undermine the results of past research. Over and above the ferocious polemics between the two tendencies, it is certainly clear that archaeology has become an independent discipline, whose results must be accepted even if and when they contradict the books of the Bible. This happens all too often, particularly when it comes to the narratives of the Exodus, the entry of the Hebrews into the Land, and the birth of the monarchy.

THE ARRIVAL OF THE HEBREWS

What exactly happened at the turn of the twelfth century B.C. in the territory of Canaan, at the presumed moment of the arrival of the Hebrews? It is very difficult to formulate a precise answer to this question. We have no extra-biblical documentation for this period that might help us discover the facts. Do the archaeological finds permit us to advance any further? Archaeological research, carried out on an extended area (one might call this regional archaeology) has shown that there was indeed a transformation in the region that took place around the year 1200, especially in a number of towns in the mountains of Ephraim, Benjamin, and Manasseh. One piece of evidence is the disappearance in this period of the remains of pigs, possibly linked to a religious prohibition, unlike the finds in the Philistine coastal towns. Might the population that settled at that time be the beginnings of what will become Israel? Israel Finkelstein, an Israeli archaeologist, and others have proposed that this might indeed be the case. "Archaeology has revealed that complex social transformations among the pastoral people of the Canaanite highlands were—far more than the later biblical concepts of sin and redemption—the most formative forces in the birth of Israel."[27]

In this case the books of Joshua and Judges must be interpreted as a rereading of history, long removed in time from the original events they are supposed to describe. Various theories, in contradiction with one another, have been proposed in order to explain the entry of the Hebrews into Palestine. From the 1920s, Albrecht Alt imagined that pastoral nomads peacefully infiltrated the Land, living in diverse groups on the margins of the existing society.[28] Norman Gottwald sought the ancestors of Israel among the peasants who had been dispossessed of their land and who consequently rebelled, fleeing into the forested highlands.[29] These are hypothetical solutions to the problem, but they are based primarily upon what can be scientifically gleaned from the lay of the land. The experience of a sole God, memorized by some nomadic travelers, the "Hapiru" (the Hebrews?), having their origin in Egypt, might indeed have offered a certain spiritual framework to those in Canaan. However, we have no indication outside of the Bible that those who left Egypt were "about six hundred thousand men on foot, besides children" (Ex 12:37).

THE VILLAGE OF JERUSALEM

Archaeological excavations in Jerusalem have raised many questions about the actual location of Jerusalem in the eleventh and tenth centuries B.C. Whereas the biblical texts give the impression that Jerusalem was a sumptuous, royal city with luxurious palaces and an extravagant temple, the archaeological findings seem to point in a very different direction:

> The converging findings obtained by different authors raise doubts about the existence of a developed urban structure in Jerusalem before the end of the eighth century B.C. This is clearly very consequential for the historical criticism and interpretation of the narratives concerning David and Solomon in the books of Samuel and Kings as well as for the literary criticism of the Pentateuch. A "source theory" presuming the existence of a Yahwist document written in Jerusalem by educated scribes during the reign of David or Solomon is incompatible with the archaeological findings that reduce Jerusalem to a simple village at the beginning of the tenth century.[30]

The Surprise of the Excavations in Jericho

The town of Jericho attracted the archaeologists more than most other towns. As early as 1867, Captain Charles Warren dug some wells there. An Austrian-German team excavated in Jericho between 1907 and 1909. This was followed by the digs of John Garstang from 1930 to 1936. He believed that he had identified traces of the city destroyed by the Israelites on their entry into the Land. Apologetic literature proudly reproduced the photograph of a collapsed wall, a physical trace of the effects of the trumpets of Jericho. Finally, a British archaeologist, Kathleen Kenyon, took up digging there again in 1951. She reached the conclusion that Jericho was in fact uninhabited at the presumed time of the entry of the Israelites into the Land. Archaeology, which was supposed to confirm the adventure of Joshua, had failed to do so. "It is best to frankly admit that for the moment the diggers' pick has left the enigma of Jericho even more obscure than it was before. We await a Prometheus who will shed some light on this problem."[31]

What consequences can be derived from this "disappointment"? What is described in the Book of Joshua is undoubtedly not historical. Rather, the Bible seems to narrate a liturgical procession, mimicking and thus making real a conquest that never took place. From this we might indeed wisely conclude: "Archaeological evidence is often fragmentary and isolated and it only has meaning when the archaeologist gives it meaning. The vigorous debates and differences of opinion will continue and this is quite logical and the final conclusions will be very few in number. Total unanimity will be the exception rather than the rule. The interpretation of the archaeological find is never definitive. It calls for a permanent reinterpretation especially in the light of new discoveries. Opinions, held sometimes for a very long time, might be mistaken and must be modified and even abandoned."[32]

These discoveries motivate exegetes to reread the biblical accounts with greater attention to detail. J. Briend, a French exegete, in a study published in 2006, carried out a literary analysis of the first ten chapters of the Book of Joshua.[33] Pointing out the logical difficulties in these chapters, he shows that the text is marked by later rereadings. He concludes that the oaths to deal favorably with the clan of Rahab ("Swear to me by the Lord that you in turn will deal kindly with my family. Give me a sign of good faith that you will spare my father and mother, my brothers and sisters and all who belong to them and deliver our lives from death," Jos 2:12–13) and with the Gibeonites ("The Israelites did not attack them, because the leaders of the congregation had sworn to them by the Lord, the God of Israel," Jos 9:18) are indications of a rereading that justifies the presence of these two non-Israelite clans in the midst of the people at a time when the presence of non-Israelites was being contested. The historicity of these chapters does not refer to the events described but, rather, reflects much later sociological realties: accepting, despite resistance, the presence of non-Israelites in the midst of the community of Israel.

How does this long, complicated history, now viewed through the prism of historical criticism and archaeological research, affect our reading of past and contemporary events? How does it affect our reading of the Land? John Chrysostom believed that the Scriptures provided proof of the definitive expulsion of the Jews from the Land. Recent history has shown that he was wrong. This lesson must not be forgotten. We must be careful not to summon up the Scriptures too quickly in order to legitimate a particular event. How should we read the contemporary "return" of the Jews to the Land of their ancestors? How should the Bible be used in evaluating this? Our reading has been transformed in the twentieth century. It is heavily colored by historical events, particularly the catastrophe of the Shoah and the creation of the State of Israel. However, by the same token, it cannot exclude either the ongoing suffering of the Palestine people, unjustly deprived of their land. How should we interpret this history of the twentieth century in Israel and in Palestine? The task is rendered even more difficult because this story involves men and women of flesh and blood who make claims that seem totally irreconcilable.

Part III
The Land in the Contemporary Documents of the Catholic Church

Against the background of what we have presented up to this point, where biblical interpretation, theology, history, hermeneutics, and geo-theology intertwine, how should the Church and Christians position themselves with regard to the Land that some call Israel and some call Palestine today? The previous traditional discourse of the Church attributed the exile of the Jewish people expressly to God; should we now, according to this same theological logic, interpret the return of the Jews to the Land as the result of a direct intervention of God? Some Christians seem to think so, seeing the return of the Jewish people to the Land of their ancestors as a sign that the biblical promises are being accomplished. Is it possible to develop a different reading of history from the vantage point of the Palestinians? Such a view would analyze the events that led to the return of the Jews as a grave injustice that progressively deprived the Palestinian people of their land, the result of a form of nineteenth-century colonialism that alone has survived into the twenty-first century. This point of view arrives at conclusions that are diametrically opposed to the first option. This diversity of perspective explains the fact that today Christians are to be found on both sides of the divide, among the most convinced partisans of the Palestinian cause as well as among the most enthusiastic supporters of Zionism. Without pushing the issue to its extreme limits, it is clear that most Christians have a difficult time taking a stand. Many are sensitive both to the tragic destiny of the Jewish people and to the continued suffering and injustices inflicted on the Palestinians. The diversity of possible readings clearly underlines the complexity of the problem. Faith alone, even when inspired by the Scriptures, is insufficient and even more so when the individual is marked by the incapacity or even refusal to overcome emotions and passions.

Face to face with such complexity, we might understand better why the teaching of the Church on this subject is so delicate, at times appearing hesitant and perhaps even lacking in resounding coherence. One German theologian commented that the State of Israel represents a theological crux for the Church.[1] In this chapter, we seek to present the development of the Church's attitude with regard to the Land claimed by both Israelis and Palestinians. The point of departure here is the Second Vatican Council (1962–65) because of the significant changes it introduced with regard to the Church's involvement in the modern world, her relationship with non-Christian religions, and the importance of the Bible in her life and thought. Arguably, the 1984 declaration of Pope John Paul II on Jerusalem, *Redemptionis anno*, represents the post–Vatican II Church's developed position on the Land and its peoples.[2] This apostolic letter reflects the complexity and multiple strands in the Church's position. The pope addresses all the central issues that define the specificity and uniqueness of this land. A careful reading of the letter delineates five areas that Church teaching seeks to take into account with regard to the Land:

(1) The traditional Christian attachment to the Holy Land as historical heritage and sacramental figure of the history of salvation: The holy places, venerated throughout Christian history, are not only dead stones and monuments to past events. They preserve the memory of those who sacrificed themselves, often in the midst of great trials, to keep the memory of Jesus Christ alive there. Today, the living stones that are the Christian communities that continue to live in the Land animate them. The Holy Land and Jerusalem, mother of the Churches, constitute a sacramental reference point for all Christians.

(2) The interpretation of the Land in the Bible, particularly the promise and gift of the Land: What does the Bible tell the Christian about the Land? How should the passages about the gift of the Land to God's people be interpreted today? Here the focus is on the correct interpretation of these passages in the light of modern exegesis (including the historical-critical approach) and the contemporary issues raised in political and fundamentalist manipulations of the biblical text.

(3 and 4) Interreligious dialogue: How should Christians respond to the Jewish claims on the Land after having, for so long, used the Scriptures to justify Jewish exile from the Land? Can or should Christians attribute a theological meaning to the settlement of Jews in the Land that became the State of Israel in 1948?

And how should Christians respond to the Muslim claim on the Land, a claim that is often also formulated in religious terms? Muslims constitute the vast majority of the Palestinian people that also includes a Christian minority.

These claims and counterclaims are the core of the conflict between Israel and the Arab world, but also constitute an important area of dialogue between Catholics and Jews on the one hand and Catholic and Muslims on the other.

(5) The pursuit of peace and justice in the Middle East in general and in Israel-Palestine in particular: How can and should Christians engage in the search for peace and justice in the Holy Land? How should Christians respond to Israeli and Palestinian claims on the Land without overlooking the legitimate rights of each side? This raises questions about Vatican policy with regard to states in general and also involves relations between the Church and the representatives of the Israeli and Palestinian peoples, respectively.

In examining each of these domains separately, we seek to present a Catholic position on the Land that takes into account all five domains.[3] We will argue here that all the above-mentioned factors must be taken into account, as one complements and clarifies another as the Church tries to advance the interests of justice and peace.

6. TRADITIONAL CHRISTIAN ATTACHMENT TO THE LAND

In the Good Friday 1984 apostolic letter *Redemptionis anno* on Jerusalem, John Paul II writes: "Although I cannot be there physically, I nevertheless feel that I am spiritually a pilgrim in that land where our reconciliation with God was brought about. . . . Christians honor (Jerusalem) with a religious and intent concern because there the words of Christ so often resounded, there the great events of the Redemption were accomplished: the Passion, Death and Resurrection of the Lord. In the city of Jerusalem the first Christian community sprang up and remained throughout the centuries a continual ecclesial presence despite difficulties."[1]

Since the first centuries A.D., many Christians have referred to the Land not as Israel or Palestine, but as the Holy Land. They continue to see it as a place of pilgrimage, where the memory of Christ and his ancestors and disciples can be venerated. However, unlike for Jews and for Muslims, for Christians, the biblical land of Israel is not a constitutive element of Christian faith. In his letter on pilgrimage to the places connected to the history of salvation, John Paul II points out: "God is equally present in every corner of the earth so that the whole world may be considered the "temple" of his presence."[2] However, manifesting sensitivity to popular religious sentiment, he adds: "Yet this does not take away from the fact that, just as time can be marked by *kairoi*, by special moments of grace, space too may, by analogy, bear the stamp of particular saving actions of God."[3]

After the failure of the Crusades, the Holy Land lost its central role in the Christian imagination. Furthermore, in the spirit of Jesus' preaching and in the newness introduced by his resurrection, centuries of Christian tradition sanctified other lands. The Holy Land became one holy land among others, even if a distinctly privileged one. The rediscovery of the Holy Land in the nineteenth century by Western travelers gave rise to a renewal of interest in the symbolic importance of the Land for Christians. As transportation improved, pilgrims and tourists, driven by romantic, literary, religious, and political motivations and often in search of their spiritual roots, flocked again to the Land. The archaeological excavations in the Holy Land excited the imagination of many Christians, raising hopes that the ground of the Holy Land would reveal the truths behind the biblical narratives. Muhammad Ali's rise to power in Syria-Palestine in the first half of the nineteenth century made the Holy Land a safe destination, more and more popular among European and North American travelers. Taking advantage of the weakening of Ottoman central power, the great European powers (France, England, Germany, Russia, Austro-Hungary) established themselves in the Land, each one declaring itself protector of different religious communities and holy places. Particularly active, the French established a consulate in Jerusalem in 1843. The reestablishment of the Latin Patriarchate of Jerusalem in 1847 was followed by the arrival of many Catholic religious congregations, most protected by the French authorities, whose anti-clericalism stopped at the frontiers of the French state. New churches were built that incorporated the archaeological finds at biblical sites and accommodated the new waves of visitors. In France, the Assumptionist Fathers contributed to the organization of large groups of pilgrims. By 1882, they were able to bring as many as 1000 pilgrims at one time to the Holy Land, signifying the rebirth of the traditional pilgrimages that continue until this day despite wars and unrest.

One cannot forget that in the twentieth century the Holy Land became the arena of a protracted conflict that put the biblical heartland back at the forefront of Christian consciousness. It was within this context that Christians became aware too of the difficult circumstances in which their coreligionists, the Christians of the Holy Land, predominantly Palestinian Arabs, lived. These two concerns, the traditional Holy Places and solidarity with the local Christian population, have both been reference points in all official Catholic statements on the Land.

Pope Paul VI became the first Roman pontiff to make a pilgrimage to the Holy Land in 1964. His pilgrimage took place predominantly within the borders of the Hashemite Kingdom of Jordan that ruled both the historical east part of Jerusalem and Bethlehem at that time. He did cross over, for one day, into the State of Israel, visiting Nazareth, Tabor, Megiddo, and other holy sites. Avoiding any reference to the political situation, his visit focused primarily on the Holy Places and the local Christian churches. The highlight of the visit was not the meetings with the Arab and Jewish political authorities but rather the historic encounter with the Greek Orthodox Ecumenical Patriarch of Constantinople, Athenagoras, and his Jerusalem counterpart, Jerusalem Patriarch Benedictos.[4] In February 2000, Pope John Paul II made his own pilgrimage to the Holy Land. Thirty-six years after the visit of Pope Paul VI, the situation had greatly changed. This time the pope arrived at a time when negotiations between Israel and the Palestinians, under U.S. patronage, had given birth to new hopes for peace in the region.

During his visit, Pope John Paul II focused explicitly on relations with Jews and Muslims as well as on the Israeli and Palestinian peoples. However, the pope appeared first and foremost as a pilgrim, come to pray at the holy places. He underlined the Church's attachment to both the holy places and to the Christian communities of faithful in the Land. In a touching address to the local Christian community, the pope said:

" 'Do not be afraid'—These words resound through the pages of Scripture. They are divine words spoken by Jesus himself after he arose from the dead: Do not be afraid. They are the words of the Church to you today. Do not be afraid to preserve your Christian presence and heritage in the very place where the Savior was born."[5]

The pope's words are faithful to the tradition of the Church in Rome, manifesting her constant solicitude for the Christian communities, reduced to minority status after centuries of non-Christian rule. Since the conquest of Jerusalem by the Muslim Arabs in the middle of the seventh century and up until 1948, there have been only two relatively short periods of non-Muslim rule in the Holy Land. The first was the Crusader period, which left sad memories of violence and oppression among the non-Christian (Muslim and Jewish) as well as non-Catholic (predominantly Orthodox) inhabitants. The second was between 1917 and 1948, when Palestine came under the British Mandate, seen by both Arabs and Jews as a foreign colonial power.

After the violent events of 1948, which led to the establishment of the State of Israel, Israel and Jordan became the authorities in the Land. Although some Holy Places were looted, Israelis and Jordanians tended to respect the Holy Places of Christianity that fell under their respective control. The Holy See clearly would have preferred that the Holy Places fall under neither Arab nor Jewish rule but rather that a third party be given administration of an internationalized zone that would include both Jerusalem and Bethlehem.[6] It was the question of the local Christian population that was particularly traumatic, however. Sixty to seventy percent of the Christian population of Palestine, alongside their Muslim neighbors, became refugees after 1948. Due to ongoing war, the Holy See recognized neither the State of Israel nor the Hashemite Kingdom of Jordan, awaiting the normalization of the situation and the clear ratification of international boundaries between states.

Throughout the decades that followed 1948, the Catholic Church has been clear on the two fundamental issues:

(1) The holy places must be protected and respected.

(2) The Christian faithful must be guaranteed full rights.

The Official Status of the Churches

Since the time of the Ottomans, the churches of Jerusalem and the Holy Land benefited from a series of exemptions and privileges. France gave a juridical form to these exemptions and privileges in the text of the Agreements of Mytilene (1901) and Constantinople (1913). This involves mainly the Roman Catholic religious congregations that are of French origin. However, the Italian government followed this example for the congregations of Italian origin. These agreements were respected by the British Mandate authorities. Since the establishment of the State of Israel, both France and Italy have insisted that these agreements are also binding for the State and they have generally been respected.

On December 30, 1993, the Holy See signed a "Fundamental Agreement" with the State of Israel, followed by the signing of the "Legal Personality Agreement" on November 10, 1997. On February 15, 2000, the Holy See signed a basic agreement with the Palestinian Liberation Organization. In both cases, the agreements underlined that neither one could prejudice the agreements that had been signed with a third party. As this book goes to press, the negotiations between Israel and the Holy See continue, not without difficulties, trying to work out an economic agreement between Israel and the Church.

7. The Interpretation of the Bible

In his 1984 apostolic letter *Redemptionis anno*, John Paul II writes: "It is a land, which we call holy, indeed the land which is the earthly homeland of Christ, who walked about it 'preaching the gospel of the kingdom and healing every disease and infirmity' (Mt 4:23). . . . I think, especially, of the city of Jerusalem, where Jesus, offering his life 'has made us both one, and has broken down the dividing wall of hostility . . . bringing the hostility to an end (Ep 2:13).'"[1]

In this reference to the geographic roots of the historical figure of Jesus, his preaching and his activity, John Paul II continued the teaching of the Second Vatican Council. The Council was profoundly marked by a return to biblical roots. The influential Council document, the *Apostolic Constitution on Divine Revelation* (*Dei verbum*), had a profound effect not only on theologians and exegetes, but also on the Catholic faithful, who once again took up their Bibles with enthusiasm. Reaffirmed in their awareness of the integral unity of the Old and New Testaments, Catholics were encouraged to read the Old Testament and deepen their sensitivity to the stages of the history of salvation that preceded the birth of Jesus: "The plan of salvation, foretold by the sacred authors, recounted and explained by them, is found as the true word of God in the books of the Old Testament: these books, therefore, written under divine inspiration, remain permanently valuable. . . . Now the books of the Old Testament, in accordance with the state of mankind before the time of salvation established by Christ, reveal to all men the knowledge of God and of man and the ways in which God, just and merciful, deals with men."[2]

This renewed exposure to the history of the biblical people of Israel would bring some Christians to reflect on land and people, a reflection that would affect Catholic thinking about the contemporary troubles in the Holy Land.

In the Church, reading the Bible has revealed a diversity of interpretations that are manifest in many domains of Church teaching. The spectrum stretches from an almost biblical fundamentalism to radical scientific historical-critical approaches that focus on the original context of the production of the text. What interests us here is how the return to biblical sources influences the Church's understanding of the place of the Land in Christian teaching. For many readers, the Bible affirms Jewish sovereignty over the Land. According to the biblical text, God gave the Land to the Jews. Fidelity to biblical teaching would, thus, seem to necessitate support for Jewish Zionism. However, a position that promotes an exclusive Jewish claim on the Land, and that ignores that the Land was and is inhabited by another people, is not a faithful representation of the complexity of the biblical message on the Land and, furthermore, ignores the insights of contemporary historical-critical and other methods of biblical interpretation.

In the groundbreaking 1993 document of the Pontifical Biblical Commission, *The Interpretation of the Bible in the Church*, Catholics were warned against the dangers of a fundamentalist reading of the Bible. According to the document, biblical fundamentalism ignores "the historical character of biblical revelation" and thus is incapable of accepting "the full truth of the Incarnation itself": "It fails to recognize that the Word of God has been formulated in language and expression conditioned by various periods. It pays no attention to the literary forms and to the human ways of thinking to be found in the biblical texts, many of which are the result of a process extending over long periods of time and bearing the mark of very diverse historical periods."[3]

Critical methods teach us that the Word is always an incarnate Word, rooted in culture and language, inevitably contextualized. The document is particularly severe when it comes to Christian biblical fundamentalism:

The fundamentalist approach is dangerous, for it is attractive to people who look to the Bible for ready answers to the problems of life. It can deceive these people, offering them interpretations that are pious but illusory, instead of telling them that the Bible does not necessarily contain an immediate answer to each and every problem. Without saying as much in so many words, fundamentalism actually invites people to a kind of intellectual suicide. It injects into life a false certitude, for it unwittingly confuses the divine substance of the biblical message with what are in fact human limitations.[4]

The text makes explicit reference to the issue of the Land in an illustration of the various "rereadings" within the Bible as a whole:

> One thing that gives the Bible an inner unity, unique of its kind, is the fact that later biblical writings often depend upon earlier ones. These more recent writings allude to older ones creating "re-readings" which develop new aspects of meaning, sometimes quite different from the original sense. A text might also make explicit reference to older passages, whether it is to deepen their meaning or to make known their fulfillment. Thus it is that the inheritance of the Land, promised by God to Abraham for his offspring (Gn 15:7.18) becomes entrance into the sanctuary of God (Ex 15:7), a participation in God's "rest" (Ps 132:7–8) reserved for those who truly have faith (Ps 95:8–11, Heb 3:7–4:11) and finally, entrance into the heavenly sanctuary (Heb 6:12.18–20), the "eternal inheritance" (Heb 9:15).[5]

Although the question of the Land is peripheral to the document, the suggestions on how to read the Bible are precious pointers to avoiding an ideological manipulation of the Bible that favors one party over another in the present struggle in the Holy Land.

In the 2001 document of the Pontifical Biblical Commission, *The Jewish People and Their Sacred Scriptures in the Christian Bible*, there is a great respect for the Jewish reading of the biblical text, explaining that "Christians can and ought to admit that the Jewish reading of the Bible is a possible one, in continuity with the Jewish Sacred Scriptures from the Second Temple period, a reading analogous to the Christian reading which developed in parallel fashion."[6] Christians are encouraged to respect the Jewish reading and learn from it. This is a new approach in the Church, rooted in the Vatican II opening to Judaism and other religions, which seeks to correct the centuries-long attitude of contempt for the Jewish reading of the Bible. This goal is clear right in the opening phrases of the document: "Modern times have made Christians more aware of the close fraternal bonds that unite them to the Jewish people. During the Second World War (1939–45), tragic events, or more precisely, abominable crimes subjected the Jewish people to a terrible ordeal that threatened their very existence throughout most of Europe. In those circumstances, some Christians failed to exhibit the spiritual resistance to be expected from disciples of Christ."[7]

One of the many ways in which anti-Jewish sentiment was fostered by Christian attitudes was in the assumption that Jews misread their own Scriptures and were thus unable to see that these very Scriptures promised the coming of Jesus of Nazareth as the Messiah of Israel. Their eyes veiled, the Jews had rejected their own savior. It is in seeking a corrective to this perspective that the Commission expresses its respect for the Jewish reading of Scripture. However, the document does not suggest that Christians, in respecting their own Jewish origins, should then read the Bible exactly as Jews might do: "To read the Bible as Judaism does necessarily involves an implicit acceptance of all its presuppositions, that is the full acceptance of what Judaism is, in particular, the authority of its writings and Rabbinic traditions, which exclude faith in Jesus as Messiah and Son of God. . . . Both [Jewish and Christian] readings are bound up with the vision of their respective faiths, of which the readings are the result and expression. Consequently both are irreducible."[8]

The document, in presenting the Christian reading of the Old Testament, insists that the promises of God to Israel are to be re-read by the Christian in the light of Jesus Christ in the New Testament: "Many of the promises made by God in the Old Testament are re-read in the light of Jesus Christ in the New Testament. This poses real and delicate questions, which touch the dialogue between Jews and Christians; they concern the legitimacy of an interpretation of the promises over and above their original, obvious meaning. Who exactly are the descendants of Abraham? Is the Promised Land first and foremost a geographical location? What future horizon does the God of revelation reserve for Israel, the people originally chosen? What becomes of the wait for the kingdom of God? And for the Messiah?"[9]

Significant here is the explicit mention of the Land. The document proposes a basic continuity between the Old and the New Testaments in which the history of Jesus is embedded in the history of the people chosen by God. However, the document also underlines the universal perspective that must be maintained in a Christian reflection on the specificity described in the Old Testament. From this universal dimension, the particularity of Israel extends beyond itself: "This opens up for the chosen people wonderful future horizons: posterity (promised to Abraham), living space (a territory), survival beyond crises and testings (due to God's fidelity) and the establishment of the ideal political order (the reign of God, Messianism). From the beginning, a reign, universal in its scope, is envisaged for the blessing given to Abraham. The salvation bestowed by God will spread to the ends of the earth. Indeed, it is Jesus Christ who offers salvation to the entire world."[10]

With regard to the Land, the document is pointedly explicit: "Every human group wishes to inhabit territory in a permanent manner. Otherwise, reduced to the status of stranger or refugee, it finds itself, at best, tolerated, or at worst, exploited and continually oppressed. Israel was freed from slavery in Egypt and received from God the promise of land. Its realization required time and gave rise to many problems throughout the course of its history. For the people of the Bible, even after the return from the Babylonian Exile, the land remained an object of hope: "Those blessed by the Lord will possess the land" (Ps 37:22)."[11]

This is followed by a survey of the entire Christian Bible, examining the meaning of the Land at each step in the history of salvation. The document seeks to provide a hermeneutic with which to read the stories and laws regarding the entry of the people into the Land. Aware that these stories, with their graphic violence, could be understood as justifying ethnic cleansing in present times, the document clearly proposes a historical-critical approach to the text:

> The theme of the land should not be allowed to overshadow the manner in which the Book of Joshua recounts the entry to the Promised Land. Many texts speak of consecrating to God the fruits of victory, called the ban (*herem*). To prevent all foreign religious contamination, the ban imposed the obligation of destroying all places and objects of pagan cults (Dt 7:5), as well as of all living beings (20:15–18). The same applies when an Israelite town succumbs to idolatry, Dt 13:16–18 prescribes that all its inhabitants be put to death and that the town itself be burnt down.
>
> At the time when Deuteronomy was written—as well as the Book of Joshua—the ban was a theoretical postulate, since non-

Israelite populations no longer existed in Judah. The ban then could be the result of a projection into the past of later preoccupations. Indeed, Deuteronomy is anxious to reinforce the religious identity of a people exposed to the danger of foreign cults and mixed marriages. Therefore, to appreciate the ban, three factors must be taken into account in interpretation; theological, moral, and one mainly sociological: the recognition of the land as the inalienable domain of the Lord; the necessity of guarding the people from all temptation which would compromise their fidelity to God; finally, the all too human temptation of mingling with religion the worst forms of resorting to violence.[12]

It is clear that in this precaution, the Commission is expressing an awareness of the current tragic situation in the Holy Land, awash in the blood of the victims of the ongoing violence. While insisting that the New Testament dynamic regarding the Land is founded in the Old Testament, the document also clearly outlines the change in perspective brought about by Jesus:

> The New Testament does not develop much further the theme of the Promised Land. The flight of Jesus and his parents to Egypt and their return to the "land of promise" (Mt 2:20–21) clearly retraces the journey of the ancestors; a theological typology undergirds this narrative. In Stephen's discourse which recalls their history, the word "promise" or "promised" is found side by side with "land" and "heritage" (Ac 7:2–7). Although not found in the Old Testament, the expression "land of promise" is found in the New (Heb 11:9), in a passage which, undoubtedly, recalls the historical experience of Abraham to better underline its provisional and incomplete character, and its orientation towards the absolute future of the world and history. For the author, the "land" of Israel is only a symbolic pointer towards a very different land, a "heavenly homeland." One of the beatitudes transforms the geographical and historical meaning into a more open-ended one, "the meek shall possess the land" (Mt 5:5); "the land" is equivalent here to "the kingdom of heaven" (5:3,10) in an eschatological horizon that is both present and future.
>
> The authors of the New Testament are only deepening a symbolic process already at work in the Old Testament and in intertestamental Judaism. It should not be forgotten, however, that a

specific land was promised by God to Israel and received as a heritage; this gift of the land was on condition of fidelity to the covenant (Lv 26; Dt 28).[13]

The inherent tension between promise and gift on the one hand and conditions of fidelity on the other is an important reminder of the complexity of the theme of the Land in the biblical narrative. In understanding the Land within contemporary Catholic interpretation of the Bible, the document warns against two dangers that manifest themselves in Christian interpretation. One is allegorization that totally spiritualizes history and in which concrete realities, like the Land, dissolve. The document critiques a certain extreme of allegorization by pointing out the danger of "detaching each detail from its context and severing the relationship between the biblical text and the concrete reality of salvation history. Interpretation then becomes arbitrary."[14] Although allegorization is a venerable part of the Christian tradition of interpretation, the Christian reader of the Bible cannot today ignore the literal meaning of the biblical text. However, the document further points out, a second danger is that of denying the legitimacy of a Christian reading of the Old Testament and the Christological interpretation that it implies. With regard to the Land, holding in perspective the entire Christian Bible as a unity is an important key to Christian interpretation, especially within the context of the conflict that besets the Holy Land today.

The Churches in the Holy Land have had to confront the question of the Land in the Bible not only theoretically but as part of a life-and-death struggle to survive. In the conflict between Israelis and Palestinians, the Zionist interpretation of the Bible, which vindicates Jewish claims on the Land, threatens to silence all other readings. Written predominantly for Christian Palestinians, the Roman Catholic Church in the Holy Land published a 1993 pastoral letter entitled *Reading the Bible in the Land of the Bible.* The burning issue in the letter is to explain why Palestinian Christians must not reject the Old Testament even though it seems to favor Israeli territorial claims: "For the Palestinian Christian, the Bible is an integral part of his faith and religious heritage. One reads it and meditates upon it individually or in community (catechism, liturgy, prayer groups). During the time of conflict, the questions raised by such reading and prayer have been numerous. These questions persist until now.[15]"

The Latin Patriarch of Jerusalem, Michel Sabbah, poses the leading questions at the beginning of his letter:

How is the Old Testament to be understood? What is the relationship between the Old and the New Testament? . . . What is the relationship between ancient biblical history and our contemporary history? Is biblical Israel the same as the contemporary State of Israel? What is the meaning of the promises, the election, the covenant and in particular the *"promise and gift of the Land"* to Abraham and his descendants? Does the Bible justify present political claims? Could we be victims of our own salvation history, which seems to favor the Jewish people and condemn us? Is that truly the will of God to which we must inexorably bow down, demanding that we deprive ourselves in favor of another people, with no possibility of appeal or discussion?[16]

The patriarch draws attention to the fact that "some [Jews], by what they say and sincerely believe seem to confirm the fears and anguish of the Palestinians."[17] Furthermore, there are some fundamentalist Christians, who "directly link all of the present history with the fulfillment of specific biblical prophecies. They even accuse local Christians who do not agree with their views as being 'unbiblical' and not true believers."[18] Thus the letter seeks to shed light on the "spiritual confusion and religious rebellion among those who have been driven away from their homes and their land." The Latin Patriarch expresses the problematic with great poignancy:

The essential question asked by the Palestinian Christian and by every believer in the Bible is this: does the Bible, as the Word of God, give the right to the Jewish people today to appropriate the land for themselves and, in doing so, dispossess the Palestinian people? The Jewish believer, the Jewish people and the State of Israel are faced with a dilemma. On one hand, this land is the holy land for them. God promised it to Abraham and to his descendants. In this land, they have found security from the nations that have persecuted them in the diaspora. For them, God, people and land, form the triangle of their security and peace. But on the other hand, for centuries this land has belonged to another people, the Palestinian people. Even in the biblical times, this land was also the land of another people who always coexisted with the Jewish people. Furthermore, this land is the cradle and the place of most important events of Christianity. It is Christianity's holy land *"par excellence"* It is also the holy land for Islam. It is then the holy land for all believers: Jews, Christians and Muslims.[19]

At the end of the letter, the patriarch seeks to both affirm the ultimate importance of the Word of God in the Old Testament that cannot be refused because this would be "a refusal to accept a part of the revealed Book and a denial of God's Word."[20] However, he warns against the type of political manipulation of the Bible that perpetuates injustice and violence. Here in the Holy Land itself just as anywhere else in the world touched by conflict, a solution can only be achieved through dialogue and a commitment to justice and peace as preached by the prophets throughout the Old Testament.

8. Interreligious Dialogue

The Second Vatican Council inaugurated a new era in the history of the Church's relations with non-Christians. The Church reflected positively on the fact that she shared the world with peoples of faiths different than her own. Together with them she is called to work for peace and justice. The gathering of religious leaders to pray for peace at Assisi in 1986, where Pope John Paul II sought to gather all leaders of the world religions, gave a palpable vision of this striving for a world built on peace, justice, and reconciliation, in which there would be no more wars.

With regard to the Holy Land, the Church has repeatedly stressed since the Council that she cannot ignore the religious sentiments of Jews, Muslims, and Christians too toward the Land they all regard as holy. In his apostolic letter of 1984, *Redemptionis anno,* Pope John Paul II recognized the attachment of Jews to Jerusalem: "Jews ardently love [Jerusalem] and in every age venerate her memory, abundant as she is in many remains and monuments from the time of David who chose her as the capital, and of Solomon who built the Temple there. Therefore, they turn their minds to her daily, one may say, and point to her as the sign of their nation."[1]

This paragraph was followed by a paragraph that was also sensitive to the Muslim perspective on Jerusalem: "Muslims also call Jerusalem "holy," with a profound attachment that goes back to the origins of Islam and springs from the fact that they have there many special places of pilgrimage and for more than a thousand years have dwelt there almost without interruption."[2]

Since Vatican II, dialogue with both Jews and Muslims has witnessed important progress. With regard to the dialogue with Muslims, the manifestation of radical political Islamic trends has obligated the Church to deepen her reflection on the true spiritual nature of Islam. With regard to the Jews, repeatedly referred to as "the older brother" of the Christian, the dialogue conforms to a different reality because of the tragic past that the Church seeks to make amends for. However, the question of the Land, so present in the Jewish tradition and at the heart of the conflict between Jews and Arabs, raises complex issues for the Church's teaching on dialogue with both Jews and Muslims.

JEWISH-CATHOLIC DIALOGUE

The second half of the twentieth century, after centuries of ignorance and contempt, can be characterized as a golden age for the dialogue between Jews and Christians. Many Western Christian Churches have engaged in a review of their teachings about Jews and Judaism in order to eradicate the "contempt of Judaism"[3] that historically characterized much of Christian thinking. We cannot review all the extensive literature, both official documents of the Vatican and local churches as well as theological treatises that touch this subject here. We will focus only on the most significant declarations, especially those that deal with the Land, which is one of the most sensitive issues for many Jews, whether religious or secular, in their relationship with Christians. In order to measure the dramatic changes in the attitude of the Church, we can evoke the 1904 meeting between Pope Pius X and Theodor Herzl, founding father of modern political Zionism, who was seeking Catholic support for the settlement of Jews in Palestine. Herzl later wrote in his diary that the pope had responded: "The Jews have not recognized our Lord, therefore we cannot recognize the Jewish people."[4]

It was in the period after the Holocaust that the tone of the Church changed radically. Pope John XXIII, remembered fondly as "good Pope John," inaugurated a new relationship with Jews and Judaism by personally listening to Jewish spokespeople right from the beginning of his pontificate, thus initiating a new epoch with regard to the Jews even before the Council was convened. His successor, Paul VI, visited the Holy Land in the midst of the Council; the first time a pope had done so since ancient times. He spent one day in the State of Israel, visiting the holy sites that fell under Israeli jurisdiction. In his official arrival

and departure addresses, on January 5, 1964, the pope, addressing Israeli President Shazar, made no mention of the political realities in the
land. He referred to himself as a "pilgrim of peace" and insisted on
the religious freedom of Catholics in the country without addressing
the delicate question of Jewish or Arab claims to the Land.[5]

The 1965 *Declaration on the Relationship of the Church to Non-
Christian Religions (Nostra aetate)* rooted the transformation of the
Church's theological perspective with regard to the world religions in
general and Judaism and the Jewish people in particular. Paragraph 4[6]
of this document begins by underlining "the spiritual bond linking the
people of the New Covenant with Abraham's stock." This, the longest
paragraph in the document, outlines the various scriptural and historical
links between Jews and Christians and condemns all forms of persecution. The document is formulated uniquely from the Christian perspective on the Jewish people and says nothing about how the Jewish people
see themselves. Jews are presented within the context of their relationship with Christians and how Christians have seen, in the past, and
should see them, in the present and future. It is not surprising then that
the document says nothing about the Land or about the State of Israel.
In fact, it says nothing about the developments of Judaism after the period of Jesus of Nazareth except with regard to the difficult relationships between Jews and Christians through centuries of shared history.

However, this document had an important impact on the later formulation of the Vatican's position on the Land as it insisted that "the Jews
should not be presented as repudiated or cursed by God, as if such
views followed from Holy Scriptures." This negative view of the Jews
had been a major factor in the justification of the Jewish dispersion, far
from the land of their ancestors. The Council added that the Jewish people remains dear to God, citing Saint Paul: "He does not repent of the
gifts He makes nor of the call He issues" (Rm 11:29).[7]

The fundamental change in official Catholic attitude, discourse, and
behavior toward Jews and Judaism was palpable after the Council. The
post-conciliar Church sees the dialogue with the Jews in a category of
its own and as a preferential option among the various interreligious
dialogue possibilities. At present, dialogue with the Jewish people does
not fall under the Pontifical Council for Interreligious Dialogue in the
Vatican, but rather under a pontifical council within the office that
works for the unity of all Christians.[8] Two predominant themes appear
in all the official documents published in the aftermath of *Nostra aetate*.

The first theme is the recognition of the Jewish roots of Christianity. Catholic teaching insists that Jesus was himself a Jew.[9] The refocus on the Bible, particularly on the importance of the Old Testament for understanding the New, is often the context in which Christians first discover Jews and Judaism. The second theme is repentance for the Church's past omissions and the "teaching of contempt" with regard to the Jewish people. This motivated Christians, especially in Europe, to become aware of their part in the responsibility for the suffering of the Jewish people that culminated in the Shoah. The period after the Council saw the emergence of numerous Catholic groups that promoted a positive teaching on Judaism and active support for the Jewish people.

The Church, ever prudent, however, resisted translating this new attitude toward the Jewish people into a political position with regard to the events in the Middle East, particularly with regard to Jewish claims to the Land and the status of the State of Israel. Between 1965 and 1993, the Holy See insisted on keeping the dialogue with Judaism separate from what was seen as the political claims of the Jewish people to the Land.

The 1973 declaration of the Commission for Relations with Judaism of the French Bishops, *The Christian Attitude towards Judaism: Pastoral Orientations of the Episcopal Committee for Relations with Judaism*, marked another important step in development of Church discourse on the Jews. This was the first official Catholic document to insist that the way Jews see themselves must be taken into account by Christians. Christians "must seek to understand" Jews "as they understand themselves, instead of judging them by Christian ways of thinking."[10] It was within this context that the document went on to explicitly formulate a position on the Jewish national claim to the Land. In a long paragraph consecrated to the subject of the Land, the document stated:

> Today more than ever, it is difficult to pronounce a well-considered theological opinion on the return of the Jewish people to "its" land. In this context, we, Christians, must first of all not forget the gift once made by God to the people of Israel of a land where it was called to be reunited (Gn 12:7, 26:3–4, 28:13; Is 43:5–7, Jer 16:15, Zep 3:20).
>
> Throughout history, Jewish existence has always been divided between life among the nations and the wish for national existence on that land. This aspiration poses numerous problems even

to Jews. To understand it, as well as all dimensions of the resulting discussion, Christians must not be carried away by interpretations that would ignore the forms of Jewish communal and religious life, or by political positions that, though generous, are nonetheless hastily arrived at. Christians must take into account the interpretation given by Jews to their ingathering around Jerusalem, which, according to their faith, is considered a blessing. Justice is put to the test by this return and its repercussions. On the political level, it has caused confrontations between the various claims for justice. Beyond the legitimate divergence of political opinions, the conscience of the world community cannot refuse the Jewish people, who had to submit to many vicissitudes in the course of its history, the right and means for a political existence among the nations. At the same time, this right and the possibilities for existence cannot be refused to those who, in the course of local conflicts resulting from this return, are now victims of grave injustice.

Let us then turn our eyes toward this land visited by God and let us actively hope that it may become a place where one day all its inhabitants, Jews and non-Jews, can live together in peace. It is an essential question, faced by Christians as well as Jews, whether or not the ingathering of the dispersed Jewish people— which took place under pressure of persecution and by the way of political forces—will, despite so many tragic events, prove to be one of the final ways of God's justice for the Jewish people and, at the same time, for all the nations of the earth. How could Christians remain indifferent to what is now decided in that land?[11]

This was followed by the expression of the hope that those who have been victims of injustice because of the Jewish return might also be granted the right to political and national existence.

The text was very favorably received both by Christian communities in France and the Jewish community too. The Chief Rabbinate in France published a statement expressing its great esteem for the document, "highly appreciated in letter and in spirit."[12] The text was not greeted everywhere with enthusiasm, however, especially not among the Christians in the Arab world and those in solidarity with them. The authors, fearing this polarization, sought to neutralize a political interpretation of the letter and published a communiqué that stressed that

the document should be read within the religious context.[13] It was precisely the biblical argument that aroused the fiercest debates. Interestingly, the text also did not designate the Palestinian people by name but
rather chose to adopt the popular Jewish terminology of Jews and non-
Jews. More than thirty years later it is instructive to reread the arguments of the defenders and opponents of the document. The letter of
support that came from the Hebrew-speaking Catholics in Israel thanking the bishops for their perspective beyond ideology and coming from
faith and hope[14] was contrasted by the letter signed by forty Jesuits in
Lebanon that expressed the fear that such orientations would only contribute further to the despair and hate that the bishops should seek to
lessen.[15] In retrospect, though, this letter was a turning point in the development of a Church discourse on the Land that wrestled with the
complexity of the issues involved and tried to respect the multiplicity
of partners involved in the question.

   In 1974, the Vatican's Commission for Religious Relations with Judaism, founded at that time, published its "foundational charter" *Ori-*
entations and Suggestions for the Application of the Council
Declaration Nostra Aetate.[16] Unlike the document of the French bishops, it said nothing about the Land; however, it was sensitive to the
question of how the Jews see themselves and did not impose Christian
interpretations upon Judaism: "Christians must therefore strive to acquire a better knowledge of the basic components of the religious tradition of Judaism; they must strive to learn by what essential traits the
Jews define themselves in the light of their own religious experience."[17]

   This important development implied that Catholics had to face the
fact that most Jews insisted on their connection to the land of Israel and
sought the Church's recognition of this. The silence of the document
on the question of the Land provoked some negative reactions to the
document in Jewish circles. This was expressed by the General Secretary of the World Jewish Congress, G. Riegner, in an audience with
Pope Paul VI, shortly after the publication of the document: "We are
pleased with the invitation issued to Christians to look for and learn 'by
what essential traits the Jews define themselves in their lived religious
reality.'" We hope that this effort will lead to a greater appreciation of
the essential place that people and land hold in the Jewish faith."[18]

   This provoked a response from the secretary of the Commission,
Father de Contenson, who explained on Vatican Radio: "Some commentators, while appreciating the general tone of the document, deplore

the fact that there is no mention of the attachment of the Jewish people to the Land nor of the meaning that the Land has in Jewish tradition. . . . The Jews, themselves, must say who they are. . . . We must listen to the Jews in order to understand them."[19]

How should the Church position itself with regard to the State of Israel and the Jewish national movement, Zionism, on the one hand, and the Palestinian people, their suffering and national rights, on the other hand?

A 1975 U.S. Bishops Conference statement on Jewish-Christian relations illustrated the new perspective of taking into account Jewish self-perception, however, reminding the faithful of the need for impartiality and respect for all parties: "In dialogue with Christians, Jews have explained that they do not consider themselves as a church, a sect, or a denomination, as is the case among Christian communities, but rather as a peoplehood that is not solely racial, ethnic or religious, but in a sense a composite of all these. It is for such reasons that an overwhelming majority of Jews see themselves bound in one way or another to the Land of Israel. Most Jews see this tie to the land as essential to their Jewishness."[20]

Marking a difference with their French colleagues, the American bishops kept their distance from the Jewish vision of the Land, insisting on a spiritual perspective. "Whatever difficulties Christians may experience in sharing this view they should strive to understand this link between land and people, which Jews have expressed in their writings and worship throughout two millennia as a longing for the homeland, holy Zion. Appreciation of this link is not to give assent to any particular religious interpretation of this bond. Nor is this affirmation meant to deny the legitimate rights of other parties in the region, or to adopt any political stance in the controversies over the Middle East, which lie beyond the purview of this statement."[21]

This formulation has been formative in later Vatican formulation of the problematic.

An important impetus was given to Catholic-Jewish dialogue with the election of John Paul II, a Pole, to the chair of Saint Peter in 1978. Karol Wojtyla had grown up in the town of Wadowice, which had had a Jewish population of between 20 to 30 percent. He had Jewish childhood friends with whom he remained in contact until the end of his life. In addition, as a young priest during the war, he had a personal experience of the Nazi Holocaust in which almost the entire Polish Jewish population of over 3 million had been exterminated. Through his words and his gests, this pope would contribute to the acceleration of change in the traditional Catholic mentality about Jews. In an early address, in 1980, to the Jewish community in Mainz, Germany, John Paul II explained his vision of the Jewish-Christian dialogue: "The first dimension of this dialogue, that is, the meeting between the people of God of the Old Covenant, never revoked by God [cf. Rom. 11:29], and that of the New Covenant, is at the same time a dialogue within our Church, that is to say, between the first and the second part of her Bible."[22]

This statement aroused controversy among both Jews and Catholics but hinted at the commitment of the new pope to the dialogue with Judaism. He continued: "It is important here "that Christians—to continue the post-conciliar directives—should aim at understanding better the fundamental elements of the religious tradition of Judaism, and learn what fundamental lines are essential for the religious reality lived by the Jews, according to their own understanding."[23]

Making the words of the 1974 document his own, he was to contribute greatly to the developing dialogue. He became the first pope to make an official visit to a synagogue (in Rome in 1986[24]) and frequently expressed repentance for the centuries of anti-Judaic teaching in the Church. The peak of this movement came when he visited the State of Israel (in 2000), going not only to the traditional Christian sites but also to the Western Wall, the Dome of the Rock, the memorial to the Holocaust (Yad VaShem) and the Chief Rabbinate of Israel. However, John Paul II was cautious too about the Land and the implications of the dialogue in positioning the Church with regard to Israelis and Palestinians. However, almost ninety years after Pope Pius X expressed his reticence about Zionism to Theodor Herzl, Pope John Paul II, in his address to the Jewish community in Brasilia during his official visit to Brazil in 1991, said: "May our Jewish brothers and sisters, who have been led 'out from among the peoples and gathered from the foreign lands' and brought back 'to their own country' (Ez 34:13), to the land of their ancestors, be able to live there in peace and security on the 'mountains of Israel' guarded by God, their true shepherd."[25]

The 1985 *Notes on the Correct Way to Present Jews and Judaism in Preaching and Catechesis in the Roman Catholic Church* presented for the first time a teaching on the Land and the State issued by the Holy See.[26] Published by the Commission for Religious Relations with Judaism on the twentieth anniversary of the publication of *Nostra aetate,* the document clarified various points about the relationship with the Jewish people after twenty years of experience of the dialogue. In its final paragraph on "Judaism and Christianity in History," the document states with regard to the Jewish attachment to the Land:

> The history of Israel did not end in A.D. 70. It continued especially in a numerous Diaspora which allowed Israel to carry to the whole world a witness—often heroic—of its fidelity to the one God and to "exalt Him in the presence of all the living" (Tobit 13:4), while preserving the memory of the land of their forefathers at the heart of their hope (Passover seder).
>
> Christians are invited to understand this religious attachment which finds its roots in biblical tradition, without however making their own any particular religious interpretation of this relationship (cf. Declaration of the U.S. Conference of Catholic Bishops, November, 20, 1975).
>
> The existence of the State of Israel and its political options should be envisaged not in a perspective, which is in itself religious, but in their reference to the common principles of international law.
>
> The permanence of Israel (while so many ancient peoples have disappeared without trace) is a historic fact and a sign to be interpreted within God's design. We must in any case rid ourselves of the traditional idea of a people punished, preserved as a living argument for Christian apologetic.[27]

The influence of the 1975 U.S. bishops' statement is clear. In the Catholic reflection, the justification for Zionism and the State of Israel is not to be theological, but rather emerges from the Jewish self-definition. The fact that Israel has survived throughout the centuries is presented as a fact and as a sign that must be received. The Israeli representative on the International Jewish Committee for Interreligious Consultation, Dr. G. Wigoder, expressed his dissatisfaction with the Notes during the twelfth meeting of the International Committee in Rome that year: "We regret certain omissions and in particular the two thousand years of Jewish history that are not mentioned. . . . God's promise to the Patriarchs to give them a land is a central element of the covenant. If then, the first covenant has not been annulled, do not all its clauses preserve their religious value? The Notes rejects the theory of punishment: the exile of the Jews thus can no longer be interpreted theologically. How then can we lose the Promised Land?"[28]

Between 1965 and 1993, appeals were constantly issued by Jews for the Church to establish diplomatic relations with the State of Israel and recognize the Jewish connection to the Land.[29] Finally, in the light of the budding peace process between Israelis and Palestinians, the Vatican and Israel established full diplomatic relations in 1993. The preamble of the Fundamental Agreement[30] between the two political entities recognized though the unique character of the moment with regard to the relations between Jews and Christians. The signers were "aware of the unique nature of the relationship between the Catholic Church and the Jewish people, and of the historic process of reconciliation and growth in mutual understanding and friendship between Catholics and Jews."[31] This is a decisive moment in the long road that began at Vatican II. At this point in time, it is incumbent upon the Church to establish a working relationship with the State of Israel, where Jews are a dominant majority. This too would have important implications for how the Church might relate to the Jewish and Palestinian claims on the Land. Seven years later (on February 15, 2000), the Church established a parallel accord with the Palestine Liberation Organization, awaiting the establishment of a Palestinian state in the lands occupied by Israel in 1967.

From the time of the diplomatic recognition of the State of Israel, the Holy See has resisted pressures from those (Jews and Christians) who want the Church to adopt the attitude of religious Zionist Jews, attributing theological value to the link of Jews to the Land today.[32] Many of the Jewish partners in the developing dialogue have continued to call the Church to take a position favorable to Jewish national claims on the Land. They have argued that Zionism, the Jewish national movement, is a major component to Jewish identity in our times and dialogue with Jews presupposes acceptance of Jewish claims on the Land. In 2000, 170 Jewish scholars signed a document, *Dabru emet* (Speak the truth), that expressed a Jewish position on dialogue with Christians, a response to the growing openness to dialogue with Jews in many Christian churches. This document tried to enunciate how Jews view Christianity, outlining the major points of agreement and discord. One of the more controversial paragraphs of the document dealt with the Jewish claim to the Land:

> Christians can respect the claim of the Jewish people upon the Land of Israel. The most important event for Jews since the Holo-

caust has been the reestablishment of a Jewish state in the Promised Land. As members of a biblically based religion, Christians appreciate that Israel was promised—and given—to Jews as the physical center of the covenant between them and God. Many Christians support the State of Israel for reasons far more profound than mere politics. As Jews, we applaud this support. We also recognize that Jewish tradition mandates justice for all non-Jews who reside in a Jewish state.[33]

Some Catholic scholars have taken up this challenge and tried to present what meaning the Land of Israel, repopulated and cultivated by the Jews, might have for Christians.[34] However, the link between the ongoing Jewish-Catholic dialogue and the Jewish claims to the Land has been one of the most sensitive aspects of the dialogue between Jews and Catholics in modern times. It is no longer a question of Catholic resistance to Jewish national sovereignty per se but rather Catholic concern for the application of principles of international law that guarantee justice for the Palestinians as well as rights and security for all Christians in the area.

Jewish partners in the dialogue with the Catholic Church have continued to present the centrality of the Land to their identity. At the eighteenth international meeting of the Catholic-Jewish Liaison Committee in Buenos Aires in July 2004, the final declaration, signed by both Jews and Catholics, drew a parallel between anti-Semitism and anti-Zionism: "We draw encouragement from the fruits of our collective strivings, which include the recognition of the unique and unbroken covenantal relationship between God and the Jewish People and the total rejection of anti-Semitism in all its forms, including anti-Zionism as a more recent manifestation of anti-Semitism."[35]

The statement, however, provoked opposition in some Catholic circles. Certain spokesmen made clear that equivalence between anti-Semitism and anti-Zionism was not the intention of the Catholic side of the meeting.[36] The context for Catholics, it was argued, for understanding the statement on anti-Zionism was to be the 1988 document of the Pontifical Commission for Justice and Peace, *The Church Face to Face with Racism*. This document had included a special paragraph that dealt with anti-Semitism. Toward the conclusion of this paragraph, a sentence was introduced that dealt with anti-Zionism too: "Anti-Zionism, which is not in the same category [as anti-Semitism] because it is an opposition to the State of Israel and its policies, sometimes serves as a cover for anti-Semitism, is nourished by it and brings it in its wake."[37] This formulation clearly avoided the problematic parallel.

Before concluding this survey of the theme of the Land in the dialogue between Western Catholics and Jews, it is important to focus on the attempts to establish an ongoing dialogue between indigenous Catholics and Jews in the Land itself. An official document of the Synod of the Catholic Churches in the Holy Land defined the contours of this dialogue in a pioneering document on interreligious dialogue published in 2000 that did not hide the difficulties in the dialogue:

> The political struggle and the concomitant continuous tensions make sincere action for truth, justice, and peace an essential element of any true relationship. This can be accomplished through collaboration with movements for peace and justice within Jewish society, and with all those of good will who seek justice and peace. . . . Religious differences and the political circumstances in which we live permit racist attitudes on both sides and these must be eradicated so that the true face of the other can be seen. This means that we must distinguish between what is political and what is religious, between Judaism as a religion and Zionism as a political ideology, between the Israeli people and the policies of its government.[38]

In December 2003, the Latin Patriarch of Jerusalem, Michel Sabbah, published a letter to his faithful in which he explained the local context of the dialogue between Catholics and Jews.

> Our contemporary context is unique: we are the only Local Church that encounters the Jewish people in a State that is defined as Jewish and where the Jews are the dominant and empowered majority, a reality that dates from 1948. Furthermore, the ongoing conflict between the State of Israel and the Arab world, and in particular between Israelis and Palestinians, means that the national identity of the majority of our faithful is locked in conflict with the national identity of the majority of the Jews. . . . As Church, we witness the continued Israeli military occupation of Palestinian lands and the bloody violence between the two peoples. Together with all men and women of peace and goodwill, including many Israeli and Palestinian Muslims, Christians and

Jews, we are called to be both a voice of truth and a healing presence. . . . The Church is called to be a prophetic witness in our particular context, a witness that dares imagine a different future: freedom, justice, security, peace and prosperity for all inhabitants of the Holy Land that is first and foremost the Lord's.[39]

An authentic dialogue between indigenous Palestinian Catholics and Israeli Jews in Jerusalem might indeed shed new light on the contentious issue of the Land.

The sensitive issue of the attitude to the Land goes beyond the context of the dialogue between Jews and Catholics. The implications of any official Catholic stand on the Land touch on fundamental questions of justice and peace, relations with the Muslims as well as support for the Church in the Holy Land and the protection of the Holy Places. As important, however, are the theological implications of such support for the future relations between Jews and Catholics throughout the world they are called upon to share with others.

MUSLIM-CATHOLIC DIALOGUE

In general, the dialogue between Catholics and Muslims does not focus on the same themes as the dialogue between Catholics and Jews, as the latter share a common biblical tradition represented by the Old Testament. However, it would be a mistake to underestimate the importance of the Holy Land and the Israeli-Arab conflict in the history of Islam, an importance appreciated by the Catholic Church. In Islam, the three holy cities are Mecca and Medina (in the Arabian Peninsular) and Jerusalem, known in Muslim tradition as "al-Quds"—the Holy. The sanctity and importance of Jerusalem, rooted in the biblical traditions which Muslims venerate, is founded on two distinct Muslim traditions. The first is that Muhammad, prophet and founder of Islam, fixed Jerusalem as the first direction of prayer (*qibla*) before deciding in favor of Mecca later in his life. The second is that Mohammed made a miraculous night journey from Arabia to Jerusalem, where he ascended into heaven to speak with the prophets from the Old and New Testaments, an event recorded in the Quran (17:1). In addition to the importance of Jerusalem within the context of Islam, Muslims the world over tend to be in solidarity with the Palestinian Arabs in the Holy Land, most of whom are Muslim too. The importance of the Arab world in Islam is linked not only to the historic center of Islam being situated in the Arab world, but also to the dominant place of Arabic language in the Muslim religion. Arabic is the language of the Quran (the Muslim holy book) and the language of theology and tradition. The developing dialogue between Christians and Muslims, particularly important today in Europe and the United States, cannot avoid the importance of the Land called Holy in the conflict between Jews and Arabs.

During the Second Vatican Council, the Church committed itself to an ongoing dialogue with Islam and Muslims.[40] Paragraph 3 of the 1965 *Declaration on the Relationship of the Church to Non-Christian Religions (Nostra aetate)*, stated that the Church "looks with esteem" upon the Muslims. The Pontifical Council for Interreligious Dialogue founded in the wake of the Council began to build relations with Muslims, and a symbolic reminder of this dialogue has been the annual greetings for the end of the Muslim month of fasting (Ramadan) that has been published every year. In the relations between Muslims and Christians, one must not forget the long history that includes dark periods like the Crusades and the European colonization of the Muslim world. Christians remember the Arab conquests and threats to the lands of Christendom. Stereotypes, prejudices, and fears that persist cause difficulties for the presence of Muslims in the lands traditionally identified with European Christendom as they do for Christians in Muslim lands. Contemporary Islamic political extremism, as manifested, for example, in the September 11, 2001 attacks in the United States, provoke the Christian imagination, leading to generalized projections on all Muslims everywhere.

Defining a series of common elements in Christianity and Islam, the Second Vatican Council urged both Christians and Muslims "to forget the past and to strive sincerely for mutual understanding" for the benefit of justice, peace, and freedom in the world. In 1974, Pope Paul VI announced the creation of the Commission for Religious Relations with Muslims and the Commission for Religious Relations with the Jews. The linking of the two in the formal allocution of the pope is revealing of the continual attempt to preserve a diplomatic symmetry in the dialogue with Jews and the dialogue with Muslims. The Pope identified 1974 as a turning point in the Vatican dialogue with Islam. He cited a number of important meetings between high Vatican officials and Muslim authorities, including the establishment of the first contacts between the Church of Rome and al-Azhar University in Cairo, an institution carrying much authority in an Islamic world that has no centralized authority.[41] That year, the pope himself received a group of Muslim religious leaders from Saudi Arabia, stressing in his greeting that these contacts indicated a new era in relations between Christians and Muslims.[42]

Pope John Paul II has been a pioneer in the field of Muslim-Christian relations too. His fourth voyage after becoming Pope took him to Turkey, a country with a Muslim majority.[43] In 1985, John Paul II went to Morocco, an Arab Muslim country with almost no indigenous Christians. There he addressed a large assembly of Muslim youth, stressing the common religious elements and values that Christianity and Islam share.[44] In 1997, he visited Lebanon, a country with a Muslim majority and a substantial Christian community and where Muslim-Christian relations are sometimes particularly fraught.[45] Later, during the third millennial celebrations, the pope would visit a series of Arab countries with Muslim majorities: Egypt, Jordan, the Palestinian Territories, and Syria. These visits were occasions to plead the cause of continued and strengthened dialogue between Muslims and Christians.

There is little explicit mention of the Holy Land in the official Church documents that address the dialogue with Muslims. Pope John Paul II avoided any overt reference to the political situation in Israel/Palestine when he met with Muslim leaders in the Haram ash-Sharif, Jerusalem's most sacred Muslim holy place, as well as when he addressed Muslims in Egypt on his visit to the al-Azhar Mosque and in Syria on his visit to the Omayad Mosque in Damascus. Early in his pontificate, Pope John Paul II enunciated principles that are guidelines for the dialogue between Catholics and Muslims regarding the Holy Land. In April 1980, King Hassan II of Morocco, representing the Tenth Islamic Conference's Committee on Jerusalem, visited the pope and expressed the Muslim world's view on the question of Jerusalem and the situation in the Holy Land. The pope responded to the Moroccan king:

> You are here as the spokesperson of a great number of Islamic countries who seek to make known their feelings with regard to the problem of Jerusalem. . . . I consider this meeting very useful. It seems to me that the Holy City represents a truly sacred patrimony for all faithful of the three great monotheistic faiths and for the entire world and principally for the populations who live on its territory. We must find a new élan, a new approach, that will

permit, instead of accentuating the differences, translation into acts of more fundamental fraternity and arrival, with the help of God, at a solution, possibly original but imminent, definitive, guaranteed and respectful of the rights of all.[46]

In other official meetings between Catholics and Muslims, spokespeople of the Church have stressed Catholic insistence on finding a solution to the problems in the Holy Land based upon the respect of all sides. A typical statement on the Holy Land was issued at the end of the 2002 meeting of the Islamic-Catholic Liaison Committee: "We are convinced that violence breeds violence. The circle of violence must be stopped. We attest and assert that dialogue is the only way out of the present impasse. We therefore call for negotiations that will lead to a just and lasting peace for Israelis and Palestinians alike, allowing them to live in freedom, security and peace within their own respective independent States."[47]

One constituent of the dialogue on the Holy Land between Muslims and Catholics that cannot be ignored are the Christian Arabs in the Middle East itself. Muslims and Christians define themselves as one people within the framework of Arab nationalism, which has played an important part in the modernization of the Middle East. Solidarity with the plight of the Palestinians has always been an essential element in this national unity. In 1994, at the peak of the optimism regarding the peace process that had begun between Israelis and Palestinians, the Council of Catholic Patriarchs of the East, composed of all the heads of the various Catholic Churches in the Arab countries, published a pastoral letter entitled *Together before God.*[48] This letter defined the contours of the dialogue between Christians and Muslims in the Arab world, emphasizing that both belong to the same Arab people and are engaged in a common struggle to construct a better future. Possibly because of the reigning optimism at the time, the letter hardly touched upon the divisive subject of the Holy Land. However, six years later, the Diocesan Synod of the Catholic Churches in the Holy Land insisted: "The reality of the ongoing struggle [between Palestinians and Israelis] has a negative influence on mutual relations [between Christian Arabs and Israeli Jews]. Christians in this region are united in fate with their Muslim brothers and sisters, carrying on their bodies the scars of exile, forced dispersion, confiscation of land and civil discrimination as well as the violation of legitimate human rights."[49]

The Latin Patriarch of Jerusalem, Michel Sabbah, issued a document on the subject of relations with Jews and Muslims that addressed the problematic of the Land in clear terms: "We are deeply conscious of the vocation of the Church of Jerusalem to be a Christian presence in the midst of society, be it Muslim Arab or Jewish Israeli. We believe that we are called to be leaven, contributing to the positive resolution of the crises that we are passing through. We are a voice from within our societies whose history, language and culture we share. We seek to be a presence that promotes reconciliation, helping all peoples toward a dialogue that promotes understanding and that will ultimately lead to peace in the Land."[50]

9. Peace and Justice

The longest part of the 1984 papal document *Redemptionis anno* deals
with peace and justice in the Middle East. At the end, the letter issues
a call for peaceful coexistence between Israelis and Palestinians:

> Jerusalem stands out as a symbol of coming together, of union,
> and of universal peace for the human family. The Holy City,
> therefore, strongly urges peace for the whole human race, espe-
> cially for those who worship the one, great God, the merciful
> Father of the peoples. But it must be acknowledged that Jerusa-
> lem continues to be the cause of daily conflict, violence and parti-
> san reprisals. . . . The Roman pontiffs, especially in this century,
> have witnessed with an ever-anxious solicitude the violent events
> which have afflicted Jerusalem for many decades, and they have
> followed closely with watchful care the declarations of the United
> Nations, which have dealt with the fate of the Holy City.[1]

The Pope continues, pointing out that the Holy See has always called
for a just solution, one that will guarantee the rights of all parties to
the conflict. He expresses his confidence that the shared monotheism of
Christians, Jews, and Muslims will eventually lead to peace in Jerusalem. The Pope explicitly mentions here the rights of both Jews and
Palestinians:

> For the Jewish people who live in the State of Israel and who pre-
> serve in that land such precious testimonies to their history and

their faith, we must ask for the desired security and the due tranquility that is the prerogative of every nation and condition of life and of progress for every society. The Palestinian people, who find their historical roots in that land and who for decades have been dispersed, have the natural right in justice to find once more a homeland and to be able to live in peace and tranquility with the other peoples of the area.[2]

The clear symmetry that is expressed here has been a constant feature of Vatican diplomacy in the search for justice and peace. There is a discernible difference between the documents that directly address the questions of justice and peace in the Holy Land and those that deal with the Bible or interreligious dialogue. The Holy See's Secretariat of State, the office that deals with the relations between the Church and the world's political authorities, has always formulated a policy rooted in international law and human rights rather than in transcendent spiritual terms. Here, we will not be able to give a full history of the complex development of Vatican policy with regard to the Holy Land.[3] Our main purpose is to show how Church teaching on peace and justice in the Holy Land attempts to steer a course of reconciliation and dialogue between the two warring parties.

Undoubtedly, a major element in the Church's position on the conflict between Israelis and Palestinians concerns human rights. At the Second Vatican Council, the Church formulated its position on religious freedom in an important document that derived its terminology from contemporary discourse on human rights. The Catholic Church has become one of the main defenders of the rights of oppressed national groups, protesting state injustice and failure to follow legal process. Although we cannot give a full survey of the development of Catholic teaching on human rights, it is important to acknowledge the importance of this domain for the Church's position on the conflict. Archbishop Jean-Louis Tauran, then Vatican Assistant Secretary of State, pointed this out in a press conference in 1998: "It is wrong to claim that the Holy See is only interested in the religious aspect or aspects of the city [of Jerusalem] and overlooks the territorial and political aspect. The Holy See is indeed interested in this aspect and has the right and duty to be, especially insofar as the matter remains unresolved and is the cause of conflict, injustice, human rights violations, restrictions of religious freedom and conscience, fear and personal insecurity."[4]

This recognition of the basic human rights of the Palestinian people, as well as that of the Israelis, is a thread that runs right through the discourse of the Church. Pope John Paul II gave repeated expression to this concern, as he did once again in his *Angelus* message of October 24, 1989, during the first uprising of the Palestinians against Israeli occupation:

> From the Holy Land pleas for help and solidarity are arriving from the inhabitants of the West Bank and the Gaza. They are the cries of the entire people who are being particularly tried today, and who feel weaker after decades of conflict with another people bound by their history and faith to the same land. One cannot be indifferent to these pleas and to the daily suffering of so many people. To them I would like to express my deepest solidarity, assuring them that the pope continues to make his own their legitimate request to live in peace in a homeland of their own, respecting the right of every other people to enjoy the necessary security and tranquility.[5]

DIPLOMATIC EFFORTS

Recognition of the new Israeli and Palestinian realities was a slow process in Vatican circles. Traditional Catholic views on Jews and Judaism created a mindset in which the reconstitution of Jewish political independence in the Holy Land was regarded with suspicion and even hostility. The Jews were in exile because of their sin of refusing Jesus of Nazareth as the Messiah. Furthermore, the displacement of Christian communities during the war of 1948 created sympathy for the Palestinian Arab cause and refusal of the newborn Jewish state. Some of the most important spokespeople for the Palestinian cause have been Christian Palestinian Arabs. Concern for the Christian Arab communities in the rest of the Arab world has also influenced policy, as it was feared that recognition of the new Jewish state might compromise the status of Christian faithful in countries that were in a state of war with Israel. Officially, the issue of recognition was explained in legal terms: the borders of the state proclaimed in 1948 were in dispute[6] and the large Palestinian Arab refugee population had not been allowed to return to their homes. Reticence to give official recognition to the new situation in the Holy Land was particularly evident when Pope Paul VI crossed into Israeli territory during his official visit to the Holy Land in 1964. Even though he was received by the Israeli State President in Megiddo, the pope made no reference to the State of Israel or the political situation in the Holy Land.

From 1948 until the Second Vatican Council (1962–65), Vatican policy regarding the Holy Land focused on Christian interests, protecting the Holy Places and the local Christian communities.[7] Fully absorbed in humanitarian aid to the Palestinian refugees after 1948, the Palestinians were seen more as refugees deserving of pity than as a people with rights. Suspicious of Zionism and its political program, the Church was unwilling to relinquish the idea of international control of Jerusalem and Bethlehem, where most Holy Places were situated and many Christians lived. Sensitive to the fragile interreligious equilibrium in Lebanon, the Church was also supremely conscious of how instability in the Holy Land affected the rest of the region. This state of affairs continued on even after the 1967 War when Israel occupied the rest of the Palestinian areas that had been formerly under Egyptian (Gaza Strip) and Jordanian (West Bank) control. Slowly but surely however official Vatican discourse began to change due to ongoing dialogue with both Jews and Arabs that became more intense after the Second Vatican Council. There was a slow recognition that the two communities in conflict, Jewish Israelis and Palestinian Arabs, had been born in traumatic circumstances in the middle of the twentieth century. For Jews, the Holocaust in Europe has been an incomparable experience of suffering and Catholics were called upon to appreciate this in their interactions with Jews. For Palestinians, the loss of their homeland in 1948 was an injustice that has to be rectified if lasting peace is to be achieved in the Holy Land. However, beyond the recognition of the traumatic genesis of the two peoples, the Church was very cautious in taking a stand that proffered recognition of particular rights in the Holy Land to either people.

Slow developments eventually led to parallel dialogues and mutual recognition between the Vatican and the State of Israel on the one hand and the Vatican and the Palestinian people on the other hand. The establishment of full diplomatic relations with the State of Israel had to overcome many obstacles. The Vatican has been clearly concerned that political recognition of the State of Israel not be confused with theological questions regarding the dialogue with the Jewish people. Furthermore, Israel's control of the Holy Places and its rule over the Christian minority in Israel raised further questions involving the freedom of religious practice and the recognition of traditional Christian privileges in the Holy Land. On the other hand, Vatican policy was also concerned with the unresolved issue of Palestinian national aspirations and the refugee problem.

Jewish participants in the Jewish-Catholic dialogue constantly called for diplomatic ties to be established by the Vatican with Israel. The Second Vatican Council removed the theological obstacles to accepting Jewish sovereignty, although it did not remove the diplomatic and legal barriers that stood in the way of full diplomatic relations. The Vatican did recognize the State of Israel de facto as numerous events show, including the negotiations that annulled the sale of Notre Dame de Jerusalem in the early 1970s and the visit of Golda Meir, prime minister of Israel, to Pope Paul VI in 1973.[8] The first peace initiatives between Israel and the Arab world led to a further shift in Vatican policy. The Vatican publicly and enthusiastically supported the peace initiative of Egyptian president Sadat and all the subsequent peace initiatives introduced by the different parties to the conflict.[9]

THE PONTIFICATE OF JOHN PAUL II

The pontificate of John Paul II saw significant changes in the position of the Holy See. John Paul II made important speeches at the beginning of his pontificate that defined the Church's position on the conflict. At the United Nations, in October 1979, he related directly to the Middle East conflict and in particular the situation in the Holy Land. Slowly the dimension of peace and justice that the Church was proposing became clear, alongside the attempts to build dialogue with both Jews and Muslims. In the developing dialogue with the Jewish people, the Church recognized fully the suffering of the Jewish people in history; however, the Church insisted that peace would only be possible through a recognition of Palestinian suffering too and the just settling of the Palestinian issue. As the pope pointed out in his apostolic letter of 1984, *Redemptionis anno*: "The Palestinian people, who find their historical roots in that land and who, for decades, have been dispersed, have the natural right in justice to find once more a homeland and to be able to live in peace and tranquility with the other peoples of the area."[10]

After the convening of the Madrid Peace Conference between the State of Israel and the Palestine Liberation Organization, the Vatican began formal steps to establish full diplomatic relations with both political entities. After the conclusion of the Oslo II accords in September 1993, all was ready for the inauguration of full diplomatic relations between Israel and the Vatican. The signing of the *Fundamental Agreement between the Holy See and the State of Israel* in December 1993 marked a turning point in the relations between the Holy See and the State of Israel.[11] The official document reflects not only the political reality of two political entities but also the significant progress in religious dialogue between Jews and Catholics. Are these accords a simple diplomatic agreement between two states or do they in fact take into account the rather unique nature of an agreement between the Catholic Church and an entity that speaks in the name of the Jewish people? Israeli Jews and Christians committed to Jewish-Christian dialogue have insisted on the theological significance of the document. Indeed, the preamble of the document, referring to "the unique character and universal meaning of the Holy Land," goes on to point out that the signers of the accord are conscious of "the unique nature of relations between the Catholic Church and the Jewish people."[12] Even though theology is not totally absent from the language of the document, far more prominent is the language of diplomatic accord between two political entities. Most of the articles of the accord address the guarantee of freedom for the local Christian population and the rights of Church institutions.

With regard to the Palestinians, it was only in 1974, when the Catholic university in Bethlehem in the West Bank was inaugurated, that Pope Paul VI explicitly affirmed the Palestinians as a people rather than as a group of refugees. This was also clearly expressed in Pope Paul VI's Christmas message of 1975: "Although we are conscious of the still very recent tragedies which led the Jewish people to search for safe protection in a state of its own, sovereign and independent, and in fact precisely because we are aware of this, we would like to ask the sons of this people to recognize the rights and legitimate aspirations of another people, which have also suffered for a long time, the Palestinian people."[13]

In 1982 and 1988 Pope John Paul II met with Yasser Arafat, leader of the Palestinian Liberation Organization, both times exposing himself to severe criticism from Israeli and Jewish figures, who condemned Arafat as a terrorist. These meetings were important signposts on the way to full recognition of the Palestinian people and its national rights in the Holy Land.

In 1987 John Paul II named the first Christian Palestinian Arab, Michel Sabbah, a native of Nazareth, to the post of Roman Catholic Patriarch of Jerusalem, the highest-ranking Roman Catholic cleric in the Church in the Holy Land and a post held until that time by Italians.[14] During the pope's 2000 pilgrimage to Bethlehem, he took a further and particularly dramatic symbolic step in recognizing the suffering of the Palestinians and their right to a homeland by paying a visit to the Deheisheh refugee camp. Addressing the refugees, the pope said:

> You have been deprived of many things that represent basic needs of the human person: proper housing, health care, education and work. Above all, you bear the sad memory of what you were forced to leave behind, not just material possessions but your freedom, the closeness of relatives, and the familiar surrounding and cultural traditions that nourish your personal and family life. . . . Only a resolute effort on the part of leaders in the Middle East and in the international community as a whole, inspired by a higher vision of politics as service of the common good, can remove the causes of the present situation.[15]

This visit must be seen as part of the delicate symmetrical series of symbolic acts that punctuated the pope's visit to the Holy Land and preceded his visit to Yad VaShem, the Israeli Holocaust memorial, to the Israeli chief rabbinate and to the home of the Israeli State president.

The *Basic Agreement between the Holy See and the Palestine Liberation Organization* was signed in February 2000.[16] It is important to note at the outset that this document echoes the one signed with Israel in 1993. In the very first paragraph, the two parties recognize that the Holy Land is "a privileged space for inter-religious dialogue between the followers of the three monotheistic religions."[17] However, more importantly, in this document the Vatican recognized "the inalienable national legitimate rights and aspirations of the Palestinian people" and declared that "an equitable solution for the issue of Jerusalem, based upon international resolutions is fundamental for a just and lasting peace in the Middle East."

Although the Vatican now has full diplomatic relations with both parties to the conflict, relations with both sides have continued to be complicated and tense at times. Catholics from Europe and the United States, involved in dialogue with Jews, have pressured the Vatican to go further in recognizing Zionism as constituting an essential element in modern Jewish identity. This leads to tensions with the Arab world and particularly with the Christians among them. The Church in the Holy Land and throughout the Middle East is overwhelmingly Arab and expresses a basic solidarity with the Palestinian people, leading to inevitable tensions with Israel.[18] However, the main reason for Vatican reticence remains the lack of justice and peace for the Palestinian people in the ongoing conflict. The establishment of full diplomatic relations though allows the Catholic Church to address both parties, encouraging them to bridge their differences and work for a resolution to the conflict.

THE LOCAL CHURCH

Before concluding our discussion of the importance of the search for justice and peace in the Holy Land in the Church's contemporary attitude toward the Land, it is important to note the role that local Christians have had in influencing Church teaching. The appointment of a Palestinian Arab, Michel Sabbah, as Roman Catholic Patriarch of Jerusalem has already been noted. Michel Sabbah, together with other priests and lay people, have produced an important literature on how Christian Arabs see the contemporary struggle in the Holy Land, and these works have influenced the formulation of Church positions on the Land beyond the boundaries of Israel and Palestine.[19] Christian Palestinians promoting the rights of the Palestinian people and the restoration of justice in order to promote peace have helped steer the Church away from a purely transcendent approach to the conflict. These Christians are addressing the problems of peace and justice not from a distance but from the very heart of the conflict. These voices maintain that Christian survival in the Holy Land depends on the resolution of the conflict and on dialogue and reconciliation.

The Church's concerned and balanced position for justice and peace in the Holy Land might be summed up most eloquently in one of the pope's annual peace messages, published for January 1. In the 2002 message, John Paul II wrote:

> Reflecting on forgiveness, our minds turn naturally to certain situations of conflict, which endlessly feed deep and divisive hatreds and a seemingly unstoppable sequence of personal and collective tragedies. I refer especially to what is happening in the Holy

Land, that blessed place of God's encounter with man, where Jesus, the Prince of Peace, lived, died and rose from the dead. The present troubled international situation prompts a more intense call to resolve the Arab-Israeli conflict, which has now been going on for more than fifty years, with alternate phases of greater or lesser tension. The continuous recourse to acts of terror and war, which aggravate the situation and diminish hope on all sides, must finally give way to a negotiated solution. The rights and demands of each party can be taken into proper account and balanced in an equitable way, if and when there is a will to let justice and reconciliation prevail. Once more I urge the beloved peoples of the Holy Land to work for a new era of mutual respect and constructive accord (n. 11).[20]

This overview enables one to perceive the considerable changes in Catholic teaching that were provoked by the Second Vatican Council, especially with regard to the Jewish people. However, it also sheds light on new questions born out of contemporary events, particularly the creation of the State of Israel and the concomitant injustices endured by the Palestinian people, leading to awareness of both Jewish and Palestinian identity and national claims. History has always constituted an important arena of theological reflection, necessarily influencing theological formulation. This is shown by the historical events that have unfolded in the Land during the twentieth century, particularly the events of 1948 that led to the creation of the State of Israel and the birth of the Palestinian refugee problem. Today, the Land is one of the most delicate points in the developing dialogue with Jews, on the one hand, and with Muslims, on the other. The challenge is to reach a dialogue in which the perspective of the other is understood and respected (without it being necessarily adopted) in order to build new relations founded on trust, cooperation, and friendship. Within the dialogue, the Church then might bear witness to the values of justice, pardon, reconciliation, and peace for all peoples.

The abyss that often seems to separate the two sides in the contemporary conflict in the Holy Land, confirmed by the repeated failures of negotiations, might lead to profound discouragement and despair. Monsignor Jean-Louis Tauran, then secretary for the Holy See's relations with States, declared: "The Arab Middle East, as a zone of convergence of great civilizations, religions and complex problems, defies easy understanding by anyone."[21] This Land is a sacred place, loaded with symbolic value accumulated over thousands of years. Two peoples and three religions have privileged ties with this land; ties that too often are claimed to be exclusive and to exclude the others. This Land, where God and violence are too often seen to interconnect, reveals humans who vocally dispute with one another in the name of a God who is now silent. In this cradle of religions, the best is side by side with the worst of religious manifestations. In the position of the Catholic Church surveyed here, we dare see some seeds of hope in a clear call for mutual respect, listening to difference, sensitivity to the dimension of justice, and consciousness of sharing a religious heritage that is common to all the children of Abraham, through whom all nations are to be blessed. In answer to the many questions raised, the Bible does not give ready-made answers. It reminds us rather, page after page, what this land of covenant is called to become, not only for those called to live there, but for all who serve God and neighbor. For the Land and all lands, as the Bible reminds us, are God's.

Conclusion
Holy Lands: Yesterday and Today

We have arrived at the end of our journey, which has taken us through the Christian Bible, Old Testament and New, studying its texts, its theology, and its spirituality, as well as its posterity in the history of the Church and in society until our present day. Our guiding theme has been that of the Land. This journey has been a very selective one. We have chosen to give an overview of all the literature rather than focus on any particular Old or New Testament text or Church document that deals with the Land. It has been likewise selective because we, the authors, have made a conscious choice to read the Old and New Testaments from a Christian point of view[1] and, as far as Church sources go, from a Catholic perspective. Nevertheless, we do hope that other readers, whether Christians, Jews, Muslims, or simply seekers of peace and justice, might find here information and reflections that are helpful in clarifying the complex issue of the Land. We would indeed be satisfied if, after reading these pages, the reader might consciously avoid the overly simplistic judgments that characterize so much of the contemporary discourse on the conflict in the Holy Land, so often stimulated by emotions and ignorance. We hope that our survey reflects the complexity of the issues at stake. In this final chapter, we would like to propose some concluding thoughts that are more personal and that take up various ideas that are found in the preceding pages. We hope to open new vistas with regard to contemporary perspectives on the Land.

The Land at the Heart of the Scriptures

In the literary and theological writings of the second and first millennia before Christ and until the first century after Christ, the biblical people of Israel developed their identity and produced their historical reflections. One constant element in their writing was the meaning and need of Land as a living space where their personal and community life with all its social, political, economic, religious, and spiritual dimensions could unfold. The entire Old Testament, from Genesis to Malachi, echoes the physical and geographical Land that "flows with milk and honey," both heritage and home of Israel. This Land had been promised to Abraham, the father of all believers, hoped for and awaited by Moses and the people going out of Egypt, given over to and conquered by Joshua, lost at the time of the exile, regained and reconstructed in the epoch of Cyrus and Ezra and then lost again at the beginning of the Christian era. Advancing stage by stage, through the repetitions, progressions and transformations in the biblical narrative, we have been able to underline the constant and outstanding importance of the Land in Israel's reflection.

This concrete dimension of rootedness in the Land is all the more precious in most of the Old Testament when measured against the nothingness of what comes after life in this world. In fact, for most of the Old Testament, the void that comes after death was contrasted with life in the Land of the living. "Are not the days of my life few? Let me alone that I might find a little comfort before I go, never to return, to the land of gloom and deep darkness, the land of gloom and chaos, where light is like darkness" (Jb 10:20–22). Within this perspective, the Land given by God is the space in which the human person and the community can find the fullness of their joy. "The Lord will love you, bless you and multiply you, he will bless the fruit of your womb and the fruit of your ground, your grain and your wine and your oil, the increase of your cattle and the issue of your flock, in the Land that he swore to your ancestors to give you" (Dt 7:13). However, throughout the Bible, this happiness, which is to be realized in the Land, depends upon the disposition of the human person. "If you will only obey the Lord your God by diligently observing all his commandments" (Dt 28:1). Land and Torah are inseparable.

In a literary and historical production as diverse as the Bible, it is not surprising to discover the diversity of attitudes regarding the Land;

attitudes sometimes even in contradiction with one another. Some texts preserve a memory of violence committed by Israel against the inhabitants who preceded them in the Land. This violence is often described as being an initiative of God himself, who exhorts the people of Israel to massacre and expel. "You must not let anything that breathes remain alive. You shall annihilate them . . . just as the Lord your God has commanded" (Dt 20:16–17). Even though contemporary biblical commentators doubt the actual application of these laws and the historicity of the massacres described in the Book of Joshua, these texts retain their shocking aspect for the contemporary reader. This is even more problematic when the texts are read literally. However, in this day and age, the Catholic Church accepts the refining fire of the historical-critical method that helps the reader discern between the human and the divine elements contained in the sacred Scriptures constituted as Word of God. This method situates the text in the milieu of its production, relating the written word to the circumstances it was commenting on. Thus, for example, it is as important to understand that the events described in the Book of Joshua are related to the reforms of King Josiah in the late seventh century and the exile in the sixth century even more than to the history of the Land in the thirteenth century, purportedly described by the author. Likewise, the Book of Joshua takes on its meaning within a wider theological context that stretches from the Book of Deuteronomy through the Books of Joshua, Judges, Samuel, and right until the end of the two Books of Kings. This consciousness regarding the history of the production of the text and its literary forms prevents us from imagining that the Word of God is to be found in the Bible in a raw, unmediated and pure state, normative in its most literal sense for our world today.

LAND FOR THE COVENANT

However, the diversity of the biblical heritage and its complex formation should not conceal the profound coherence and dynamism of God's design for the earth. This project is revealed as we pass from book to book in the development of the biblical story. Israel's attitude to the Land is already foreshadowed in the figure of Abraham. The Land is promised to his descendants as a place where hopefully they will succeed, unlike Adam and Eve, who failed in the Garden of Eden. In Abraham, the promise of a particular Land is linked to Abraham being a blessing for all the nations of the earth. The Land of promise where the Word of God is realized will begin the process of restoration by which all lands will once again become a space for holy living. With the Exodus, the promise of the Land is close to realization and yet the hesitating and painful progress toward the Land falls short of an entry: the people fear at Qadesh Barnea and are forced back into the wilderness where that entire generation must die. From there Moses leads the people as far as the eastern banks of the Jordan River before he too must die outside the borders of the Land.

At the center of this slow development in the Pentateuch is not the Land but the Law (Torah) given at Sinai, outside the borders of the Land, in the wilderness. The most intimate meeting between God and his people takes place on a holy mountain in a wilderness and there the conditions for successful living in the Land are enunciated. The Land that Israel is about to enter must be and must remain a Land of obedient fulfillment of the Law and covenant, where righteousness and justice between God and humanity and between man and man must reign. Israel's worship is a constant proclamation of these values and reaches a peak in the laws of the Sabbath. Israel's *Shabbat* is a constant reminder of the covenant undertaken at Sinai. With regard to the Land, the *Shabbat* serves to prevent Israel from forgetting its salvation history and transforming the Land into a land like all others. *Shabbat* guarantees remembering and acknowledging God as Creator and Redeemer but it also ensures that the powerful do not oppress brother or sister, widow, orphan, and disenfranchised without limit. "Remember that you were a slave in the land of Egypt and the Lord your God brought you out from there with a mighty hand and an outstretched arm; therefore the Lord your God commanded you to keep the Sabbath day" (Dt 5:15). Under Israel, the Land that is God's must not become Egypt, the land of a tyrannical Pharaoh.

We would like to propose here that with regard to our theme the Old Testament is less a celebration of the conquest of the Land than a profound and heartrending confession of a people ever conscious of their failure to recognize and acknowledge God's overwhelming generosity. Israel teaches humanity how to ask for pardon in the face of human weakness and sin. The Land meant to be a space for holy living becomes a place of repeated transgression, both against God and against neighbor, especially the weakest among them. The counterpoint to the Land of blessing is exile depicted as wilderness, its shadow is to be felt throughout the biblical narrative that deals with the Land. Although at first glance, the Bible seems to depict Land as the place of blessing and wilderness as the place of curse and punishment, a deeper meditation on their significance reveals the full ambivalence of the two spaces. Certainly, the Land, "flowing with milk and honey," is a garden of delight, whereas the wilderness, place of "thorns and thistles" represents a primordial punishment for Adam's disobedience. However, the Land, rich and fertile, is a constant trap for human nature that tends toward idolatry and self-glorification. Whereas the Land should provoke an attitude of thanksgiving to God for the blessings showered on the human person, it becomes a place where the human person congratulates himself on his prowess and bows down before the gods he has created. Whereas the wilderness is imposed as a punishment, the very fact that there the human person is directly dependent on God for all his needs leads him to rediscover the loving God he had abandoned in the Land, making this place of emptiness a space for renewed intimacy with God. Thus, the wilderness becomes the place of nuptial celebration and renewal of fidelity (cf. Hos 2:16ff). This fundamental ambivalence is never far from the narratives of Land and wilderness throughout the biblical tradition.

The Pentateuch ends very significantly outside the Land, thus insisting not on the Land that is a gift promised, but on the Torah (the revealed Law), which is the expression of the will of God for the human person. The editing of the Pentateuch, that began during exile and was completed probably by Ezra the priestly scribe in the period of reconstruction, clarified a choice that had been made at the time of the fall of Jerusalem:

> In Babylonia after the news had arrived in 587 B.C. that Jerusalem had fallen and the temple been destroyed, some elders went to the prophet Ezekiel and asked him the pertinent question: "*Ek nihyeh? How shall we live?*" (cf. Ez 33:10). In what now does our experience obtain? What now is our identity? The answer finally came in the form of the Pentateuch and the laws. . . . And that was when we knew that our true identity, the Torah *par excellence*, included the conquest neither of Canaan [Joshua] nor of Jerusalem [David] but that Sinai which we never possessed was that which we would never lose.[2]

Whereas the Torah in the Pentateuch is the constitution for holy living in the Land that God has given, the history books mostly tell of the failure to apply this constitution. Beginning with the triumphal entry of Joshua into the Land, they reach their tragic crescendo with the catastrophic destruction of the Temple and the exit from the Land into exile at the end of 2 Kings. The Land that had been given has now been taken away. Israel has met with the same fate as the nations that dwelt in the Land before her and for the same reasons. The Land is the Lord's (cf. Lv 25:23) and he gives it as a space for intimate life with him. Only those who enter into the intimacy of a relationship with him can stay in the Land. However, the Lord, in his constant search for the human person, makes the promise of the Land a central element of his fidelity.

In this story, the prophet plays an essential role. The people are constantly tempted to desecrate the Land of the covenant through infidelity to God and injustice committed against brother and neighbor, especially after the crowning of a human king over Israel. The prophet arises as the defender both of the rights of God and of the rights of the weak. He (or sometimes she) is there to point out the sin that is hidden, condemning faithlessness and injustice, and protesting the spilling of the blood of innocents that contaminates the Land. "You eat flesh with the blood and lift up your eyes to your idols, and shed blood; shall you then possess the Land? You depend on your swords, you commit abominations and each of you defiles his neighbor's wife; shall you then possess the Land?" (Ez 33:25–26).

In the ups and downs that alternate as the Land is promised, gained, lost, and reclaimed, Israel deepens its understanding of Land and exile. Ezekiel shows how the glory of God, leaving the temple and Jerusalem, accompanies the people into exile (Ez 10–11). Despite the loss of Land, Temple, and king, he proclaims that God is not absent. In the desolation of the exile, Israel cries out a lament for what has been lost and ponders how this has come about. The Land vomits out those who do not live in thanksgiving and adoration of God according to the will of the one who has created the Land as a garden of blessing. It is in the wilderness and in exile that Israel experiences, despite its own unfaithfulness, that God is always faithful. It is in exile that Israel is called back to faithfulness and receives the promise once again.

JESUS AND THE LAND

One cannot disassociate Jesus and his message from the Land of Israel where he appeared. Without rootedness in his Land and his people,

Jesus' life and message lose their concrete and embodied dimension, risking the transformation of Christ and gospel into simply another ideology. Jesus is a child of the Land, in which he was born and where he grew up. He traversed its length and its breadth, its mountains and its plains; he undertook exhausting voyages that enabled him to discover the contrasting beauty of the summits of Upper Galilee and the Golan under the snow of winter, the green rolling hills of the regions around the Sea of Galilee and the arid ruggedness of Judea. His teaching bears the traces of the images he saw, drawing on the Land's flora and fauna, its seasons and agriculture. For Jesus, the Land is bearer of all its symbolic weight, accumulated during the long centuries of salvation history that preceded his appearance.

Led into the wilderness and tempted there, Jesus turns to the Book of Deuteronomy, a series of discourses placed in the mouth of Moses that constitutes an exhortation to transform the Land about to be given into a Land for the covenant. The temptations Jesus faced are a programmatic summary of those faced by Israel in the Land: self-congratulation and glorification as well as idolatry. Deuteronomy is the book of the Land par excellence. In responding to Satan in the words of Deuteronomy, "one does not live by bread alone," he gives meaning to the long march through the centuries of salvation history, resumed as parallel to the forty years in the wilderness. "Remember the long way the Lord your God has led you these forty years in the wilderness, in order to humble you, testing you to know what was in your heart, whether or not you would keep his commandments. He humbled you by letting you hunger, then by feeding you with manna, with which neither you nor your ancestors were acquainted in order to make you understand that one does not live by bread alone, but by every word that comes from the mouth of the Lord" (Dt 8:2–3). There where Israel faltered, Jesus, son of Israel, reveals himself to be an obedient son whose food is to do the will of the Father.

Yet, Jesus also reminds his disciples of the universal dimension hidden in the particularity of the borders of the Land. In his teaching, the Good News echoes beyond the borders of this land, preached to the ends of the earth. The blessing Abraham was called to become reaches fulfillment in Jesus, "son of Abraham" (Mt 1:1). While his earthly life might have been spent in the limited space available to Israel in a Land promised to his ancestors, the Risen Christ calls his disciples to go beyond the borders of Israel, making the entire surface of the earth a Land promised for intimate living with God the Father. By his resurrection, Jesus Christ comes to all men and women, wherever they might be, inaugurating a reality where "there is no longer Jew or Greek, there is no longer slave or free, there is no longer male and female" (Ga 3:28). The first believers in him drew the logical conclusions: Jerusalem and the Land made holy, while remaining symbolic places of reference, cease to have the central importance they had enjoyed since the time of the promise to Abraham. Overshadowing the Land, it is now the resurrected Jesus Christ who offers his body as a meeting place for those called to lives of holiness from all the lands sanctified by his disciples. The borders of the kingdom stretch to the furthest corners of the earth.

THE CHURCH, THE JEWS, AND THE LAND

Although Jesus lived in the Land among his people, the Church that was born after his death and resurrection was faced with a new historical situation: the destruction of the Temple in Jerusalem (in A.D. 70) and the subsequent dispersion of the Jews throughout the Jewish Diaspora. Even though limited to a restricted number of major figures from among the Fathers of the Church, the texts we have cited are eloquent witnesses to how, for centuries, the Church interpreted the situation of the Jewish people in exile. Despite the fact that these texts echo the classic interpretations found in the prophets of Israel, seeing exile as a divine punishment, the prophets spoke with burning love from within the people of Israel whereas many of the later Christian commentators, speaking from a Christian perspective, judged the Jews with contempt. Confronting the people from within its own ranks, the prophets' sorrow and rage were legitimate expressions of God's own desolation and anger, confronted with his people's sinfulness. The Church Fathers, however, sought to lock Israel in the role of perfidious sinner and unrepentant murderer of Christ, presenting the Church as the "new Israel," proud and pure and far from the faults of the Old Testament Israel. According to their vision of salvation history, the coming of Jesus, his death and resurrection, should have opened the eyes of the Jews. Having rejected Jesus, the Jews are now condemned to eternal exile, destined to wander the earth forever, rejected by God. If they are a permanent fixture of history, it is only because in their state of misery they bear witness to the Christian truth, carrying testimony to the promise throughout the entire world, to all the lands in which they are dispersed. According to the formula of Saint Augustine, "The Jews carry our books. . . . We receive the writings of our enemies in order to confuse all our other enemies."[3]

Living, as we do, on a completely different horizon, we are able to perceive the limits and the dangers of the interpretation of the Church Fathers. This is particularly evident when depraved men and political authorities exploit the biblical texts accompanied by the commentaries of the Church Fathers as was the case throughout the centuries of Christendom's history, particularly in Europe, reaching a tragic crescendo in the Nazi period. In a gesture of repentance, the Church, in the document *We Remember*, discussed its responsibility, asking: "whether the Nazi persecution of the Jews was not made easier by the anti-Jewish prejudices imbedded in some Christian minds and hearts?"[4] The convulsions set in motion in the nineteenth century by the birth of Zionism and the parallel emergence of Palestinian nationalism, the development of anti-Semitism, culminating in the genocide of six million Jews in the death camps during the Second World War and the genesis of the Palestinian refugee problem, have led the Church to slowly modify its attitude toward its Jewish brothers and sisters and toward the Land and its contemporary inhabitants. The Second Vatican Council saw the formulation of a new discourse on Jews and Judaism after twenty centuries during which ignorance and a teaching of contempt had too often dominated. The creation of the State of Israel also created a new situation, simultaneously offering Jews from all over the world a national state and a safe refuge and producing the drama of a new refugee problem, that of the Palestinian people. It is against this backdrop that we must try to understand the contemporary discourse of the Church with regard to the Middle East in general and the Land, seen as holy by Jews, Muslims, and Christians in particular.

WORDS FOR OUR TIMES

Although the issue of the Land is profoundly rooted in the Bible, we are supremely conscious that the Bible does not offer us ready-made solutions to resolve our contemporary conflicts. The present situation in the Holy Land is the result of many of the complex political, social, economic, human, and religious factors we have evoked. It is a situation that must be resolved politically through the involvement of all parties, including the international community. This task, however, is not directly ours. We do believe nonetheless that the sacred Scriptures and the communities they inspire have an essential role to play in a future breakthrough that will enable us to embark on new paths of hope.

Respect for Complexity

History has witnessed and continues to witness many conflicts that involve the tracing of borders among neighbors or between adjacent territories that are in dispute. The territorial imperative and the conflicts it engenders have always been an element of the history of humankind. The situation in Israel and Palestine, then, is not unique. With regard to this Holy Land, many, as a function of their past, their sensibilities, their identity, and their level of formation, propose variant and diverse readings of the situation and sometimes even suggest solutions. For our part, we have no intention of taking the place of the politicians and political leaders who must search for possible solutions that will bring about the necessary compromise for justice and peace.

We believe, however, that the present discourse of the Church does provide possibilities and openings that might inspire Christians and all people of good faith in approaching what seems like an inextricable conflict between Israelis and Palestinians. We propose that the fundamental insights of the Apostolic Letter *Redemptionis anno*, published by the late Pope John Paul II in 1984 on Jerusalem as sacred heritage of all believers, is a coherent starting point. In its conclusion, this letter reviews all the aspects of the Land and particularly the city of Jerusalem that a Christian must take into account. These aspects include the particular status of the holy places, the situation of the local Christians in the Land, the role of the Bible in clarifying the vocation of the Holy Land, the tragic history of the Jewish people and the creation of the State of Israel, the dramatic situation of the Palestinian people with the burning issue of the refugees, the importance of Islam and the place of Muslims in the ongoing debate, and finally the requirements of justice for lasting peace. In the light of the multiple and complex claims and requirements, each observer is called to examine how his or her own reading of the situation might be partial, focusing on one element, be it, for example, the question of justice for the Palestinians or reconciliation with the Jews. Taking into account all the elements might stretch us beyond simplistic and single-minded ideologies. Remaining true to the multiple elements involved is at the root of a prophetic stance that must be the Church's as all men and women of good will continue to search for ways to bring peace and justice, pardon and reconciliation, prosperity and security for all the inhabitants of God's Land.[5]

THE IMPASSE OF FUNDAMENTALISM

Our presentation of the Church Fathers demonstrated that their commentaries were marked by the times they lived in. They were led to interpret the exile of the Jewish people from the Land as a permanent and irreversible punishment from God. One might have thought that the entry into modernity and particularly the application of a historical-critical approach to the Scriptures would have corrected this and similar literal interpretations and applications of the Bible. This, however, has not been the case. In fact, one can note the exact opposite in many religious traditions; the return of religion, often in its most irrational forms, is linked, in many cases, to what we call "fundamentalism."

Fundamentalism, a literal and uncritical contemporary reading of sacred text, often hostile to modernity and pluralism, has taken root in present-day religion. It has found many adepts in the Holy Land too, among Jews, Christians, and Muslims. The fundamentalist reads both history and current events as the direct function of a literal interpretation of the foundational texts of his religious community, considering them the direct revelation of absolute truth derived directly from his God and uncompromising in the face of the complexities of the real world. Thus, within the present situation in the Holy Land, some Jews are led to read their texts as forbidding a territorial compromise that would enable the establishment of a Palestinian state under any circumstances, thus blocking progress toward the goals of peace, justice, and reconciliation. Some Jews even propose the construction of the Third Temple, implying the destruction of the Islamic holy sites within the *Haram al-Sharif* ("the noble sanctuary") that have existed on the ancient site of the Temple since the seventh century. Also, some Muslims justify horrendous acts of violence against their perceived enemies, defined in Quranic terms as infidels, inspired by a literal reading of their sacred texts. The Muslim fundamentalist portrayal of Jews and Christians as subservient and distorters of the revealed truth is an obstacle to the dream of a democratic and modern society in the lands where Islam is the majority religion. Muslim fundamentalist intransigence in the face of the reality of Jewish life in the Holy Land endangers the prospective for a deepening of dialogue between Israelis and Palestinians in search of a better future.

Among Christians there is also a fundamentalist movement that has its roots in the nineteenth century among Protestants in England and the United States. Many in this movement interpret the contemporary history of the State of Israel, particularly the wars of 1948 and 1967, as a sign that the Redemption promised for the End of Days is in the process of unfolding before our eyes. In order to accelerate the coming of the Messiah (the return of Christ), some Christian Zionists, with their powerful political influence in the United States and their vast financial assets, support Israeli expansionism in the occupied Palestinian territories, opposing territorial compromise with the Palestinians in the name of the approaching End of Time. Our presentation of the position of the Catholic Church is in radical opposition to this kind of fundamentalist discourse that focuses on eschatological and apocalyptic themes, often ignoring the biblical values of peace, justice, and pardon. The Church tradition we have presented is one that values human activity in history and believes that the human person is able to strive for justice and peace through dialogue, reconciliation, and the struggle to pardon and be pardoned. Most traditional Christian churches, whether Catholic, Protestant, or Orthodox, refuse to interpret history, particularly the history of events in the contemporary Middle East, from the vantage point of a literal reading of the Scriptures (whether they be Jewish, Christian, or Muslim).[6]

What Is Christian Zionism?

"In developing a working definition of Christian Zionism, one can say it is a nineteenth and twentieth century movement within Protestant fundamentalism that supports the maximalist claims of Jewish political Zionism, including Israel's sovereignty over all of historic Palestine, including Jerusalem. The modern State of Israel, as a fulfillment of prophetic scriptures, is regarded as a necessary stage prior to the Second Coming of Jesus. Christian Zionism is marked by the following theological convictions:

God's covenant with Israel is eternal, exclusive and will not be abrogated, according to Genesis 12:1–7, 15:4–7, 17:1–8, Leviticus 26:44–45 and Deuteronomy 7:7–8.

There are two distinct and parallel covenants in the Bible, one with Israel that is never revoked and the other with the Church that is superseded by the covenant with Israel. The Church is a "mere parenthesis" in God's plan and as such will be removed from history during the Rapture (1 Thessalonians 4:13–17, 5:1–11). At that point, Israel, as a nation, will be restored as the primary instrument of God on earth.

Christian Zionists claim that Genesis 12:3 (I will bless those who bless you and curse those who curse you) should be interpreted literally and lead to political, economic, moral and spiritual support for the State of Israel and for the Jewish people in general.

Christian Zionists interpret the Bible literally and have a hermeneutic understanding of Apocalyptic texts—the book of Daniel, Zachariah 9–14, Ezekiel 37–38, 1 Thessalonians 4–5 and the book of Revelation—and assume their messages will be fulfilled in the future. . . .

Christian Zionists . . . have a pessimistic view of history and wait in eager anticipation for the unfolding of a series of wars and tragedies pointing to the return of Jesus. The establishment of the State of Israel, the rebuilding of the Third Temple, the rise of the Antichrist and the buildup of armies poised to attack Israel, are among the signs leading to the final battle and Jesus' return. Leading Christian Zionist authorities in biblical prophecy seek to interpret political developments according to the prophetic schedule of events that should unfold according to their view of Scripture. As an apocalyptic and dualistic type of theology, the movement looks in history for the escalation of power and influence of satanic forces aligned to the Antichrist, who, as the end draws near, will do battle with Israel and those aligned with it. Judgment will befall nations and individuals according to how they 'bless Israel'" (Gn 12:3).

. . . With its pessimistic view of history, Christian Zionism seeks to provide simple and clear answers through a literal and predictive approach to the Bible."[7]

—D. Wagner, "Christian Zionists, Israel, and the Second Coming"

THE HOLY LAND: AN EXEMPLARY LAND

For Christians, the Holy Land represents a place of reference where salvation history has unfolded. Wherever he or she might live, the disciple of Jesus Christ preserves a vibrant memory of this parcel of land. There, Christ took on flesh, gave his life for all humanity and was resurrected by the Father. Throughout the ups and downs of history, this has been the justification for the preservation of the Holy Places, looked after, in the name of the Catholic Church, by the Franciscans who were named custodians of the Holy Land in the thirteenth century. Pilgrimage to the Holy Land, especially to the Holy Sepulcher of Christ and the other sites linked with his life, constitute important moments of initiation in the lives of many Christians. The faithful have always sought to "walk in the footsteps of Jesus" in order to find the roots of their faith. Visits to the Land are also the occasion to come into contact with the Mother Church of Jerusalem, which, for centuries, has maintained an often precarious presence in the Land of salvation history. The Land is not only the site of multiple religious sanctuaries but is also home to living communities of Christian believers from a mind-boggling variety of churches and affiliations.

We began this book by evoking the meaning of the Land in the Old Testament of our Christian Bible. The modern reader, often shocked by the violence that characterizes the story told as the Children of Israel enter the Land, evicting previous occupants and destroying the societies that had been there, must also struggle with what to do with texts that present not only the human person, but also God as "a man of war" (cf. Ex 15:3). A tradition of "sacred violence" runs through the history of religions. However, for those who accept to enter into the dynamism that runs through the Holy Scriptures, the Land, as it is described in the biblical narrative, takes on an exemplary value for all humanity in all times. Even today, we still witness human dramas linked to questions of land: territories in dispute among nations; refugees driven out of their homes and countries by wars, famine, or persecution; and lands devastated by powerful interest groups. In many different places all over the globe, the land, instead of being a place of covenant and reconciliation, is still a place of exploitation and injustice. This reality is not alien to the Bible, which might be revealing something normative and definitive for all the inhabitants of the earth in its reading of Land and covenant.

Being rooted in a land is essential for any human being; the Bible eloquently shows this in underlining the concrete dimension of a land "that flows with milk and honey." The Land is given to Israel as land is given to all people in order that it might become a land of fraternity, justice, and reconciliation. In the Psalms, the poor of God dream of a Land where righteousness and justice reign. The reign of men and women has the reign of God as its model. "The Lord is king; let the peoples tremble! He sits enthroned upon the cherubim; let the earth quake. . . . Mighty King, lover of justice, you have established equity"

(Ps 99:1.4). Attributing to God righteousness and justice, the Bible transforms categories of human law, equity, and justice into the very grounds of divine revelation itself. These qualities of human govern- ment on earth are sacred in the eyes of God. For those who have power on earth, this constitutes a constant call to respect the earth and all those who live on it. "Blessed are the meek for they shall inherit the Land" (Mt 5:5). In this beatitude, Jesus takes up the theme of Psalm 37, plac- ing himself in the long line of prophets calling for a new Land, repre- senting the kingdom, "already here" but "not yet fully realized." In this kingdom, the poor and the meek occupy the first places. The bibli- cal land of Israel prefigures this kingdom. However, it is in all lands that this kingdom must be realized. This is the tremendous challenge, so often an exasperating one. The disciples of Jesus must show that this utopian kingdom has already begun to be realized on earth.

Appendix: Redemptionis anno

APOSTOLIC LETTER OF POPE JOHN PAUL II
(April 20, 1984)

Revered Brothers and Beloved Sons,
Health and Apostolic Blessing.

As the Jubilee Year of Redemption draws to a close, my thoughts go to that special land which is located in that place where Europe, Asia and Africa meet in which the Redemption of the human race was accomplished "once and for all" (Rom 6:10, Heb 7:27, 9:12, 10:10).

It is a land which we call holy, indeed the land which was the earthly homeland of Christ who walked about it "preaching the gospel of the kingdom and healing every disease and every infirmity" (Matt 4:23).

This year especially I was pleased to be touched by the same sentiment and the same joy as my predecessor, Pope Paul VI, when he visited the Holy Land and Jerusalem in 1964.

Although I cannot be there physically, I nevertheless feel that I am spiritually a pilgrim in that land where our reconciliation with God was brought about, to beg the Prince of Peace for the gift of redemption and of peace which is so earnestly desired by the hearts of people, families and nations—in a special way by the nations which inhabit this very area.

I think especially of the city of Jerusalem, where Jesus, offering his life, "has made us both one, and has broken down the dividing wall of hostility . . . bringing the hostility to an end" (Eph 2:14.16).

Before it was the city of Jesus the Redeemer, Jerusalem was the historic site of the biblical revelation of God, the meeting place, as it were, of heaven and earth, in which more than in any other place the word of God was brought to men.

Christians honor her with a religious and intent concern because there the words of Christ so often resounded, there the great events of the Redemption were accomplished: the Passion, Death and Resurrection of the Lord. In the city of Jerusalem the first Christian community sprang up and remained throughout the centuries a continual ecclesial presence despite difficulties.

Jews ardently love her and in every age venerate her memory, abundant as she is in many remains and monuments from the time of David who chose her as the capital, and of Solomon who built the temple there. Therefore, they turn their minds to her daily, one may say, and point to her as the sign of their nation.

Muslims also call Jerusalem "holy," with a profound attachment that goes back to the origins of Islam and springs from the fact that they have there many special places of pilgrimage and for more than a thousand years have dwelt there, almost without interruption.

Besides these exceptional and outstanding testimonies, Jerusalem contains communities of believers full of life, whose presence the peoples of the whole world regard as a sign and a source of hope—especially those who consider the holy city to be in a certain way their spiritual heritage and a symbol of peace and harmony.

Indeed, insofar as she is the homeland of the hearts of all the spiritual descendants of Abraham who hold her very dear, and the place where, according to faith, the created things of earth encounter the infinite transcendence of God, Jerusalem stands out as a symbol of coming together, of union, and of universal peace for the human family.

The holy city, therefore, strongly urges peace for the whole human race, especially for those who worship the one, great God, the merciful Father of the peoples. But it must be acknowledged that Jerusalem continues to be the cause of daily conflict, violence, and partisan reprisal.

This situation and these considerations cause these words of the Prophet to spring to the lips: "For Zion's sake I will not keep silent, and for Jerusalem's sake I will not rest, until her vindication goes forth as brightness and her salvation as a burning torch" (Is 62:1).

I think of and long for the day on which we shall all be so "taught by God" (John 6:45) that we shall listen to these messages of peace and reconciliation. I think of the day on which Jews, Christians, and Muslims will greet each other in the city of Jerusalem with the same greeting of peace with which Christ greeted the disciples after the Resurrection: "Peace be with you" (John 20:19).

The Roman pontiffs, especially in this century, have witnessed with an ever-anxious solicitude the violent events which have afflicted Jerusalem for many decades, and they have followed closely with watchful care the declarations of the United Nations which have dealt with the fate of the holy city.

On many occasions the Holy See has called for reflection and urged that an adequate solution be found to this difficult and complex situation. The Holy See has done this because she is concerned for peace among people no less than for spiritual, historical, and cultural reasons of a nature eminently religious.

The entire human race, and especially the people and nations who have in Jerusalem brothers in faith—Christians, Jews and Muslims—have reason to feel themselves involved in this matter and to do everything possible to preserve the unique and sacred character of the city. Not only the monuments or the sacred places but the whole historical Jerusalem and the existence of religious communities, their situation and future cannot but affect everyone and interest everyone.

Indeed, there should be found, with goodwill and farsightedness a concrete and just solution by which different interests and aspirations can be provided for in a harmonious and stable form, and be safeguarded in an adequate and efficacious manner by a special statute internationally guaranteed so that no party could jeopardize it.

I also feel it an urgent duty, in the presence of the Christian communities, of those who believe in the One God and who are committed to the defense of fundamental human values, to repeat that the question of Jerusalem is fundamental for a just peace in the Middle East. It is my conviction that the religious identity of the city and particularly the common tradition of monotheistic faith can pave the way to promote harmony among all those who in different ways consider the holy city as their own.

I am convinced that the failure to find an adequate solution to the question of Jerusalem, and the resigned postponement of the problem, only compromises further the longed for peaceful and just settlement of the crisis of the whole Middle East.

It is natural in this context to recall that in the area two peoples, the Israelis and the Palestinians, have been opposed to each other for decades in an antagonism that appears insoluble.

The Church, which looks at Christ the Redeemer and sees his image in the face of every man, invokes peace and reconciliation for the people of the land that was his.

For the Jewish people who live in the State of Israel and who preserve in that land such precious testimonies to their history and their faith, we must ask for the desired security and the due tranquility that is the prerogative of every nation and condition of life and of progress for every society.

The Palestinian people, who find their historical roots in that land and who, for decades, have been dispersed, have the natural right in justice to find once more a homeland and to be able to live in peace and tranquility with the other peoples of the area.

All the peoples of the Middle East, each with its own heritage of spiritual values, will not be able to overcome the tragic events in which they are involved—I am thinking of Lebanon so sorely tried—unless they discover again the true sense of their history which, through faith in the One God, calls them to live together faithfully in mutual cooperation.

I desire, therefore, to draw the attention of politicians, of all those who are responsible for the destiny of peoples, of those who are in charge of international organizations, to the plight of the city of Jerusalem and of the communities who live there. In fact, it escapes no one that the different expressions of faith and of culture in the holy city can and should be an effective aid to concord and peace.

On this Good Friday, when we solemnly recall the Passion and the Death of the Savior, we invite you all reverend brothers in the Episcopate and all priests, men and women religious, and the faithful of the whole world to include among the special intentions of your prayers the petition for a just solution to the problem of Jerusalem and the Holy Land and for the return of peace to the Middle East.

As this Jubilee Year of Redemption draws to a close, a year which we have celebrated with great spiritual joy, whether in Rome or in all dioceses of the universal Church, Jerusalem has been the ideal goal, the natural place to which we direct our thoughts of love and thankfulness for the great gift of the Redemption which the Son of Man accomplished for all people in the holy city.

And since the fruit of Redemption is the reconciliation of man with God and of every man with his brother, we ought to pray that also in Jerusalem, in the Holy Land of Jesus, those who believe in God might find reconciliation and peace after such sorrowful division and strife.

This peace proclaimed by Jesus Christ in the name of the Father who is in heaven thus makes Jerusalem the living sign of the great ideal of unity, of brotherhood, and of agreement among peoples according to the illuminating words of the Book of Isaiah: "Many peoples shall come and say: Come, let us go up to the mountain of the Lord, to the house of the God of Jacob; that he may teach us his ways and that we might walk in his paths" (Is 2:3).

Finally, we gladly impart our apostolic blessing.

Given in Rome at Saint Peter's on Good Friday, 20 April 1984, the sixth year of our pontificate.

Notes

PART I: INTERPRETING THE LAND IN THE BIBLE

1. One example of difference between these two presentations, Christian and Jewish, of canon is that the Christian canon of the Old Testament ends with the eschatological text of Malachi containing the promise to send Elijah to visit the Land. The Jewish canon, on the other hand, ends with 2 Chronicles and the invitation extended by Cyrus, King of Persia, to the Jewish exiles in Babylon to return to the Land and to rebuild the Temple.

CHAPTER 1: THE LAND IN THE OLD TESTAMENT

1. All biblical citations are taken from the NRSV (1989). Throughout, the Hebrew word *aretz* and the Greek word *ge* have been translated as "land." When the authors have preferred to translate from the original this will be noted in the text.

2. P. Trible suggests an evocative translation for *adam*: "the earth creature," see P. Trible, *God and the Rhetoric of Sexuality* (Philadelphia, 1978), 79.

3. The word "covenant" (Hebrew *berith*) is used for the first time with regard to Noah; however, Jesus ben Sira, the author of Ecclesiasticus, might be attributing an original covenant to *Adam* (cf. Sir 17:12).

4. "These words, of course, contain an expression of a relationship to the land which is characteristic of Israel. While, as far as we can see, the peoples around about lay strong emphasis upon their autochthonism—for them the possession of the land was a primary religious datum—Israel never lost the memory that she had been led to her land in a special way and only then invested with it in fief by Jahweh." See G. von Rad, *Theology of the Old Testament*, vol. 1 (New York, 1962), 1:26.

5. The Hebrew here is in the imperative form of a commandment.

6. The biblical text implies that more than 400 years have passed in the interim, cf. Gn 15:13 and Ex 12:40.

7. Moses' mediating role, as prophet, is established within the *Torah* (Dt 18:15–20). Moses' role in the Pentateuch is a fascinating one as he moves between God and the people, consigned to a space between the two, a space that will be inherited by the prophets after him. At first, this was a temporary mission given to Moses by God, who sent Moses to lead the people out of Egypt. Israel, as blessing for the nations, was supposed to assume this role of mediation between God and the nations. As of Ex 20, this is a role established for the prophet by the people, who fear to meet God directly.

8. According to historical-critical analysis, these writings are attributed to the priestly writer, who seems less concerned with Land and more concerned with sacred cultic space and practice.

9. The laws for the construction of the tent end with the laws of the Sabbath (Ex 31:12–17, cf. 35:2–3), implying that the construction itself is a new act of creation.

10. The centralization of the cult in Jerusalem is a particular concern of the Deuteronomist.

11. This is inspired by the discussion in W. Brueggemann, *The Land* (Minneapolis, 2002), 56–62.

12. Ibid., 58.

13. Ibid., 60.

14. The act of sanctifying is central to Leviticus cf. 11:45, 19:2, 20:7.8.26, 21:8, 22:9.32.

15. This is lyrically repeated in the Psalms, too (Ps 78:54–55, 80:8, 105:43–44), in a celebration of God as Lord of history.

16. With regard to Ammonites and Moabites, it is significant that in the history books of the Old Testament, both a Moabite woman (Ruth) and an Ammonite chief (Akhior) are presented not only as models of faith but as entering fully the people of God in the Books of Ruth and Judith, respectively. They prepare us for similar unexpected models of faith from outside of Israel in the Gospels, for example the Syro-Phoenician woman (Mk 7:24–30, interestingly presented as a Canaanite in Mt 15:21–28).

17. I. Pardes, *The Biography of Ancient Israel: National Narratives in the Bible* (Berkeley, 2000), 158.

18. Once Jericho is destroyed, Joshua pronounces a curse on it: "Cursed before the Lord be anyone who tries to build this city—this Jericho! At the cost of his firstborn he shall lay its foundation, and at the cost of his youngest he shall set up its gates" (Jos 6:26). Later, the biblical reader discovers that Jericho was indeed rebuilt, a sign of how far Israel had strayed from the way of the Lord. In the text that introduces Ahab, king of Israel, who "did more to provoke the anger of the Lord, the God of Israel, than had all the kings of Israel who were before him" (1 Kgs 16:33), the reconstruction of Jericho is mentioned too. "In his days, Hiel of Bethel built Jericho; he laid its foundations at the cost of Abiram his firstborn, and set up its gates at the cost of his youngest son, Segub, according to the word of the Lord, which he spoke by Joshua son of Nun" (1 Kgs 16:34). The new Jericho, it seems, was founded on child sacrifice, the peak of the sinfulness of the pagan nations, now practiced by Israel in the Land.

19. In Jewish tradition, Ruth is among the Five Scrolls within the third part of the TaNaKh, the Writings.

20. R. Alter, *The Art of Biblical Narrative* (New York, 1981), 58–60.

21. Ibid., 59.

22. In the midst of the narrative relating David's sin, and quite unexpectedly, the text refers to Abimelekh, first king in the Land, and his ignoble demise (2 Sam 11:21, cf. Jgs 9).

23. In the history narrative of the Books of Chronicles, containing its own perspectives on Land, Temple and kingship, it is interesting to note that a different reason for God's refusal that David build Him a temple is given. David explains to the officials of the people that God had said to him: "You are not to build a house for My name, for you have been a man of war and have shed blood" (1Chr 28:3). The biblical text here seems to be echoing a developing sense of unease with the violent narratives of the conquest of the Land.

24. This sin is also portrayed in the prophetic literature from the period of the Deuteronomist writer, cf. Jer 32:35 and Ez 20:31, 23:37 (accusations of the people).

25. The priestly writer who produced the texts that concern cult, sacrifice, priestly office, and purity in the *Torah* is also from this period.

26. It is important to note, however, that despite this seemingly particularist extremism, the same period produced the Books of Ruth and Jonah with a very universal message.

27. It is interesting to note that in the Jewish canon of the Bible, the books known as historical books (i.e., Jos, Jgs, Sam, and Kgs) are called "First Prophets" distinguished from the "Latter Prophets" (Is, Jer, Ez, and the Twelve). This reminds the readers that only a prophet is capable of understanding and writing sacred history.

28. Solomon was made king in order to exercise righteousness and justice, but we know how far from this he went astray.

29. Or again: "This is because they have abandoned me, have profaned this place, have offered incense here to alien gods, which neither they, nor their ancestors, nor the kings of Judah, ever knew before. They have filled this place with the blood of the innocent" (Jer 19:4).

30. This is the only other text in the Bible that uses the Hebrew expression *tohu va-vohu,* the primordial chaos out of which the creation is extracted in Gn 1:2.

31. Brueggemann, *The Land,* 101–2.

32. In the midrashic literature, the rabbis identified the cry of God in Gn 3:9, "Where are you!" (in Hebrew *Ayeka*) with the cry at the beginning of Lm 1:1, "Oh, how can it be!" (in Hebrew, *Aykha*). The two cries have the same consonants in Hebrew although they are vocalized differently. See *Midrash Lamentations Rabba,* 1:1.

CHAPTER 2: THE LAND IN THE NEW TESTAMENT

1. This has been shown in the important study of W. D. Davies, *The Gospel and the Land* (Berkeley, 1974).

2. Later, we will analyze the traditional Christian reading of the dispersion of the Jews and their banishment from the Land.

3. This formulation of Saint Augustine was cited in the Second Vatican Council document *Dei Verbum*, 16, issued in 1965.

4. This is also the language used in Rv 11:2, where the Gentiles trample on the Holy City for a certain time.

5. This is a significant difference between the images used by Jesus the preacher and the preaching of the generation of apostles that succeeds him, especially Paul. The apostles, and particularly Paul, seldom use the Land-rooted images that fill Jesus' teaching. Their natural environment seems to be the cities of the extended Empire rather than the hills and plains of Galilee and the Judean wilderness.

6. "He will be called a Nazorean," words preceded by Matthew's usual fulfillment formula: "In this way the words spoken through the prophets were to be fulfilled" (Mt 2:23). However, none of the prophets speak of Nazareth or a Nazarene.

7. Jesus son of Nun is better known as Joshua. However, it is important to remember that in the ancient Greek translation of the Hebrew Scriptures, Hebrew Joshua was translated into Greek Jesus. It was this ancient Greek translation that was predominantly used as the Old Testament version behind the writing of the New.

8. W. D. Davies, *The Gospel and the Land* (Berkeley, 1974), 367–68.

CHAPTER 3: VISITING THE LAND

1. P. Maraval, *Lieux saints et pèlerinages d'Orient* (Paris, 1985), 25.

2. Particularly helpful in this regard is the series of articles by D. Attinger, "Christian Pilgrims in the Holy Land" in *Jerusalem* (Diocesan Bulletin of the Latin Patriarchate of Jerusalem), from 8/6 (2002) onward.

3. Eusebius, *Ecclesiastical history,* IV, 26, 13–14.

4. Origen, "Commentary on Saint John," VI, 204.

5. John Paul II, "Letter of the Supreme Pontiff John Paul II concerning pilgrimage to the places linked to the history of salvation, Vatican," (29.6.1999).

6. Maraval, *Lieux saints et pèlerinages d'Orient*, 34.

7. Jerome, Letter LVIII to Paulinius in *St. Jerome: Letters and Selected Works*, vol. 6 of *Nicene and Post-Nicene Fathers* (Grand Rapids, Eerdmans, reprinted from 1892), 119–20.

8. Ibid.

9. Translated from the French, P. Maraval, ed., *Récits de premiers pèlerins au Proche-Orient (IV–VIIe s.)* (Paris, 1996), 45.

10. Ibid.

11. Ibid., 46–47.

12. Translated from the French and Greek in Grégoire de Nysse, Lettre 2, *Lettres*, Sources chrétiennes (363), 111.

13. Ibid.

14. Ibid., 115.

15. Ibid., 117.

16. Ibid., 122.

17. Gregory of Nyssa, *Sources chrétiennes* (363), 123.

18. Y. Leibowitz, *Judaism, Human Values and the Jewish State* (Cambridge, 1992), 261.

19. E. Mazar, *The Temple Mount Excavations in Jerusalem 1968–1978 directed by Benjamin Mazar*, vol. 2, Qedem 43, Jerusalem, 2003. See also the short summary by the author, E. Mazar, "Monastery of the Virgins," *Biblical Archaeological Review*, 30/3 (May–June 2004), 20–33.

20. Wilkinson (1977) quoted in Mazar, ibid., 66. The identification of this site with the monastery mentioned by Theodosius is the subject of a debate. The argument does not convince Jerome Murphy O'Connor, for example, who has questioned the methodology of E. Mazar, cf. J. Murphy O'Connor in *Revue biblique*, 112 (2005) 126–30.

21. The authors are grateful to Dr. Joseph E. David for this selection of texts on Rabbinic Judaism and the Land.

22. Citation of Urban II, see N. Daniel, *Islam and the West*, 2nd ed. (Oxford, 1993), 411.

23. Translated from the French and the Latin, see Bernard de Clairvaux, *Eloge de la nouvelle chevalerie*, Sources chrétiennes (367), 59–61.

24. Muqaddasi, quoted in G. Le Strange, *History of Jerusalem under the Moslems*, 1890, 5–6.

25. Translated from the Latin and the French, "François D'Assise, Règle de 1221 ou Première règle," *Ecrits*, Sources chrétiennes (285), 151.

26. An interesting analysis of Raymond Lull and other medieval authors' attitudes to Islam can be found in N. Daniel, *Islam and the West*.

CHAPTER 4: A CHRISTIAN READING OF THE LAND UNTIL VATICAN II

1. Translated from the German, P. Lapide, *Rom und die Juden* (Frankfurt, 1967), 10.

2. John Chrysostom, Discourse V, *Discourses against Judaizing Christians* (Washington, DC, 1977), 437.

3. G. Langmuir, *Towards a Definition of Anti-Semitism* (Berkeley, 1990), 7.

4. See J. Isaac, *Has Anti-Semitism Roots in Christianity?* (New York, 1961).

5. D. Marguerat, *Le dechirement: juifs et chrétiens au premier siècle* (Geneva, 1996), 7.

6. Tertullian, "Apology," in *Apologetic Works* (Washington, DC, 1962) 7.

7. Ibid., 26.

8. Ibid., 61–62.

9. Langmuir, *Towards a Definition of Anti-Semitism*, 58.

10. Ibid., 105–6.

11. A. Pessah, K. Meyers, and C. Leighton, "How Do Jews and Christians Read the Bible?" in D. Sandmel, R. Catalano, and C. Leighton, *Irreconcilable Differences?* (Boulder, 2001), 66–67.

12. Origen, *Homilies on Joshua* (Washington, DC, 2002), 59.

13. Ibid., 34.

14. Ibid., 36.

15. Ibid., 37–38.

16. Ibid., 158.

17. Origen, *Homilies on Joshua*, 39.

18. John Chrysostom, *Discourses against Judaizing Christians*, 18.

19. Ibid., 99–100.

20. Ibid., 113.

21. Ibid., 135.

22. John Chrysostom, *Homily on Psalm 8*.

23. Augustine, *In Answer to the Jews (Adversus judaeos)*, Treatises on Marriage and Other Subjects (Washington, D.C., 1955).

24. Ibid., 414 (X, 15).

25. Augustine, "On Psalm LXV (LXIV)" in "Expositions on the Book of Psalms," *Nicene and Post-Nicene Fathers* (New York, 1894), 8:268.

26. Ibid.

27. Augustine, "On Psalm CIX (CVIII)," ibid., 536.

28. Augustine, *City of God* (Book XVIII, ch. 46) (Edinburgh, 1909), 201.

29. The term in Latin, *capsarius*, is used by the Romans for the servant charged with carrying the books of the child. Here, the Jews carry the book that is the Old Testament.

30. Augustine, "On Psalm XLI (XL)," in "Expositions on the Book of Psalms," ibid., 132.

31. Walafridi Strabi, "Glossa ordinaria," in *Patrologiae latinae,* 13:904. The Latin text reads: "*Benedictus* (. . .) *Deus Israel.* (AUG.) Judaei sunt casparii nostri, qui nobis codices portant; nos Israel. Aliter putassent pagani ficta quae dicuntur de Christo et Ecclesia, sed vicuntur testimonio inimicorum."

32. See A. G. Martimort, "Bossuet" in *Dictionnaire des théologiens* (Paris, 1998).

33. Translated from the French, Bossuet, Sermon pour le IX Dimanche après la Pentecôte (1653) sur la Bonté et la Rigueur de Dieu, Garnier, III, 570.

34. Pascal, *Pensées* (London, 1977), n. 640 (125).

35. Ibid., n. 638 (123).

36. Prudentius, "Apotheosis," 540–45, translated from the Latin, *Patrologiae latinae*, 59:986–87.

CHAPTER 5: SHAKING UP A FAMILIAR LANDSCAPE

1. Commission for Religious Relations with the Jews, *We Remember: A Reflection on the Shoah*, 1998.

2. Ibid.

3. Ibid.

4. It is important to point out that long before the formulation of Jewish political Zionism, the idea of a Jewish "return" to the biblical Holy Land had penetrated certain Protestant circles, motivated by a literal reading of the Old Testament. Already in the nineteenth century some great literary figures gave expression to this idea, like George Eliot, Herman Melville, and Mark Twain.

5. The founder of political Zionism, Theodor Herzl, an Austro-Hungarian Jew, formulated his vision of a "Jewish State" in the aftermath of the trial of Alfred Dreyfus in France. Herzl, an assimilated and completely non-religious Jew, had first dreamt of complete assimilation (even conversion to Christianity) for the Jews in Europe. The vicious anti-Semitism that showed its face during the Dreyfus trial in France convinced him that anti-Semitism was so rooted in Europe that there could be no future for Jews there. His vision of a Jewish state in Palestine was of a liberal-democratic, European-style regime where Jews were the ruling majority.

6. Cited in A. Hertzberg, *The Zionist Idea* (New York, 1977), 222.

7. Ibid., 419.

8. Cited in M. Selzer, ed., *Zionism Reconsidered* (London, 1970), 16–17.

9. Cited A. Hertzberg, *The Zionist Idea*, 461.

10. In 1913, a wide coalition of Orthodox rabbis from Eastern and Western Europe formed Agudat Yisrael (the Union of Israel) in order to oppose Zionism and warn the Jewish people of its dangers.

11. A. J. Heschel, *Israel: An Echo of Eternity* (New York, 1967), 122.

12. U. Simon, *Seek Peace and Pursue It: Topical Issues in the Light of the Bible, The Bible in the Light of Topical Issues* (translated from Hebrew) (Tel Aviv, 2002), 21–22.

13. Originally formulated by the Christian English politician Lord Shaftesbury, it was adopted and popularized by the Zionist thinker Israel Zangwill.

14. E. Said, *The Question of Palestine* (New York, 1979).

15. A. Qleibo, *Before the Mountains Disappear* (Cairo, 1992), xix.

16. E. Said, *After the Last Sky* (London, 1986), 43.

17. Michel Sabbah, Patriarch of Jerusalem, *Seek Peace and Pursue It: Questions and Answers on Justice and Peace in Our Holy Land*, 1998, n. 6.

18. Cf. 2Tm 3:15–16, 2 Pt 1:20.

19. Leo XIII, *Providentissimus Deus*, 1893, n. 21 quoting Letter lxxxii of Saint Augustine.

20. Translated from the French, a letter of June 7, 1905, cited in B. Montagnes, *Exégèse et obéissance: Correspondance Cormier-Lagrange, 1904–1916* (Paris, 1989), 72.

21. Translated from the French, a letter of December 14, 1914, ibid., 418.

22. Pontifical Biblical Commission, *The Interpretation of the Bible in the Church* (Vatican, 1993), 34.

23. W. D. Davies, *The Gospel and the Land* (Berkeley, 1974), 18–19.

24. W. Keller, *Und die Bibel hat doch recht* (Hamburg, 1955), translated into English as *The Bible as History: Archaeology confirms the Book of Books* (London, 1956).

25. W. F. Albright, *The Archaeology of Palestine and the Bible* (London, 1932), 127.

26. N. Shragai, "A careful examination, a fraud discovered," *HaAretz*, December 30, 2004. The article mentions a number of other forgeries that had created waves in the world of archaeology including a supposed ornamental pomegranate from the First Temple (touted as the only artifact from Solomon's Temple), an eighth-century-b.c. jar, and an ossuary with an inscription, initially understood as the ossuary of James, brother of Jesus of Nazareth.

27. I. Finkelstein and N. Silberman, *The Bible Unearthed* (New York, 2001), 122.

28. See A. Alt, *Old Testament History and Religion* (New York, 1968).
29. See N. Gottwald, *The Tribes of Yahweh* (London, 1980).
30. Translated from the French, O. Artus, "Archéologie, Bible, Histoire," *Cahiers Evangile* 131 (2005), 22. See also D. Jamieson-Drake, *Scribes and Schools in Monarchic Judah* (Sheffield, JSOTS, 1991).
31. R. North, *La terre sainte* (ed. J. Briend) (Paris, 2003), 344.
32. Collective, *Archaeology and Old Testament Study* (Oxford, 1967), Introduction.
33. J. Briend, "Une épopée de fiction: Jos 2.6–12," in ACFEB, *Comment la Bible saisit-elle l'histoire*, ed. D. Doré, Lectio Divina (Paris 2007).

PART III: THE LAND IN THE CONTEMPORARY DOCUMENTS OF THE CATHOLIC CHURCH

1. C. Thoma, "Der Staat Israel: Ein *Crux theologiae*" in *Bibel und Kirche*, 2/2, 1974, 48–51.
2. For this document see "Apostolic Letter of John Paul II—*Redemptionis anno*," E. Fisher and L. Klenicki, eds., *Pope John Paul II: Spiritual Pilgrimage: Texts on Jews and Judaism 1979–1995* (New York, 1997), 33–37.
3. Important studies have been written on Vatican policy in the Middle East, cf. G. Irani, *The Papacy and the Middle East: The Role of the Holy See in the Arab-Israeli Conflict 1962–1984* (Notre Dame, 1986) and A. Kreutz, *Vatican Policy on the Palestinian-Israeli Conflict* (New York, 1986).

CHAPTER 6: TRADITIONAL CHRISTIAN ATTACHMENT TO THE LAND

1. "Apostolic Letter of John Paul II—*Redemptionis anno*," 34.
2. "John Paul II, Letter concerning Pilgrimage to the Places Linked to the History of Salvation" (August 1999).
3. Ibid.
4. The traces of this visit are visible even today in three institutions that were established after the Pope's visit: the Ecumenical Institute of Tantur, the Epheta Institute for deaf and dumb children in Bethlehem, and Bethlehem University.
5. Assembly of Catholic Bishops in the Holy Land, *The Holy Land Welcomes His Holiness Pope John Paul II: 20–26 March 2000* (Jerusalem, 2000), "Homily in Bethlehem—22.3.2000," 53.
6. O'Mahony, A, "The Vatican, Palestinian Christians, Israel and Jerusalem: Religion, Politics, Diplomacy and the Holy Places, 1945–1950" in Swanson, R. N., ed., *The Holy Land, Holy Lands and Christian History* (London, 2000), 358–72.

CHAPTER 7: THE INTERPRETATION OF THE BIBLE

1. "Apostolic Letter of John Paul II—*Redemptionis anno*," Fisher and Klenicki, eds., *Pope John Paul II: Spiritual Pilgrimage,* 33–34.

2. "Apostolic Constitution on Divine Revelation," *The Documents of Vatican II* (New York, 1966), nn. 14–15 (121–22).

3. Pontifical Biblical Commission, *The Interpretation of the Bible in the Church* (Vatican, 1993), I, F (71).

4. Ibid., 72.

5. Ibid., III, A. 1 (86–87).

6. Pontifical Biblical Commission, *The Jewish People and their Sacred Scriptures in the Christian Bible* (Vatican, 2001), n. 22 (51)

7. Ibid., n. 1 (13).

8. Ibid., n. 22 (50–51).

9. Ibid., n. 54 (124–25).

10. Ibid., n. 64 (143).

11. Ibid., n. 56 (128).

12. Ibid., n. 56 (130).

13. Ibid., n. 57 (130–31).

14. Ibid., n. 20 (45).

15. Patriarch Michel Sabbah, *Reading the Bible Today in the Land of the Bible* (Jerusalem, 1993), n. 7 (10).

16. Ibid., n. 7 (10).

17. Ibid., n. 7 (11).

18. Ibid.

19. Ibid., n. 53 (54–55).

20. Ibid., n. 56 (59).

CHAPTER 8: INTERRELIGIOUS DIALOGUE

1. "Apostolic Letter of John Paul II—*Redemptionis anno*," 34.

2. Ibid.

3. The expression "teaching of contempt" appears in the writings of the French Jewish thinker Jules Isaac, who met with Pope John XXIII and convinced him of the need for a reform in the Church's attitude toward the Jews. See J. Isaac, *Has Anti-Semitism Roots in Christianity?* (New York, 1961).

4. Quoted in "Pius X" in *Encyclopedia Judaica* (Jerusalem, 1971), 13:572.

5. For the various discourses see *Documentation catholique*, 1417, 161–94. Paul VI did not use the word "Jew," "Judaism," or "Israel" nor did he mention the Palestinians by name. His entire visit to the Holy Land (both territories under Jordanian and Israeli rule) focused on traditional pilgrim themes and the dialogue with the Orthodox Church.

6. "Declaration on the Relationship of the Church with Non-Christians," n. 4, *The Documents of Vatican II* (New York, 1966), 663–67.

7. This biblical verse from the Epistle to the Romans has become a linchpin in the new attitude to the Jewish people. Quoted many times by Pope John Paul II, it has refocused attention on God's fidelity to his chosen ones. It is important to note though that in Paul's list of these gifts in Rm 9:4–5 the Land is not mentioned.

8. The commissions for dialogue with the Jewish people and with Muslims were created in 1974. The Commission for Religious Relations with the

Jews is attached to the Pontifical Council for Christian Unity, and the Commission for Religious Relations with Muslims is part of the Pontifical Council for Interreligious Dialogue.

9. See the *Catechism of the Catholic Church* (Rome, 1992), n. 423 ("Jesus of Nazareth, born a Jew of a daughter of Israel . . .), 488, 531, 574–94, 839, etc.

10. "L'attitude des chrétiens à l'égard du judaïsme: orientations pastorales du comité épiscopal pour les relations avec le judaïsme, publiées par la conférence épiscopale française (16 avril 1973)," republished in J. Dujardin, *L'Eglise catholique et le peuple juif* (Paris, 2003), 411–19. For a translation of this document see Boston College Center for Jewish-Christian Learning website (http://www.bc.edu/research/cjl/).

11. Ibid.

12. For the French text see J. Dujardin, *L'Eglise catholique et le peuple juif*, 422.

13. Ibid.

14. See the French text in *Documentation catholique,* 1635 (1.7.1973), 617.

15. Ibid., 619. An even more comprehensive documentation is available in French in *Documentation catholique*, 1648 (17.2.1974).

16. "Orientations and Suggestions for the Application of the Council Declaration *Nostra Aetate*." For a translation of this document see Boston College Center for Jewish-Christian Learning website (http://www.bc.edu/research/cjl/).

17. Ibid.

18. See the allocution of Dr. Reigner at the meeting of the Jewish-Catholic Liaison Committee, held in Rome on 10.1.1975, *Documentation catholique*, n. 1669, 111.

19. Ibid.

20. U.S. National Conference of Catholic Bishops, "Statement on Catholic-Jewish relations," 1975, for this document see Boston College Center for Jewish-Christian Learning website (http://www.bc.edu/research/cjl/).

21. Ibid.

22. "Address to Jewish Community—West Germany, 1980," Fisher and Klenicki, eds., *Pope John Paul II: Spiritual Pilgrimage,* 15.

23. Ibid.

24. On the occasion of this visit, the pope declared: "With Judaism, therefore, we have a relationship which we do not have with any other religion. You are our dearly beloved brothers, and, in a certain way, it could be said that you are our elder brothers." See "Historic visit to the Synagogue of Rome, 1986," Fisher and Klenicki, eds., *Pope John Paul II: Spiritual Pilgrimage*, 63.

25. "Visit to Brazil, 1991," *Pope John Paul II: Spiritual Pilgrimage*, 160.

26. "Notes on the Correct Way to Present Jews and Judaism in Preaching and Catechesis in the Roman Catholic Church" (1985). For a translation of this document see Boston College Center for Jewish-Christian Learning website (http://www.bc.edu/research/cjl/).

27. Ibid.

28. See reaction of Dr. Wigoder in *Documentation catholique*, n. 1965 (1985), 691–700.

29. Catholics involved in the dialogue had to try and explain Vatican policy, see E. Fisher, "The Holy See and the State of Israel: The Evolution of Attitudes and Policies," *Journal of Ecumenical Studies* 24/2 (1987), 191–211.

30. "Fundamental Agreement between the Holy See and the State of Israel," *Pope John Paul II: Spiritual Pilgrimage,* 203–8.

31. Ibid., 203.

32. One Catholic formulation of such a position might be that of Cardinal Jean-Marie Lustiger, then Archbishop of Paris, who, in an address at Tel Aviv University commemorating the Shoah, said: "The children of Israel have gathered in a State like any other—no more, no less—and this is both legitimate and necessary," see *Documentation catholique*, 2116 (1995), 481.

33. *"Dabru emet* (Speak the Truth)," *First Things,* 107 (2000), 39.

34. For a survey of English-speaking Catholic trends see "The State of Israel and Catholic Theology," in A. Kenny, *Catholics, Jews and the State of Israel* (New York, 1990), 66–80. Also the more recent M. McGarry, "The land of Israel in the Cauldron of the Middle East: A Challenge to Christian-Jewish Relations," in M. Boys, ed., *Seeing Judaism Anew: Christianity's Sacred Obligation* (Lanham, MD, 2005), 260–75. See also European writings in French and Italian, Marcel Dubois, *Rencontres avec le judaïsme en Israël* (Jerusalem, 1983); Francesco Rossi di Gasperis, *Cominciando da Gerusalemme* (Monferrato, 1997), Pierre Lenhardt, "La fin du sionisme?" *Sens,* 56/3 (2004), 99–138, Jean Dujardin, *L'Eglise catholique et le peuple juif: un autre regard* (Paris, 2003).

35. "Joint declaration of the International Catholic-Jewish Liaison Committee: Our commitment to justice is deeply rooted in both our faiths," *Zenit,* July 13, 2004.

36. See for example M. Prior, "A Disaster for Dialogue," *The Tablet,* 31.7.2004 and the response of E. Fisher, "Zionism and Michael Prior," *The Tablet*, 1.9.2004. Also "Anti-Zionism not the same as anti-Semitism say Vatican officials," *The Tablet,* 31.7.2004. Also W. Dalrymple, "The demonizing of Islam," *The Tablet,* 11.9.2004.

37. Pontifical Commission for Justice and Peace, *The Church Face to Face with Racism* (Rome, 1988), n. 15.

38. Assembly of Catholic Ordinaries in the Holy Land, *The General Pastoral Plan* (Jerusalem 2001), 156.

39. For French see *Documentation catholique*, n. 2307 (1.2.2004), 140.

40. The writings of Louis Massignon, the great French Catholic writer on Islamic mysticism and confidant of Pope Paul VI, had a great influence.

41. See *Documentation catholique*, n. 1664 (17.11.1974), 959.

42. Ibid., 960.

43. Like his predecessor Pope Paul VI, the visit focused mainly on the dialogue with the Greek Orthodox Patriarch whose seat is in Istanbul.

44. See *Documentation catholique*, n. 1903 (6.10.1985).

45. The most explicit statement concerning relations between Muslim and Christian Arabs is the Apostolic Exhortation of John Paul II, *A New Hope*

for Lebanon, issued in May 1997, after the synod of Lebanese bishops; see *Documentation catholique,* n. 2161 (1.6.1997).

46. *Documentation catholique,* n. 1785 (4.5.1980), 420.

47. *Zenit,* 20.8.2002.

48. *Documentation catholique,* n. 2113 (2.4.1995), 320–36.

49. Assembly of Catholic Ordinaries in the Holy Land, *The General Pastoral Plan,* Jerusalem 2001, 154.

50. *Documentation catholique,* n. 2307 (1.2.2004), 142.

CHAPTER 9: PEACE AND JUSTICE

1. "Apostolic Letter of John Paul II—*Redemptionis anno,*" Fisher and Klenicki, eds., *Pope John Paul II: Spiritual Pilgrimage,* 33.

2. Ibid., 36.

3. For fuller studies see M. Perko, "Toward a 'Sound and Lasting Basis': Relations between the Holy See, the Zionist Movement and Israel, 1896–1996," *Israel Studies* 2/1 (1997), 1–21; M. Breger, *The Vatican-Israel Accords* (South Bend, 2004).

4. J.-L. Tauran, "Resolving the Question of Jerusalem" *Origins* 21/28 (5.11.1998), 367. Mgr. Tauran also gave a very enlightening talk on the principles guiding Church positions in the Middle East at the Catholic University in Washington, DC (cf. *Origins* 18.3.1999). This conference is a remarkable application of the guidelines laid out in the letter *Redemptionis anno,* taking into account many of the nuances and complexities of the situation in the Middle East.

5. The Angelus message quoted in United States Bishops, "Bicentennial Meeting: Toward Peace in the Middle East," *Origins,* 25/19 (23.11.1989), 409.

6. This meant that there were no official relations between the Hashemite Kingdom of Jordan and the Vatican either. An apostolic nunciature was established in Jordan only in 1994.

7. This was formulated in the encyclicals of Pope Pius XII, *Multiplicibis curis* (1948) and *Redemptoris nostris* (1949).

8. Other visits followed: Moshe Dayan, Foreign Minister, to Pope John Paul II in 1978, Yitzhaq Shamir, Foreign Minister, in 1982, Shimon Peres, Foreign Minister, in 1985.

9. See Paul VI's enthusiastic welcome of the Sadat initiative in *L'Osservatore Romano,* 20.11.1977, 268.

10. "Apostolic Letter of John Paul II—*Redemptionis anno,*" *Pope John Paul II: Spiritual Pilgrimage,* 33.

11. "Fundamental Agreement between the Holy See and the State of Israel," *Pope John Paul II: Spiritual Pilgrimage,* 203–8.

12. Ibid., 203.

13. Translated from the French in *Documentation catholique,* n. 1690 (18.1.1976), 55–56.

14. The position of Roman Catholic or Latin Patriarch of Jerusalem had been created during the Crusades and disappeared after the Crusaders had been defeated. The position was re-established in 1847.

15. Assembly of Catholic Bishops in the Holy Land, *The Holy Land Welcomes His Holiness Pope John Paul II: 20–26 March 2000* (Jerusalem, 2000), "Speech of John Paul II in the Deheisheh Palestinian Refugee Camp— 22.3.2000," 60.

16. "Basic Agreement between the Holy See and the Palestine Liberation Organization," *Jerusalem Quarterly* n. 8 (2000).

17. Ibid.

18. In 2003, the pope named an auxiliary bishop for the Latin Patriarch of Jerusalem, Jean-Baptiste Gourion (d. 2005), a Benedictine of Jewish origin, responsible for the Hebrew-speaking Catholics in the diocese. Although this group is small in number, the symbolic value of a Hebrew-speaking community alongside the Arabic-speaking Palestinian church might be seen as another model for coexistence in the Holy Land.

19. See for example: Y. Teyssier d'Orfeuil, *Michel Sabbah: Paix sur Jérusalem* (Paris, 2002) (French); Rafiq Khoury, *The Incarnation of the Churches of the East in the Arab Tent* (Jerusalem, 1998) (Arabic); Elias Chacour, *Blood Brothers* (Eastbourne, 1984); Elias Chacour, *We Belong to the Land* (San Francisco, 1990); Naim Ateek, *Justice and Only Justice* (New York, 1989); Naim Ateek et al, *Jerusalem: What makes for Peace?* (London, 1997); Mitri Raheb, *Bethlehem Besieged* (Minneapolis, 2004). See also Gary Burge, *Whose Land? Whose Promise?* (Cleveland, 2003).

20. Pope John Paul II, *Message for the Celebration of the World Day of Peace*, Rome, 1.1.2002.

21. Conference at the Catholic University, Washington, D.C., 9.3.1999, cf. *Origins*, 18.3.1999.

CONCLUSION: HOLY LANDS: YESTERDAY AND TODAY

1. There are numerous studies on the Jewish attitude to the Land from the perspective of a Jewish reading of the biblical sources and from the perspective of Rabbinic Judaism and modern Zionism. See A. Halkin, *Zion in Jewish Literature* (New York, 1961); B. Segal, *The Land of Israel as Focus in Jewish History* (Jerusalem, 1987); A. Ravitzky, *Messianism, Zionism and Jewish Religious Radicalism* (Chicago, 1996); D. Hartman, *Israelis and the Jewish Tradition* (New Haven, 2000). A four-volume series is being prepared by M. Walzer, M. Lorberbaum, and N. Zohar entitled *The Jewish Political Tradition,* to be published by Yale University Press. J. C. Attias and E. Benbassa, *Israel: The Impossible Land* (Stanford, 2003) is an interesting Jewish parallel study to the one presented here.

2. J. Sanders, *Torah and Canon* (Philadelphia, 1972), 53.

3. *Discourses on the Psalms*, Psalm 56,9,13 (CCL 39), 669.

4. Commission for Religious Relations with the Jews, *We Remember: A Reflection on the Shoah*, 1998.

5. In order to provoke renewed reflection we have included the full text of this Apostolic Letter in the appendix of this book.

6. We mention here the noteworthy document of the Church of Scotland's "Committee on Church and Nation," *Theology of Land and Covenant,* which includes extensive notes and bibliography, 2003.

7. D. Wagner, "Christian Zionists, Israel, and the Second Coming," *Daily Star* (Lebanon), October 8, 2003.

Selected Bibliography

Alt, A. *Old Testament History and Religion*. New York: Anchor Books, 1968.

Alter, R. *The Art of Biblical Narrative*. New York: Basic Books, 1981.

Ateek, N. *Justice and Only Justice*. New York: Orbis Press, 1989.

Attias, J.-C., and E. Benbassa. *Israel: The Impossible Land*, translated by Susan Emanuel. Stanford: Stanford University Press, 2003.

Boys, M., ed. *Seeing Judaism Anew: Christianity's Sacred Obligation*. Lanham, MD: Sheed and Ward, 2005.

Breger, M. *The Vatican-Israel Accords*. South Bend, IN: Notre Dame University Press, 2004.

Brueggemann, W. *The Land*. 2nd ed. Minneapolis: Fortress Press, 2002.

Burge, G. *Whose Land? Whose Promise?* Cleveland: Pilgrim Press, 2003.

Chapman, C. *Whose Promised Land?* Oxford: Lion Books, 2002.

Church of Scotland (Committee on Church and Nation). *Theology of Land and Covenant*. Edinburgh: Church of Scotland, 2003.

Davies, W. D. *The Gospel and the Land*. San Francisco: Sheffield Academic Press, 1974.

Dujardin, J. *L'Eglise catholique et le peuple juif*. Paris: Calman-Lévy, 2003.

Finkelstein I., and N. Silberman, *The Bible Unearthed*. New York: Free Press, 2001.

Fisher, E., and L. Klenicki, eds. *Pope John Paul II: Spiritual Pilgrimage: Texts on Jews and Judaism, 1979–1995*. New York: Crossroad, 1997.

Gottwald, N. *The Tribes of Yahweh*. London: SCM Press, 1980.

Halkin, A. *Zion in Jewish Literature*. New York: Herzl Press, 1961.

Hartman, D. *Israelis and the Jewish Tradition*. New Haven: Yale University Press, 2000.

Hertzberg, A. *The Zionist Idea*. New York: Atheneum, 1977.

Heschel, A. J. *Israel: An Echo of Eternity*. New York: Farrar, Strauss and Giroux, 1967.

Irani, G. *The Papacy and the Middle East: The Role of the Holy See in the Arab-Israeli Conflict, 1962–1984*. South Bend, IN: University of Notre Dame Press, 1986.

Kenny, A. *Catholics, Jews and the State of Israel*. New York: Paulist Press, 1990.

Langmuir, G. *Towards a Definition of Anti-Semitism*. Berkeley: University of California Press, 1990.

Leibowitz, Y. *Judaism, Human Values and the Jewish State*. Cambridge: Harvard University Press, 1992.

Maraval, P. *Lieux saints et pélerinages d'Orient*. Paris: Cerf, 1985.

Maraval, P., ed. *Récits de premiers pèlerins au Proche-Orient (IV–VIIe s.)*. Paris: Cerf, 1996.

March, W. E. *Israel and the Politics of Land: A Theological Case Study*. Louisville: John Knox Press, 1994.

Merkley, P. C. *Christian Attitudes toward the State of Israel*. New York: Mc-Gill–Queens Press, 2001.

Pardes, I. *The Biography of Ancient Israel: National Narratives in the Bible*. Berkeley: University of California Press, 2000.

Qleibo, A. *Before the Mountains Disappear*. Cairo: Kloreus, 1992.

Prior, M., ed. *They Came and They Saw*. London: Melisende, 2000.

Raheb, M. *Bethlehem Besieged*. Minneapolis: Fortress, 2004.

Ravitzky, A. *Messianism, Zionism and Jewish Religious Radicalism*. Chicago: University of Chicago Press, 1996.

Reuther, R. R., and H. Reuther. *The Wrath of Jonah: The Crisis of Religious Nationalism in the Israeli–Palestinian Conflict*. San Francisco: Harper and Row, 1989.

Said, E. *After the Last Sky*. London: Faber, 1986.

———. *The Question of Palestine*. New York: Vintage Books, 1979.

Sanders, J. *Torah and Canon*. Philadelphia: Fortress Press, 1972.

Swanson, R. N., ed. *The Holy Land, Holy Lands and Christian History*. London: Boydell Press, 2000.

von Rad, G. *Theology of the Old Testament*. New York: Harper and Row, 1962 and 1965.

Wilken, R. *The Land Called Holy: Palestine in Christian History and Thought*. New York: Yale University Press, 1992.

Catholic Church Documents

Documents of the Second Vatican Council

"Apostolic Constitution on Divine Revelation" (1965).
"Declaration on the Relationship of the Church with Non-Christians" (1965).

Documents of Pope John Paul II:

"Apostolic Letter on Jerusalem" (*Redemptionis anno*) (1984).
"Letter Concerning Pilgrimage to the Places Linked to the History of Salvation" (1999).
"Discourses in the Holy Land" (2000)

Other Vatican Documents

Catechism of the Catholic Church (1992).
"Fundamental Agreement between the Holy See and the State of Israel" (1993).
"Basic Agreement between the Holy See and the Palestine Liberation Organization" (2000).

Documents of the Pontifical Biblical Commission

"The Interpretation of the Bible in the Church" (1993).
"The Jewish People and their Sacred Scriptures in the Christian Bible" (2001).

Documents of the Commission for Religious Relations with the Jews

"Orientations and Suggestions for the Application of the Council Declaration *Nostra Aetate*" (1985).
"We Remember: A Reflection on the Shoah" (1998).

Documents of the Latin Patriarchate in Jerusalem

"Patriarch Sabbah, Reading the Bible Today in the Land of the Bible" (1993).
"Patriarch Sabbah, Seek Peace and Pursue It: Questions and Answers on Justice and Peace in Our Holy Land" (1998).
Assembly of Catholic Ordinaries, *The General Pastoral Plan* (2001).

DOCUMENTS FROM OTHER EPISCOPAL CONFERENCES

"L'attitude des chrétiens à l'égard du judaïsme: orientations pastorales du comité épiscopal pour les relations avec le judaïsme, publiées par la conférence épiscopale française" (1973).
"Statement on Catholic-Jewish relations of the U.S. National Conference of Bishops" (1975).

Index

Abel, 11, 14–15
Abimelekh, 17, 35, 211
Abraham (patriarch), ix, 2, 15–20,
    21, 24, 25, 31, 46–47, 48, 57, 58,
    60, 64, 65, 73, 79, 85, 94, 134,
    137, 153, 154, 155, 156, 158,
    162, 186, 188, 189, 193, 194, 204
Adam, 7, 9–11, 12, 14, 15, 16, 19,
    29, 30, 54, 62, 69, 70, 78, 84, 85,
    189, 191, 209
Agudat Yisrael, 215
Ahab, King, 37, 40, 210
Ahasuerus, 121
Ahaz, King, 40
Akhior, 210
Al-Aqsa Mosque, 106
Al-Azhar, 173, 174
Albright, W. F., 138
Alexander II, Czar, 129
Alt, A., 140
Alter, R., 36
Amos (prophet), 49, 50, 51, 57, 83,
    130
anti-Judaism, xii, 108–24, 126, 129,
    163, 195
anti-Semitism, 2, 4, 126, 127, 170,
    171, 195, 215
Antioch, 83, 116
Antiochus IV, King, 115
Arabs, 102, 131–32, 146, 149, 175,
    179, 184

Arafat, Y., 182
archaeology, 130, 135, 137–42, 148
Arculf, 102
Assumptionists, 148
Assyria, 25, 40, 43, 58
Athanasius, 95–96
Athenagoras (patriarch), 149
Augustine, 117–19, 134, 195

Babel, 12–13, 15
Babylon, 25, 40, 41, 42, 53, 84, 118,
    136, 155, 191
Beit Shean, 138
Bernard of Clairvaux, 103
Benedictos (patriarch), 149
Bethel, 39, 138
Bethlehem, 66, 67, 68, 93, 94, 95,
    107, 149, 150, 180, 183, 216
Bethlehem University, 182, 216
Boaz, 36
Bossuet, J., 120–21
Briend, J., 142
Brueggemann, W., 23
Buber, M., 128
Byzantium, 102

Caesar of Arles, 119
Caesarea, 82
Cain, 11, 14–15
Canaan, 16, 18, 30, 46, 60, 71, 73,
    89, 130, 140, 141, 191

Capernaum, 91
Cassidorus, 119
Charles Martel, 102
Constantine, Emperor, 93, 98, 104, 108
Conteson, Rev. de, 165
Cornelius (Acts), 82
covenant, 2, 3, 11, 12, 17, 22, 23, 24, 34, 40, 44, 48, 52, 76, 84, 90, 123, 186, 190, 192, 193, 198, 200, 209
creation, ix, xi, 2, 7, 9–10, 11, 12, 14, 22, 28, 30, 38, 43–46, 49, 58, 62, 64, 79, 80, 84, 85, 210, 211
Crusades, 102–4, 106, 131, 148, 149, 173, 220
Custody of the Holy Land, 107, 199–200
Cyril of Jerusalem, 97, 188, 209
Cyrus, Emperor, 41–42, 188, 209

Dabru emet, 169–70
Daniel (prophet), 58, 59, 116
David, King, 37, 38, 39, 40, 42, 45, 47, 50, 57, 60, 68, 75, 79, 83, 101, 136, 141, 160, 191, 204, 211
Davies, W. D., 63, 137
Dayan, M., 220
Decius, Emperor, 113
Deheisheh Camp, 183
Deuteronomist, 31–32, 136, 210, 211
Dina, 16
Dome of the Rock, 106, 167
Dreyfus, A., 215

Egeria, 104
Egypt, 13, 16, 18, 20–22, 25, 27, 28, 34, 38, 39, 40, 46, 53, 56, 58, 60, 67, 68, 76, 78, 105, 106, 113, 115, 141, 155, 156, 174, 180, 181, 188, 190, 210
Elijah (prophet), 40, 59, 69, 71, 92, 209
Elisha (prophet), 69
Elliot, G., 214
Esther, Queen, 43
Eucharist, 69
Euphrates, 31, 46, 60

Eusebius, 92, 93
Eve, 10–11, 29, 189
exile, x, 4, 11, 42–43, 55, 61, 62, 69, 90, 92, 115–17, 121, 136, 145, 146, 155, 188, 192, 194, 209
Ezekiel (prophet), 51, 55, 56, 58, 129, 191, 192
Ezra (scribe), 42, 188, 191

Finkelstein, I., 140
Francis of Assisi, 106
Franciscans, 106–7, 199
fundamentalism, 4, 146, 152–53, 158, 197–99

Galilee, 66, 67, 68, 71, 72, 73, 193, 212
Gandhi, M., 128
Garstang, J., 141
Gaza, 81, 93
Gaza Strip, 133, 180
Gerizim, Mount, 77
Gideon (judge), 17, 35
Goethe, J. W. von, 122
Golan, 193
Golgotha, 95, 98, 121
Gottwald, N., 140
Gourion, J.-B., 221
Gregory of Nyssa, 96–98

Hadrian, Emperor, 90, 93
Hameiri, M. Rabbi, 101
Haram ash-Sharif, 174, 197
Hassan II, King, 174
Hebron, 19
Hegessipius, 93
Helena, Empress, 98
Herzl, Theodor, 127, 128, 161, 167, 215
Heschel, A. J., 129
Hezekiah, King, 47
Hiram, King, 38, 42
Holocaust. *See* Shoah
Holy Land, ix, 2, 3, 6, 90, 147, 148, 151
Holy Places, 91, 92, 93, 95, 96, 98–99, 104, 107, 146, 148, 149, 150, 172, 180, 196, 199
Holy See, 150, 178, 181, 185, 205

Holy Sepulcher, 95, 98–99, 103, 199
Holy Spirit, 73, 77, 81, 97, 98, 114
Horeb, 22, 92. *See also* Sinai

interreligious dialogue, 160–76
Isaac (patriarch), 19, 20, 21, 24, 60,
    65, 79, 109, 134
Isaac, J., 109, 217
Isaiah (prophet), 13, 42, 53, 57, 58,
    60, 61, 67, 84, 85, 129, 130, 207
Ibn Arabi, 105
Israel, kingdom, 17, 36, 39–41, 47,
    48
Israel, State of, xii, xiii, 2, 4, 127,
    128, 129, 131, 132–33, 143, 145,
    146, 149, 150, 158, 161, 162,
    163, 166, 167, 168, 169–72, 177–
    78, 179, 180, 181, 182, 184, 185,
    195, 196, 198, 199, 205, 206
Islam, 2, 102–3, 104, 105–6, 107,
    158, 160, 161, 172–76, 196, 197,
    204, 213. *See also* Muslims

Jacob (prophet), 16, 20, 21, 24, 60,
    65, 79, 134, 207
Jaffa, 82
James, Saint, 57, 83, 93, 215
Jereboam, King, 17
Jeremiah (prophet), 47, 50, 52,
    53–54
Jericho, 33, 141–42, 210
Jerome, 92, 94, 134
Jerusalem, x, xi, 1, 3, 5, 7, 13, 17, 22,
    23, 25, 32, 37, 38, 39, 40, 41, 42,
    43, 45, 47, 51, 53, 54, 55, 56, 57,
    58, 60, 61, 65, 66, 67, 68, 72, 73,
    74, 77, 81, 82, 83, 84, 85, 86, 90,
    91, 92, 93, 94, 95, 96, 97, 98–99,
    100, 101, 103, 104, 105, 106,
    107, 113, 114, 118, 128, 129,
    130, 133, 134, 138, 141, 146,
    147, 148, 149,150, 151, 157, 160,
    164, 171, 172, 174, 177, 178,
    180, 181, 183, 184, 191, 192,
    194, 196, 200, 203–7, 210
Jesuits, 165
Jesus, xii, 3, 4, 5, 63–81, 84, 85, 93,
    151, 154, 163, 192–93, 212
Jews, ix, x, xiii, 1, 5, 90–91, 100,
    108, 109, 110–24, 125, 126, 127,

132, 133, 137, 145, 146, 149,
    152, 153–54, 157, 158, 160, 161–
    72, 177, 179, 181, 182, 194–95,
    196, 197
Jezebel, Queen, 40
Job, 44
John XXIII (pope), 161, 217
John of Acre, Saint, 107
John the Baptist, 67, 98
John Chrysostom, 108, 113, 115–17,
    121, 142
John Paul II (pope), 93, 146, 147,
    149, 151, 160, 166–67, 172, 179,
    181–83, 184–85, 196, 203, 204,
    217, 220
Jonah (prophet), 70–71
Jordan River, 31, 60, 66, 67, 68–69,
    113, 190
Jordan, kingdom, 149, 150, 174, 180,
    217, 220
Jose, Rabbi, 101
Joseph (Genesis), 16, 21
Joshua, 30–34, 37, 42, 47, 56, 65,
    69, 78, 79, 114, 141, 188, 191,
    192, 210, 212
Josiah, King, 23, 47, 72, 92, 189
Judah, 17, 39, 41, 53, 60, 156
Judah, Rabbi, 101
Judaism, 2, 99, 100–1, 115, 121,
    122, 123, 125, 127, 128, 136,
    153, 154, 161–72, 179
Judas (disciple), 108, 118
Judith, 43
Justin Martyr, 93, 112
Justinian, 99

Kenyon, K., 141
Kook, A. I., Rabbi, 127

Lachish, 138
Lagrange, M.-J., 134–35
Langmuir, G., 109
Lapide, P., 108
Latin patriarchate of Jerusalem, 148,
    220
law. *See* Torah
Lebanon, 60, 165, 174, 180, 206
Leibowitz, Y., 99
Leo XIII (pope), 134
Levites, 23

Lull, R., 107
Lydda, 81

Maccabees, 43, 90
Manasseh, King, 40
Marguerat, D., 109
Mary, Virgin, 67, 68, 72, 99
Massignon, Louis, 219
Mazar, B., 100
Mazar, E., 100
Mecca and Medinah, 106, 172
Megiddo, 138, 149, 180
Meir, G., 181
Melito of Sardis, 92
Melville, H., 214
Mesopotamia, 18, 60
Micah (prophet), 57, 68
Muhammad, 5, 104, 172
Muhammad Ali, 148
Moses (prophet), 21–30, 31, 33, 35,
    42, 47, 48, 59, 60, 69, 71, 78, 79,
    92, 105, 113, 114, 115, 188, 190,
    193, 210
Mount of Olives, 95, 98, 99
Muslims, xiii, 1, 4, 5, 102, 103,
    105–6, 107, 124, 131, 133, 146,
    147, 149, 158, 160, 161, 171,
    172–76, 177, 181, 185, 187, 195,
    196, 197, 204, 205, 210, 217. See
    also Islam

Nablus. See Shechem
Naomi, 36
Nathan (prophet), 37, 38
Nazareth, 66, 67–68, 72, 91, 149,
    212
Nazism, 126, 195
Nebo, Mount, 29, 30, 31
Nebuchadnezzar, King, 54, 115
Nehemiah, governor, 42
Nineveh, 13
Noah, 12, 55, 209
Notre Dame de Jerusalem, 181

Origen, 92, 113–15

Palestine, Palestinians, xii, xiii, 2, 4,
    124, 128, 130–33, 139, 143, 145,
    146, 148, 149, 157, 165, 166,
    167, 169, 170, 172, 177, 178,
    179, 180, 181, 183, 184, 185,
    195, 196, 197, 205
Palestine Exploration Fund, 138
Palestine Liberation Organization
    (PLO), 131–32, 150, 169, 181,
    182, 183
Pascal, B., 119, 120–21,
Paul, apostle, 73, 80, 82, 83, 212
Paul VI (pope), 148–49, 161, 165,
    173, 179–80, 181, 182, 203, 217,
    219
Paulinus of Nola, 94
Peres, S., 220
Persia, 41, 43
Peter, apostle, 71, 82, 83, 95, 99
Pharaoh, 20, 35, 38, 190
Pharisees, 122
Philip, Deacon, 82, 93
Pilgrim of Bordeaux, 122
Pius X (pope), 161, 167
Pompei, 137
Pontifical Biblical Commission, 135,
    152, 153, 156
Pontius Pilate, 74, 75, 77–78
Priestly writer, 136, 210, 211
Prudentius, 121

Qadesh Barnea, 28, 190
Qumran, 122, 172, 173, 197
Quran, 105

Rahab of Jericho, 36, 142
Rebecca (matriarch), 119
Reformation, 96
Resurrection, xii, 3, 4, 63, 64, 65,
    72–73, 81, 84, 90, 115, 147, 148,
    194, 204
Riegner, G., 165
Robinson, E., 138
Rome, 83, 90, 92
Ruth the Moabite, 35–36, 210

Sabbah, M., 133, 157–59, 171–72,
    176, 183, 184
Sabbath, 10, 23, 42, 78, 79, 190
Sadat, A., 181
Said, E., 131, 132
Samuel (prophet), 36
Sarah (matriarch), 19, 48

Saul, King, 37
Saulcy, F. de, 138
Schliemann, H., 137
Schneerson, S., 128
Sea of Galilee, 70–71
Second Vatican Council. *See* Vatican
    II
Shaftesbury, Lord, 215
Shamir, Y., 220
Shazar, S. Z., 162
Shechem, 16–17
Shelley, P., 122
Shoah, 4, 109, 123, 125–26, 129,
    132, 143, 161, 163, 166–67, 180
Simon (high priest), 47
Sinai, 17, 21–27, 71, 89, 190, 191
Smith, E., 138
Sodom and Gomorrah, 13, 19, 37,
    53, 57, 138
Solomon, King, 32, 38–39, 42, 45–
    46, 136, 141, 160, 204, 211
Stephen, Deacon, 73, 81, 83, 99, 156
Syria, 174

Tabor, Mount, 149
Talmud, 100–1
Tauran, J.-L., 178, 185, 220
Temple, x, xi, 4, 22–23, 37–39, 41–
    42, 55, 72, 73, 84, 85, 86, 99, 100,
    106, 122, 128, 129, 130, 160,
    192, 194, 197, 204, 209, 211
Tent of Meeting, 22–23, 38
Tertullian, 10–111
Theodosius, 100
Titus, 120
Tobit, 43, 93
Torah, x, 10, 11, 12, 20, 21–30, 34,
    35, 37, 39, 41, 43, 45, 47, 49, 57,

58, 59, 61, 62, 63, 66, 71, 81,
    122, 128, 190, 191, 210, 211
Troy, 137
Twain, M., 214

Umar, 105
United Nations, 132, 205
Urban II, 103

Vatican II, xii, 4, 7, 109, 123, 125,
    134, 145–46, 151, 153, 160, 161,
    169, 173, 178, 180, 181, 185,
    195, 212
Vulgate, 92

Wandering Jew, 121–22
Warren, C., 141
West Bank, 133, 179, 180, 182
Western Wall, 167
wilderness, 11, 28–29, 32, 43, 55,
    66, 69–70, 73, 79, 190–91, 192,
    193
Wigoder, G., 168
Wisdom, x, xi, 14, 43–48, 49, 61–62

Yad VaShem, 167, 183
Yahwist, 141
Yavneh, 65
Yehoash, King, 139

Zangwill, I, 215
Zenobius, 98
Zera, Rabbi, 101
Zionism, 127–30, 145, 152, 157,
    161, 166, 167, 170, 171, 180,
    183–84, 195, 214–15
Zionism, Christian, 198–99

Index of Biblical Citations

OLD TESTAMENT

Genesis   ix, 2, 9–20
Gn 1–2   7, 9, 211
Gn 1:1–2:4   9
Gn 1:1   9
Gn 1:1–5   14
Gn 1:9–10   9
Gn 1:26   9
Gn 1:28   9
Gn 2:3   10
Gn 2:4–3:24   10, 17
Gn 2:8–9   14, 69
Gn 2:10   85
Gn 2:15   10
Gn 2:16–17   10, 11, 14
Gn 3–11   10
Gn 3:9   11, 54
Gn 3:14   11
Gn 3:17   11, 70
Gn 3:18   9
Gn 4:1–16   11, 15
Gn 4:1   11
Gn 4:14   11
Gn 6:7   12
Gn 6:18   2
Gn 8:21   12
Gn 9:1   12
Gn 9:9–11   15
Gn 10–11   12
Gn 11:4   13

Gn 11:8–9   15
Gn 11:30   16
Gn 12:1–7   198
Gn 12:1   15, 130
Gn 12:2   15
Gn 12:3   199
Gn 12:6   16
Gn 12:7   16, 163
Gn 13:9   17
Gn 13:17   18
Gn 15:4–7   198
Gn 15:4–5   18
Gn 15:7   153
Gn 15:8   31
Gn 15:13   209
Gn 15:18–21   18, 25, 60, 153
Gn 17:1–8   198
Gn 17:5   15, 18
Gn 17:8   18, 60
Gn 18:19   19
Gn 19   13
Gn 20:7   48
Gn 22:16–18   19
Gn 23:1–24   19–20
Gn 25:23   119
Gn 26:3–4   20, 163
Gn 28:13   20, 163
Gn 28:14   20
Gn 34:30   16
Gn 35:12   20
Gn 37:12   16

Exodus	55	
Ex 1:1–4	20	
Ex 1:7	20	
Ex 1:8	21	
Ex 1:9	20	
Ex 3	21	
Ex 3:6	103	
Ex 3:8	21, 25	
Ex 3:12	22	
Ex 6:2–4	25	
Ex 6:8	21	
Ex 12:37	141	
Ex 12:40	209	
Ex 15:3	200	
Ex 15:7	153	
Ex 15:18	21, 35	
Ex 19:10–11	32	
Ex 19:11	21	
Ex 20	210	
Ex 20:1–17	22	
Ex 20:11	10	
Ex 20:19	22	
Ex 23	25	
Ex 23:17	114	
Ex 23:23–33	25	
Ex 25–40	38	
Ex 31:12–17	210	
Ex 32	48	
Ex 33:1–3	25	
Ex 34:11–15	25	
Ex 35:2–3	210	
Leviticus		
Lv 11:45	210	
Lv 18:21	40	
Lv 18:24–30	26	
Lv 18:28	27	
Lv 19:2	24, 210	
Lv 20:7–8	210	
Lv 20:26	210	
Lv 21:8	210	
Lv 22:9	210	
Lv 22:32	210	
Lv 25:23	14, 24, 192	
Lv 25:38	101	
Lv 26	25, 157	
Lv 26:11–13	25	
Lv 26:44–45	198	
Numbers		
Nm 10:10	21	
Nm 12:7	48	
Nm 14:32–33	69	
Nm 21:1–3	25	
Nm 21:21–35	25	
Nm 34:1–12	31, 60	
Nm 33:50–56	25	
Deuteronomy	155, 156, 193	
Dt 1:2	27	
Dt 1:6	65	
Dt 2–3	33	
Dt 2:33–36	25	
Dt 5:15	190	
Dt 7:1–6	25	
Dt 7:1	25	
Dt 7:4	26	
Dt 7:5	155	
Dt 7:6	52	
Dt 7:7–8	198	
Dt 7:16–24	25, 26	
Dt 7:13	188	
Dt 7:17–19	28	
Dt 7:21	28	
Dt 8:2–5	29, 69–70, 193	
Dt 8:7–10	29–30	
Dt 8:8	66	
Dt 8:19–20	27, 52	
Dt 9:1–6	25	
Dt 9:3	26	
Dt 9:4–5	26	
Dt 10:8	23	
Dt 10:9	23	
Dt 10:19	27	
Dt 11:10	21	
Dt 11:24	65	
Dt 12:8–10	61	
Dt 12:31	26	
Dt 13:12–18	27, 155	
Dt 13:15	27	
Dt 16:16	92	
Dt 17:16–19	39	
Dt 18:2	23	
Dt 18:10	40	
Dt 18:15–20	210	
Dt 20:15–18	25, 155	
Dt 20:16–17	189	
Dt 23:3–6	26	
Dt 23:7	27	
Dt 23:8	27	
Dt 26:1–11	80	
Dt 26:2	25	

Dt 26:10   80
Dt 28   25, 157
Dt 28:1   188
Dt 30:16–20   24
Dt 32:28   28
Dt 32:47   59
Dt 34:1–4   29, 31, 60
Dt 34:5   60
Dt 34:7   30
Dt 34:10   48

Joshua   140, 141, 155, 189
Jos 1:2   30, 114
Jos 1:3–4   60, 65
Jos 1:7–8   31
Jos 1:12–18   32
Jos 2:12–13   142
Jos 4:23–24   32
Jos 5:11–12   33
Jos 5:13–15   33
Jos 6:21   33
Jos 6:26   210
Jos 8:1–29   33
Jos 9:18   142
Jos 12   33
Jos 13:1   33
Jos 14:9   65
Jos 21:43–45   34
Jos 21:44   30, 61
Jos 21:45   30
Jos 22:4   61
Jos 23:1   61
Jos 24:13–14   34

Judges   140
Jgs 2:1–3   34–35
Jgs 2:10–16   35
Jgs 2:20–21   35
Jgs 8:23   35
Jgs 9   17, 211
Jgs 21:25   35

Ruth   35–36, 210, 211

1 Samuel
1Sam 1   92
1Sam 8:5   36
1Sam 8:6–9   48
1Sam 8:15   50
1Sam 8:17   36
1Sam 8:19–20   36

1Sam 17:1   68
1Sam 17:18   68
1Sam 26:19   101

2 Samuel
2Sam 7:1   61
2Sam 7:5–6   38
2Sam 11:21   211
2Sam 12:9   37

1 Kings
1Kgs 3:11–12   38, 46
1Kgs 4:31   46
1Kgs 5:7   46
1Kgs 5:18   61
1Kgs 7:1–12   38
1Kgs 8:41–43   39
1Kgs 11:6   39
1Kgs 12   17, 32
1Kgs 15:26   37
1Kgs 16:30   37
1Kgs 16:33   210
1Kgs 16:34   210
1Kgs 19:8–15   92
1Kgs 21   40
1Kgs 21:19   40

2 Kings   192
2Kgs 5   92
2Kgs 12   139
2Kgs 16:2–4   40
2Kgs 17:7–23   32
2Kgs 17:7–9   40–41
2Kgs 17:17   41
2Kgs 17:18–19   41
2Kgs 21:6   40
2Kgs 21:11ff   32
2Kgs 22–23   72
2Kgs 23:26–27   32
2Kgs 24:20   41

1 Chronicles
1Chr 28:3   211

2 Chronicles   209
2Chr 33:6   40
2Chr 36:23   42

Ezra
Ezr 9:10–12   42
Ezr 10:10–11   42

Nehemiah
Neh 5:3–5   42
Neh 11:25–35   60
Neh 13:15–18   42
Neh 13:23–25   42

Tobit   x
Tb 1:6   93
Tb 13:4   168

Judith   210

Esther   x
Es 1:3 (Gr.)   43

Maccabees   x

Job   ix
Jb 1:1   44
Jb 10:20–22   188
Jb 12:24   28
Jb 28:28   44

Psalms   ix, 200
Ps 1:2   43
Ps 37   201
Ps 37:3   76
Ps 37:9–11   76
Ps 37:22 1   55
Ps 42   44
Ps 44:2   44
Ps 44:3   44
Ps 44:11   44
Ps 44:23   44–45
Ps 45:5   103
Ps 47   45
Ps 48   45
Ps 60   45
Ps 68   45
Ps 74   45
Ps 78   45
Ps 78:54–55   26, 210
Ps 79   45
Ps 80   45
Ps 80:8   26, 210
Ps 83   45
Ps 87:4–5   45
Ps 87:7   45
Ps 95:8–11   153
Ps 95:11   28, 61
Ps 99:1   200
Ps 99:2   50

Ps 99:4   200
Ps 104:27–30   62
Ps 105   45
Ps 105:43–45   26, 60, 210
Ps 106   45
Ps 107:40   28
Ps 108   45, 118
Ps 119:1   43
Ps 126:1–2   45, 130
Ps 132:7–8   153
Ps 135   45
Ps 137   45

Proverbs   46

Ecclesiastes 46

Song of Songs 46
Cant 2:7   101
Cant 3:5   101

Wisdom
Wis 12:3–7   46
Wis 15:1–6   46
Wis 15:2   46

Jesus Son of Sirach (Ecclesiasticus)
Sir 16:29   46
Sir 17:1   46
Sir 17:12   209
Sir 17:23   46
Sir 24:6–8   47–48
Sir 24:23   47
Sir 24:34   48
Sir 33:10   46
Sir 36:17–22   46
Sir 44:21   46
Sir 46:6   7
Sir 48:18   47
Sir 49:4–6   47
Sir 49:7   47

Isaiah
Is 2:1–5   57
Is 1:7–10   53
Is 1:10   13
Is 1:23   13
Is 2:3   207
Is 3:9   13
Is 5:1–7   66
Is 9:6–9   70
Is 19:23–25   58, 60–61

Is 24:1	52		Ez 16:46–56	13
Is 32:15–18	50–51		Ez 20:31	211
Is 33:5	50		Ez 23:37	211
Is 34:11	28		Ez 33:10	191
Is 41:18–20	58		Ez 33:25–26	50, 192
Is 43:5–7	163		Ez 34:25–31	58
Is 43:19–20	58		Ez 34:13 1	67
Is 45:1	42		Ez 36:24–38	56
Is 45:8	58		Ez 37–38	199
Is 47	13		Ez 37:1–14	56
Is 47:4–7	57		Ez 37:12	56
Is 51:3	17, 56			
Is 54:7–10	55		**Daniel**	199
Is 56:7	39, 57		Dn 7:13–14	59
Is 59:8–12	50			
Is 61:1–2	67		**Hosea**	
Is 62:1	204		Hos 1:12	66
Is 65:17	84		Hos 2:14	29
Is 66:1–2	61		Hos 2:16	56, 191
Is 66:18–24	58–59		Hos 4:3	52
			Hos 11:1	68
Jeremiah			Hos 11:9	56
Jer 4:6–7	53		Hos 14:8	66
Jer 4:23–26	52			
Jer 5:17	66		**Joel**	
Jer 7:4	95		Jl 2:3–4	2
Jer 8:13	66		Jl 2:22	66
Jer 9:11–12	54		Jl 4:18–21	56
Jer 9:13–14	54			
Jer 9:24	0		**Amos**	
Jer 16:15	163		Am 2:4–8	51
Jer 17:19–27	52		Am 3:2	52
Jer 19:4	211		Am 3:7	49
Jer 22:3	50		Am 4:11	13
Jer 23:14	13		Am 4:13	49
Jer 27:11	61		Am 5:24	50
Jer 27:19ff	101		Am 5:7	50
Jer 27:22	101		Am 8:4–6	52
Jer 32:35	211		Am 9:11–12	57, 83
Jer 44:6–8	53		Am 9:12 (Gr.)	57
Jer 49:18	13		Am 9:13–14	66
Jer 50:7	47			
Jer 50:40	13		**Jonah**	211
Lamentations	54		**Micah**	
Lm 1:1–2	54, 211		Mi 4:1–5	57
Lm 5:2	54		Mi 5:2	68
Ezekiel			**Nahum**	19
Ez 9:9	50		**Habakkuk**	
Ez 10–11	55, 192		Hab 1:5–11	53
			Hab 1:6–9	54–55

Hab 3:2	55
Hab 3:5	55

Zephaniah

Zep 1:2–3	52
Zep 3:20	163

Haggai xi

Zachariah xi

Za 2:16	5
Za 7:9–10	58
Za 8:3	xi, 58
Za 9–14	199

Malachi xi, 209

Mal 3:22–24	59, 69

NEW TESTAMENT

Matthew

Mt 1:1	193
Mt 2:6	68
Mt 2:15	68
Mt 2:20–21	156
Mt 2:23	212
Mt 3:2	63
Mt 3:17	85
Mt 4:17	63
Mt 4:20	96
Mt 4:23	151, 203
Mt 5:1	71
Mt 5:3	76, 156
Mt 5:5	xii, 3, 76, 115, 156, 201
Mt 5:10	76, 156
Mt 5:17	63
Mt 8:10–11	65
Mt 10:5–6	65, 71
Mt 14:23	71
Mt 15:21–28	71, 210
Mt 15:29	71
Mt 17:1	71
Mt 19:14	76
Mt 24:1–36	66
Mt 28:19	65

Mark

Mk 1:13	70
Mk 1:15	64
Mk 3:1	91
Mk 3:7	91
Mk 4	70
Mk 5	70
Mk 7:24–30	65, 71, 210
Mk 8:27–9:13	71
Mk 9:2	91
Mk 10:14	76
Mk 11:12–14	66
Mk 11:21–22	66
Mk 12:1–12	66
Mk 13:3–32	66
Mk 16:1–9	91

Luke

Lk 1:26	67
Lk 4:21	67
Lk 4:22	70
Lk 6:20	76
Lk 6:35	80
Lk 7:37–38	96
Lk 8:1	64
Lk 9:51–19:45	68
Lk 9:51	68
Lk 10:39	96
Lk 10:42	96
Lk 13:22	68
Lk 13:28–29	65
Lk 17:11	68
Lk 17:21	95
Lk 18:16	76
Lk 19:3–8	96
Lk 19:11	68
Lk 19:22	78
Lk 21:5–33	65
Lk 21:21–24	65
Lk 24:18	92

John 122

Jn 1:46	67
Jn 1:49	74
Jn 2:13	93
Jn 4	77
Jn 4:21–24	3, 17, 77
Jn 4:22	77
Jn 4:24	95
Jn 6:15	74
Jn 6:45	204
Jn 7:10	93
Jn 12:12	93
Jn 12:13	74
Jn 14:6	75

Jn 18:20–22   121
Jn 18:36   74, 75
Jn 18:37   74, 75
Jn 20:19   205

Acts   81
Ac1:4   96
Ac 1:6   73, 82
Ac 1:7   82
Ac 1:8   61, 81, 82, 83
Ac 7:2–7   156
Ac 7:4   73
Ac 7:48–49   73
Ac 8:27   93
Ac 11:19   83
Ac 13   82
Ac 13:19   73
Ac 15   82
Ac 15:16–18   57
Ac 15:17   57, 83
Ac 16:9   83

Romans
Rm 1:16   82
Rm 6:10   203
Rm 8:11   95
Rm 9:4–5   80, 217
Rm 11:29   162, 167

1 Corinthians
1Cor 10–11   80
1Cor 14:20   114

2 Corinthians
2Cor 6:16   95

Galatians
Ga 3:28   80, 194
Ga 4:4   114
Ga 4:26   114
Ga 6:14   6

Ephesians
Eph 2:13   151
Eph 2:14   82, 203
Eph 2:16   203

1 Thessalonians
1Th 4:13–17   199
1Th 5:1–11   199

Hebrews
Heb 3–4 7   8
Heb 3:7–4:11   153
Heb 3:19   78
Heb 4:1   78
Heb 4:6–7   79
Heb 4:8   79
Heb 5:10   114
Heb 6:12   153
Heb 6:18–20   153
Heb 7:27   203
Heb 9:12   203
Heb 9:13   114
Heb 9:15   153
Heb 10:1   79
Heb 10:10   203
Heb 11:8   79
Heb 11:9   79, 156
Heb 11:13–16   79–80
Heb 13:12–14   80

1 Peter
1P 1:19   114

Revelation   2, 81, 83–84, 199
Rv 6:10   84
Rv 11:2   212
Rv 11:8   13
Rv 11:15   84
Rv 12   84
Rv 14:1   84
Rv 17:5   13, 84
Rv 18   13
Rv 19:1   84
Rv 21–22   7
Rv 21:1   84
Rev 21:2   85
Rv 21:11   13
Rv 21:22   85
Rv 22:2   85